The Hidden Army

THE HIDDEN ARMY

The Untold Story
of Japan's Military Forces

Tetsuo Maeda

Edited and with an introduction by David J. Kenney
Translated from the Japanese by Steven Karpa

edition q, inc.
Chicago, Berlin, Tokyo, and Moscow

© 1995 by edition q, inc.

© 1995 Introduction by David J. Kenney

Translated and updated from the Japanese, *Jieitai Wa Nani o Shite Kita No Ka?*, © Chikuma Shobo, 1990.

edition q, inc.
551 North Kimberly Drive
Carol Stream, Illinois 60188

Library of Congress Cataloging-In-Publication Data

Maeda, Tetsuo, 1938–
    [Jieitai wa nani o shite kita no ka? English]
    The hidden army : the untold story of Japan's military forces / Tetsuo Maeda; edited and with an introduction by David J. Kenney; translated by Steven Karpa.
       p. cm.
    Includes bibliographical references.
    ISBN 1-883695-01-5
    1. Japan—Armed Forces—History—20th century. 2. Japan—Armed Forces—Officers. 3. Japan—History, Military—1945– I. Title.
UA845.M2643   1995
355'.00952'0904—dc20

94-40937
CIP

Printed in the United States of America

Contents

Part III
The Self-Defense Forces from 1975 to the Present

Preface

After its devastating defeat in World War II, Japan adopted a constitution that renounced war as the nation's sovereign right and pledged that it would not maintain land, sea, or air forces. Today, Japan's defense budget is the world's second largest after America's, outranking that of Russia. In 1993, Japan spent about $46 billion, about one percent of its huge GNP, on defense, funding 155,000 ground soldiers and a navy larger than those of North and South Korea combined. Despite, or possibly because of, the Japanese government's semantic legerdemain in creating the Japanese Self-Defense Force (SDF), a certain air of illegitimacy surrounds it.

As a journalist, I am always tempted to use words like *shadowy* and *twilight* when I write about the Self-Defense Force because of Japan's constitutional prohibition on military forces. But a sunnier view of the early years of the Self-Defense Force is equally plausible. General Douglas MacArthur and Japan's second postwar prime minister, Shigeru Yoshida, created the Self-Defense Force in the early 1950s, when the Korean War brought a sudden prosperity to Japan. The SDF then grew into a powerful force during the golden years of the 1960s and prospered yet again as Japan became rich in the 1980s. The Self-

Defense Force may have started as Japan's illegitimate child, but with the Cold War as its father and Japan's economic miracle as its mother, the child is heir to a fortune.

The rebuilding of Japan's defenses began with the creation in 1950 of the National Police Reserve, a small ground force that was half police department, half army. Fours years later, in 1954, maritime and air branches were created and the Police Reserve was renamed the Self-Defense Force. The forty-year history of the SDF differs in almost every respect from the seventy-five-year history of Japan's prewar imperial military.

During the Imperial Army's first forty years, it put down samurai rebellions in southern Japan, suppressed riots and violent strikes around the country, invaded Taiwan, and fought full-fledged wars against imperial China and Russia. In contrast, the Self-Defense Forces have never turned their guns on fellow Japanese or fought foreign enemies. But this is not to say that the years since 1950 have been without incident. Far from it! The Japanese have argued incessantly in the political arena over every aspect of the Self-Defense Force: its very constitutionality, its weaponry, the deployment of troops, and Japan's appropriate strategic interests.

These fundamental conflicts have divided public opinion and to some degree have isolated the military from Japanese society as a whole. Further complicating the issue, the United States has often expected the Self-Defense Force to play a role in its Cold War strategies. In the view of some, the United States–Japan Security Treaty has effectively made the Self-Defense Force subject to the laws of a foreign nation.

This conflict has forced the SDF to create two contradictory faces; a domestic one that reflects the constraints of the peace constitution, and an international appearance of working hand in glove with the United States. As the SDF's budget and size have grown, this schizophrenia has become more pronounced. Increasing engagements with other Asian countries and their military problems will doubtless cause the outside world to question whether the expanding role of the SDF is a positive or a negative development.

The Japanese military is changing. The men who ushered in the birth of the SDF have been almost entirely replaced by a younger corps. Not a single Imperial Army veteran remains in the Self-Defense Forces. The new military was intended to embody the spirit of peace enshrined in Japan's postwar history and constitution in order to make a break with imperial expansionism. A graduate of the first class of the postwar Defense Academy was appointed to the Maritime Self-Defense Force's highest post in 1989, and by the summer of 1990, graduates of that first class had been promoted to the top posts of the Ground Self-Defense Force and Air Self-Defense Force as well. The oldest of these men was only twelve years old when the United States defeated Japan's Imperial Army and Imperial Navy. Although they are considered to be part of the postwar generation of officers, it would be just as accurate to call them part of the no-war generation, since these three men, who hold the highest posts in the Japanese military, have never experienced war. Ironically, they experienced bombing raids and starvation and attended the Defense Academy while enduring vilification by their peers as embarrassments and public parasites. With the promotion of these men to the SDF's highest posts, the transformation of the Japanese military was complete; the torch has been truly passed to a new generation.

As the reins of power pass to new hands, the Self-Defense Force faces a world that has undergone drastic changes. Japan is consumed with uncertainty. This world in flux is frightening, if only because it presents Japan with glimpses of a future that it has never before contemplated. North Korea's possession of nuclear weaponry has dimmed the joy produced by the Cold War's end. Still, economic factors retain priority over contests of military power.

To find out where the Self-Defense Forces are going, we need to examine where they have been and who the individuals are that compose them. These are the necessary conditions of any discussion of Japanese national security. I have written this history of Japan's Self-Defense Force with a focus on the changing of the guard within the force and on the problems that confront them today. I cannot present every detail of history because of the SDF's justifiable concern for its own security. But the quest for the truth, and only the truth, has been my guide, and I have rejected supposition and speculation as tools of inquiry. I have relied exclusively on objective sources whose reliability can be ascertained. I have tried to clarify the process of rearmament that Japan began in 1950, and to show the form and direction of that process today.

Acknowledgment

I would like to thank my editor, Masatoshi Izaki, who was also the editor of my previous book, *Nuclear War Simulation*. The genesis of this book came from a talk we had when we met serendipitously on board the *Peace Boat*. We hashed out the book's themes as we rode together from the Shimokita Peninsula to Kanazawa and on our return to Tokyo by car. The book took me over a year to complete, and I felt great joy upon getting to this point. I extend my best wishes to its first reader.

Translator's Note

For the ease of the English-language reader, Japanese names are presented given name first, family name last.

Introduction

by David J. Kenney

Japan inc. faces a problem that neither its bankers nor its technicians are apt to solve. The story is this. Far from the cool, high-tech world where Japan's commerce flowers, an ugly universe churns. Oddly, its dark side was ignored in the Land of the Chrysanthemum. North Korea's nuclear adventurism changed all of that. By accumulating primitive nuclear devices the late Kim Il Sung drove Japan into the gray-collared arena where other nations strive. No diplomatic or military moves can regain the *status quo ante*. Japan must play a new part on the stage of nuclear politics.

Since World War II's end, Japan's political society has clung almost exclusively to six axioms that have guided its foreign and military policy. It is these notions, all the more powerful for being unwritten, that must metamorphose if Japan is to maintain its economic and political preeminence. They include:

1. Shunning squabbles contributes to the world's peace. Japan's military adventures had proven disastrous.
2. A profitable mercantilist empire, backed not by military assets but by brain power and a docile work force, sustains the world's order.

3. Japan is a nuclear casualty and cannot afford a repetition thereof. The Bomb has transformed a bellicist society into one of history's pacifist nations.
4. Liberals oppose granting the Japanese military significant resources. They see the military's increased manpower and rising levels of equipment as portents of fresh disasters abroad and impediments to democracy's growth at home.
5. Conservatives, i.e., big business, believe that keeping a defense force cheap and small while accepting a junior partnership in the U.S. military alliance makes good financial and political sense.
6. The electorate gratified by peace and prosperity accepts, with rare exceptions, its leaders' decisions.

The best-executed schemes end. The belief that Japan's economic triumphs could be isolated from its international responsibilities has lost credibility. This happened because the collapse of the Soviet Union invalidated the Cold War's rules. Unexpectedly, the nuclear stand down has not brought certainty or even relief mostly because we have not gestated a new set of enforceable international habits. We are sure only that new times have abrogated old practices.

The two blocs that made the rules no longer keep the peace. The paradigm of fifty years is shattered; nations of the Northern Pacific, especially Japan, find themselves groping for new roles. For example: in Tokyo a few indistinct mutterings can be heard about deeper involvement in U.N. security matters. It is even tacitly admitted there that the terminological sleights of hand that confounded the letter of Article 9 while obeying its spirit have no further use.

The new era's realities, as ill-defined as they are, force Japan to answer four novel military challenges: the possession by North Korea of nuclear weapons deliverable now or soon on any part of Japan; the swift and massive buildup of the Chinese

military machine, the near elimination of the Soviet Union as
Asia's dominant military power and the pledge by beleaguered
Russian authorities to maintain hegemony over Siberia by force
if necessary.

Then, too, the rise of the outlaw nuclear state puts all
nations in a kind of danger that few foresaw. North Korea, Iran,
Iraq and Syria, for example, have little regard for the protocols
of international life that sustained us through the nuclear risks
that infested the Cold War.

Clearly responses to the Japanese military dilemma
demand a new mind-set from Japanese leaders. They must now
deal with chancy economic moves, innovative alliance politics,
reeducation of the electorate and strategic choices that Japan
has not faced since the 1930s. Make no mistake, the Japanese
leadership's definition of its military problem will soon affect
the way Japan lives and the level of prosperity it enjoys.

The crunch comes when proposed solutions to these problems collide with Japan's commercial aspirations, a declining
birth rate, a diminishing labor force, a frangible stock market,
notorious corruption in government, society's demands for better living and as yet little-understood limits on political power
derived from wealth. And all these sit atop the underlying need
to keep healthy a young democratic system of government.

Fundamental to any set of solutions is an admission that
even before North Korea announced its intention to procure
nuclear weapons, the Chinese buildup in nuclear arms, naval
forces and well-trained infantry had changed the balance of military power in all of Asia. The possibilities for mischief here are
almost limitless: a northern thrust to seize Siberian land and
resources from a debilitated Russia; a westward march to pacify
the irksome Moslem baronies of the old Soviet Union; a southern strike to capture the Paracels and the Spratelys; a brooding
presence on the North Vietnamese and Thai borders to ensure
Chinese commercial access to Southeast Asia or perhaps a

naval projection force to acquire parity on the petroleum lanes of the Western Pacific—all this backed by a burgeoning nuclear force. For now Chinese military and territorial aspirations do not threaten the peace or Japanese prosperity. Economic growth, Hong Kong's transfer to China and the leadership's succession are the front-burner issues there.

On the other hand, North Korean *realpolitik* backed by nuclear weaponry is a hard-edged thing. The possibility, however unlikely, that Japan might resign its economic suzerainty of the Northern Pacific, sign over part of its commercial heritage or demilitarize in return for a guarantee against nuclear attack cannot be dismissed. Japan's leaders of whatever stripe cannot believe, with certainty, that a nuclear threat to Japan would provoke an American nuclear reply. John F. Kennedy's *Ich bin ein Berliner* does not apply to Tokyo.

Should Japan respond with a massive buildup of conventional forces or perhaps sate North Korea's demands with a demeaning set of commercial and political agreements? Should Japan abandon its role as America's surrogate in the North Pacific in order to become the managing partner of a nuclear-armed Asian bloc? After all, without allies Japan might be compelled to answer threats unilaterally or not at all. Could Japan abandon or diminish the American tie in favor of a new and dependent relationship with China? China's markets tempt inordinately. And swapping Japanese technology and capital for Chinese muscle might appeal to many. Or should Japan annex Siberia's wealth by treaty and commercial agreement in order to find favor with a still-nuclear Russia? Could Japan retain its pacifist persona in the Northern Pacific, its dominant economic role in the world's affairs and its present national life if any or a combination of these events occurred? Probably not.

North Korea's born-again belligerency is not Japan's sole military problem. Not surprisingly old vexations have emerged with new twists. Just as before in this century, Russian vulnerability to anyone picking at the Siberian bear's tail is woefully clear. Does Japan stay clear of a Sino-Russian brawl? How does Japan keep its pledge to regain Sakhalin Island without destabilizing Eastern Russia and indeed derogating Moscow's capacity to govern? Does Japan benefit more from a strong Russia that counterweights the Chinese military, or should Japan opt for a weak Russia whose vast natural resources would become ripe for plucking? Earlier in this century Japan chose a military presence on the Asian mainland with, it must be said, no lasting benefit to anyone. Might Japan regain this military and political option? Or does prudence demand the conquest of new territories by force of yen alone? Or should Japan, oblivious to nuclear risk and tacitly trustful of its protectors, remain in splendid isolation, communicating with the outside world only through exports and currency transactions? Often lost in abstruse discussions of nuclear vulnerability is the unpleasant fact that outlaws can, with high-tech weaponry, sink enough Japanese tankers in a day to throw Japanese export plans into a cocked hat and Lloyd's of London into pandemonium.

When all is said, the perduring thorn in Japan's side remains that North Korea has bankrupted its people to go nuclear. Perversely, that country gives no indication of wanting to practice the appropriate modes of nuclear behavior that maintained a fragile peace during fifty years of Cold War. Kim Il Sung's successor and his colleagues have learned neither the vocabulary of nuclear usage nor acceptable forms of restraint. They remain ignorant, apparently, of the structures and practices the West has developed to accommodate this most hideous of weapons to the search for peace.

At times nuclear war almost seems for North Korea a realistic policy option. None there appears to remember that nuclear arms are not meant to be used and that under a Soviet-American nuclear umbrella the tanks did not roll and the missiles did not fly. North Korea is about to match the West's armory while replicating few if any of its restraining institutions. It is as though the nastiest bully on the block has acquired a loaded rifle to threaten the neighborhood's peace rather than to ensure its safety.

What then of Japan and its military? While Japan's military doctrine has been almost comically asymmetrical—its leader carried slingshots to the negotiating tables owned for the past fifty years by nuclear proprietors—its business leaders have whistled all the way to the bank. Now they stand a fair chance of being mugged at their own doorway. It should be quite clear to Japan's leadership that its almost self perpetuating prosperity cannot assure the outside world's friendship nor in the end its own safety. At the time of the yen's greatest strength, Japan's security has shown a fragility that should alarm the most torpid.

As is proper in democracies, civilian leaders must formulate answers to the trickiest military questions. Can Japan continue to devote 1% of its GDP to the defense of a self-centered society whose surprisingly low living standards sustain a galloping export economy? Will Japan take its place as a world leader in order to help stop nuclear arms' proliferation? Would the Japanese electorate support a strict embargo, backed by force, against the sale of North Korean nuclear weaponry to other outlaw states? Will Japan remain the U.S.'s silent and junior partner in the area's military affairs? Is Japan willing to pay the price of entry into global political affairs as it has so successfully done in its economic matters? Pride of place in the world means, inevitably, the shedding of young men's blood. Can the Japanese electorate be convinced that in some instances loss of life is a condition precedent to internal stability and not necessarily a prelude to gory adventurism?

Tetsuo Maeda has written a book that gives an impressionistic look at the convoluted logic and policy making that has resulted in today's Japanese Self-Defense Force. That nation's leaders made policy on the assumption that Japan could benefit from extraordinarily high consumers' demands abroad while remaining aloof from the mundane problems of nuclear threats, terrorism, world-wide poverty and social change. In a sense Japanese planners guessed right because under the protection of the West's nuclear umbrella none of the Soviet Union's 40,000+ nuclear weapons was ever fired in anger. While the West ran deficits to keep its defense industry well-stoked Japan's current surplus ran from ¥11 billion in 1971 to over ¥400 billion by 1985. True, Japanese interests bought urban real estate and other oddments here to palliate the American migraine; but even this move was oh-so clever because after Japanese merchants sold Americans perishable assets, such as cars and televisions, they used the proceeds to buy productive assets like factories that guarantee market share and yield an almost unending cash flow.

What now? Despite the proscriptions of Article 9, Japan has built a military force to control the air and sea space around Japan and to assist in keeping the Soviet navy bottled up in the Sea of Japan. This force, large enough to meet discreet goals and small enough to stay out of sight, served splendidly before North Korea acquired nuclear weaponry. It must be said that the Japanese defense establishment designs and builds superb military hardware equal to any other. Yet it is the wrong force for the wrong era. Modest amphibious lift limits the usefulness of the splendid Model 90 tanks. New destroyers on patrol in the Molaccas offer little protection against missiles that fire nuclear tips from 1,000 miles' distance or against North Korean infantry storming towards Seoul. Only the Japanese Air Force might offer a slender chance of hitting missile sites and blunting armored thrusts before they did their worst.

The Hidden Army's author rightly shows why the SDF finds itself at a crossroads and why the comfortable old ways no longer suit. New thinking by a reoriented bureaucracy, new strategies, new force mixes, in fact nothing less than a new military posture for Japan are clearly in order. *The Hidden Army* shows in painstaking detail why the SDF must seek new relationships with the bureaucracy and the electorate. Yet the obstacles to positive change remain enormous. Japanese politics rebuke external *stimuli*. Only rarely do jabs from the U.S., some well-publicized corruption and the odd maverick politician like Ozawa Ichiro jolt the body politic. Moreover scandal at the top and the nascent infirmities of a bureaucracy more mindful of procedure than of innovation have rendered present Japanese governments far less stable than their predecessors. Japan's exquisitely collegial method for making decisions shows itself weakest, ironically, just when Japan faces its greatest need for change since World War II's end.

Like it or not Japan has become an interested party in a dangerous universe. Icy incomprehension of it no longer excuses delay. Genuine reflection upon the world's vexations and their effects on the Japanese military, not sophists' word games, must be the order of the day. It is not enough that the SDF owns new iron, it needs new ideas as well. Nettlesome questions have to be faced: are the mechanisms of Japanese governance equal to the task of making Japan a reliable partner in nuclear games-manship? After all an adversary's passions and miscalculations can launch missiles quite without notice. Can the Japanese electorate understand and support societal changes necessitated by Japan's changed and expensive place in the world? Can Japan's political society learn how to dance safely with the nuclear devil?

Looking on from the outside, a sympathetic observer might decently suggest some changes that do not merely echo Japan's celebrated past:

1. A realistic view of the world as something to be joined and dealt with rather than shunned; a new cast of mind that accepts a world no longer bipolar and no longer responsive to

to the kinds of force that kept the peace from 1945 until now; an acknowledgment that Japan's wealth, far from being a shield against malefactors, may in fact attract them. All this means finally that Japan see itself as a normal member of the international community.

2. A new class of leaders teased out of their intellectual bunkers and comfortable in a post-détente but still-nuclear world. This new elite would assist the West in keeping international problems manageable. It would formulate justifications for a continued American alliance. It would manifest the political will and fund the combat forces needed to convince any adversary that Japan will not submit to military blackmail. It would willingly join international peace-keeping operations and preemptive military action against outlaw nuclear groups.

3. Membership in a community of Pacific nations bound by long-term interests in open markets, technology transfer, capital, energy and nuclear weaponry that will keep a balance of power among rival military and political blocs. For example, Japan might engage in a mature dialogue with America, China and Russia about the North Korean bomb, the stability of Asiatic Russia and the aspirations that China intends to fulfill in the early twenty-first century. No *a priori* linkage with economic disputes should muddy these discussions. Satisfactory economic relations will follow once a reasonable level of trust and security is obtained. A partnership with three owners of nuclear weapons might convince Japan to remain non-nuclear.

4. A flexible and pragmatic relationship with the U.S., perhaps more nearly equal than before, that will keep U.S. and Japanese markets, societies and military open to each other. Keeping an American military presence in Japan is a first priority.

5. Renegotiation of The Status of Forces Agreement, due to expire in May 1996, should provide a forum for bilateral discus-

sion about the direction and substance of the U.S.–Japanese military relationship in its broadest sense. These talks should emphasize that whatever thorny economic differences chafe the two principals, their overwhelming interests lie in concerting their strengths for universal peace. Bear in mind that any derogation of the military relationship between the two countries will automatically lessen the Northern Pacific's stability.

6. The fount of true change in Japanese foreign behavior sits in the bowels of domestic politics. Ructions in the Diet are, in the main, cosmetic and reactive. Shuffling prime ministers every four or five months embarrasses winner and loser alike and stifles genuine political movement. The present complexion of affairs brooks no delay. Japanese politicians' most important task is arguably the re-education of the electorate and of the bureaucracy to support significant shifts in their nation's life.

From time to time generals and admirals have been pilloried for errors that were not exclusively theirs. What might Japanese military leaders undertake now in order to avoid history's sour judgments?

1. At all costs the military establishment must avoid the reality or appearance of a return to prewar adventurism. Whatever happens to Article 9, its spirit of nonaggression must be preserved.
2. Within the framework of civilian rule military planners must define and publicize the military risks facing Japan in terms the electorate and the bureaucracy can understand. Their lodestar must be the world's bare reality and not the bureaucracy's foggy contrivances. The intellectual link among the people, the government and the military must be tended with infinite care. Reciprocated trust among the three is

essential to political movement. Democracy is still young in Japan and nothing should hinder its maturation.

3. It is imprudent to believe that diplomacy, the U.S. relationship and luck will shield Japan's enormous wealth from intrusion by the envious. Japan lives in a rough neighborhood. If the Japanese Self-Defense Force is to operate on the American model, it should nonetheless pursue a Japanese purpose. That said, Japan must sustain pragmatic military partnerships in order to preserve its foreign fortunes. The Northern Pacific's stability will crumble without a significant and visible American military presence in Japan.

4. Up to now, Japan's foreign aid has been calculated to shore up its commercial endeavors. It has seemed to many like a rich man throwing Twinkies to the crowds from the window of his Rolls-Royce. The reality and the myth must change. The Bank of Japan should not fall into a swoon if Japan's foreign aid spans the entire spectrum of assistance to humanity's truly needy. A Japanese face to disaster relief, peace-keeping, medical and engineering assistance would be no bad thing either. It is a sad fact that poor nations often buy guns before butter. Better that they should build infrastructure using Japanese capital and know-how. The Japanese Self-Defense Force should be part and parcel of such efforts.

5. New military planning needs new assumptions. The American nuclear umbrella that shielded Japan's mercantilist cocoon has lost its value because the principal nuclear enemy no longer exists. Similarly, America can no longer afford ubiquitous defense for the weak and the ill-favored. The neo-isolationist skewing of American politics does not help either. Clearly, Japan's permanent military stance must include the capacity to resist military blackmail alone or preferably by alliance and to prevent the transfer of nuclear weaponry to outlaw nations. The goal here is to convince possible adversaries from the outset that they will lose a nuclear or con-

ventional confrontation. We must all find ways to collaborate now in peace and not later in calamity.

Neither countries nor individuals get security on the cheap. With it come costs, some quite burdensome. *The Hidden Army* demonstrates why the legalistic formulations that permitted the SDF to function will not suffice for Japan in the twentieth century's waning years. The book is important because it shows how badly the SDF needs new legal, political and strategic justifications. A warning: there is no magic bullet here! Work, patience, trust, forbearance and a little luck accomplish far more than theorists' elegant formulations or politicians' bluster. Mindful of its responsibilities to the electorate and to its civilian leadership the Japanese Self-Defense Force can make substantial contributions to the world's order. And we shall all be grateful for that.

PART I

The Birth of the Self-Defense Forces, 1950–1955

Article 9

Aspiring sincerely to an international peace based on justice and order, the Japanese people forever renounce war as a sovereign right of the nation and the threat or use of force as a means of settling international disputes.

In order to accomplish the aim of the preceding paragraph, land, sea, and air forces, as well as other war potential, will never be maintained. The right of belligerency of the state will not be recognized.[1]

From the Japanese Constitution, Chapter 11 (Renunciation of War).

The Order to Rearm

On June 25, 1950, only five years after the end of World War II, Asian blood flowed again, this time on the Korean peninsula. On the other side of the Tsushima Strait, Japan remained at peace and under United States military occupation. The Imperial armed forces were dissolved; their officers were purged from public service and reviled for leading Japan into disaster. Charred and destroyed buildings remained very much a part of the Japanese landscape. The black market prospered. War orphans and millions of destitute returnees from Japan's colonies abroad were common sights. Japan lay in impoverished chaos. It had lost all its overseas territories and overseas markets; its eighty million people were crammed onto four desolate islands. The mere act of living from day to day was a struggle.

In 1947, Japan had ratified the peace constitution, whose Article 9 renounced war and pledged that Japan would never maintain war potential.[1] War-weary Japanese greeted their new constitution with relief. In 1950, only three years later, Japan's brief period of peace had ended. Amid the frightening news of renewed war, reports circulated that the government was forming a police reserve force. Many were concerned that Japan might return to the failed policies of the past.

Under Allied occupation Japan had no sovereign rights. Even exports of Aritayaki pottery, fired at a famous kiln with centuries of history, bore the ignominious label "Made in Occupied Japan." The General Headquarters (GHQ), under the command of United States General Douglas MacArthur, controlled all of Japan's governing institutions.* GHQ's directives were law. Weak and impotent Japan was putty waiting to be molded by the force of war in Korea. That war's impact would decisively shape the structure and direction of the nation.

The Korean War breathed economic life into Japan as the country met the extraordinary wartime demand for labor and matériel. Some towns and cities, like Sasabo, transformed themselves into workshops to support the United Nations war effort. The financial rewards to Japan were significant.[2] Additional economic benefit came in the form of a 1950 GHQ directive ordering Japan to form a police reserve force, thereby breaking the spirit of the peace constitution. This directive marked the beginnings of a stealthy tiptoe toward Japanese rearmament that quietly pushed aside some of the ideals of the infant constitution. The pacifism and disarmament that MacArthur had so forcefully and tirelessly promoted in Japan soon ended. In their place came an implacable conflict between economic prosperity and the realization of constitutional ideals that has never been fully resolved.

By 1950 the World War II alliance of the United States and the Soviet Union was a fading memory. Across Europe and Asia the gloomy front lines of East-West confrontation hardened. Many Japanese hoped that physical separation from Asia's mainland would perpetuate political separation from that continent's problems as well. As the war heated up on the Korean peninsula, the supreme commander of the allied powers in

---

*Editor's Note: Japanese lower courts retained the right to try and to sentence American service personnel for minor offenses such as traffic violations.

Japan, General Douglas MacArthur, also became the commander of the United Nations forces in Korea. Simultaneously, the policies of the Occupation army in Japan changed to reflect developments in Korea and shattered Japan's illusion of isolation from world events.

To General MacArthur, the situation in Korea appeared simple and disheartening. Defeated South Korean troops were on the run. Seoul fell on June 25, three days after the fighting began, and the North Korean army drove hard to the south, herding the South Korean army toward the southernmost city of Pusan. Surveying the battle area by air the day after Seoul fell, MacArthur saw how desperate the military situation had become. "Like Napoléon at Ratisbon, MacArthur stood on a little mound just off the road, clogged with retreating, panting columns of troops interspersed with ambulances filled with groaning, broken men, the sky resonant with shrieking missiles of death and everywhere the stench and misery and utter desolation of a stricken battlefield."[3] Barely ten years had passed since German panzer divisions had pushed the British off the beaches of Dunkirk. Now such an event might be repeated. Only American troops could save the situation, but reinforcements from the United States would arrive too late to prevent defeat. The only realistic course of action entailed the dispatch of troops already in Japan. It was a gambit born of desperation.

At that time, the United States had four divisions of troops stationed in Japan. The Seventh Division was deployed in the north, the Twenty-fifth Division in central Japan, the Twenty-fourth Division in western Japan, and the First Cavalry in Tokyo and the surrounding region. MacArthur dispatched the Twenty-fourth Division, the division that was closest to Korea, on July 3. It saw battle near Taejon and was severely mauled. By July 18, the Twenty-fifth Division and First Cavalry had landed in Korea. Three weeks after the start of the war, the only American troops remaining in Japan were the Seventh Division, in Hokkaido and northern Honshu, and the Air Force.

> MacArthur's hopes that two United States divisions could
> check the enemy had been dashed. Out of condition and out-
> numbered by as much as twenty to one, the first detachments
> to arrive were for the most part green troops; fewer than
> twenty percent had seen action in World War II. Their only
> anti-tank weapons were obsolete bazookas, hopelessly ineffec-
> tive against the very successful Soviet T-34s. Isolated and cut
> off from one another, many, including the commander of the
> Twenty-fourth Division, surrendered in the first days before
> learning that the In Min Gun, the North Korean army, took
> few prisoners. More often than not the In Min Gun tied the
> captives' hands behind their backs and bayoneted them.[4]

The fighting in Korea went badly. Predictably, the combat
ability of the troops on the Korean front lines was marginal.
The main mission of American Occupation troops in Japan
had, after all, been supervision of Japan's reconstruction and
democratic reforms. The troops were more clerks than soldiers.
Because Japanese topography was not suited to mechanized
warfare, "the sad decision had been made to commit no tanks to
the Japan forces," recalled Colonel Frank Kowalski, who was
chief of the GHQ Civil Affairs Section at that time.[5]

As ill suited for combat as these troops were, they were the
only troops available. At that point the North Koreans had almost
won the war. Finally, MacArthur ordered the Seventh Division to
Korea, and by late July, the entire American Occupation army
had crossed the straits to engage the North Korean army.[6]

As Japan emptied of American troops, MacArthur had
another matter of concern to deal with. In his memoirs, *Reminiscences*, he recalled the questions he posed to himself four
days after the start of the war:

> And what of Japan? Japan was where my primary responsibil-
> ity lay. Only a few hours before, my most recent directive
> from Washington had re-iterated that no action I took to pro-

tect South Korea should prejudice the protection of Japan. Could I denude this great bastion of troops without inviting Soviet entry from the north? Could I improvise native forces in Japan sufficient to deter any abortive seizure of that country by an enemy if I took elements of the pitifully thin American forces there and committed them to Korea?[7]

As he surveyed the front lines in Korea for the first time on June 29, it is very likely that MacArthur's idea for a Japanese native force was already forming. After all, MacArthur had already established and led an Asian army in the Philippines before, during, and after World War II. Moreover, Japanese rearmament was rapidly taking shape even as the gunfire roared across the Tsushima Strait. But it remained to write the idea into a GHQ directive in order to begin the process of forming a real Japanese military.

MacArthur delivered his "Memo on Increasing the Japanese Police Force" to Prime Minister Shigeru Yoshida[8] just after nine o'clock on the morning of July 8, 1950.[9] The actual delivery was rather matter-of-fact; Frank Rizzo, the chief of GHQ's Government Section, simply handed the memo over to the Liaison and Coordinating Department of Japan's Foreign Office. By contrast, the memo's contents were quite shocking. Chief secretary to the cabinet Katsuo Okazaki, who received the letter, immediately reported its contents to Prime Minister Yoshida, who called a cabinet meeting to consider its message and the measures necessary to implement it.

The first part of MacArthur's memo stated that Japan's police forces were small relative to the size of the population when compared to those of other democracies. He noted that Japan was peaceful and orderly despite the poverty and other misfortunes that afflicted the country, unlike its neighbors, who had fallen into violence, disorder and lawlessness. He praised Japan's effective police force and the Japanese penchant for obeying laws. The memo then moved on to its heart.

> To maintain this good situation, I believe that Japan has arrived at a point where we must increase and strengthen the Japanese police force because it is at the limit necessary for maintaining the public peace in a democratic society and safeguarding those measures that limit the opportunity for the lawless minority given to breaking laws and disturbing public peace and security. For this reason, I authorize the Japanese government to establish a national police reserve composed of seventy-five thousand members and to increase the staffing of the Maritime Safety Board by an additional eight thousand maritime security staff.

With this memo, MacArthur ordered the establishment of the National Police Reserve. The initial praise of the Japanese people and the use of expressions such as "authorize . . . to establish" did not disguise the fact that this was an order, not a response, to the Japanese government, since the Yoshida cabinet had made no request for any sort of increase. According to Osamu Kaihara, a Police Department official who would later be closely involved in the evolution of the National Police Reserve, the Security Forces, and the Self-Defense Forces, "the 'authorization' had no request connected to it. For someone not aware of the context, the message reads as though the Japanese government had asked for permission and General Headquarters had then granted it. That was not the case."[10]

The government showed a certain amount of confusion as to what GHQ intended the National Police Reserve to be. As the government of an occupied nation, the Yoshida cabinet had no authority to refuse orders from the Occupation army and it immediately set forth policies intended to comply with the directive. Specifically, it created the Police Reserve Establishment Commission. The governor of Kagawa Prefecture, Keikichi Masuhara, who happened to be in Tokyo on another matter, headed the commission, although Masuhara himself had no clear idea what the government wanted him to create. "At that time we knew that the Police Reserve should fulfill functions that the National-Rural Police and local autonomous police forces could not. So we knew that they should carry some sort of weapons, but beyond that, we knew little," Masuhara later said.[11] The phrase "National Police Reserve" translates into the Japanese language as "reserve personnel of the national police." As a consequence, some members of government felt that the memo really was simply an instruction to increase the number of police officers in existing municipal and rural police forces.

While the Japanese groped for a simple understanding of what was required of them, GHQ was plowing full steam ahead with preparations for Japanese rearmament. When GHQ sent the MacArthur memo to the Japanese government, it simultaneously announced the development to the Japanese people through a special proclamation from the GHQ Public Relations Department. The next day, July 9, Colonel Frank Kowalski asked his superior at the GHQ Civil Affairs Section, Major General Winfield Shepard, who was head of the department, for a regimental command in Korea. Shepard refused: "MacArthur has charged me with organizing a Police Reserve. The force will defend Japan, starting with four divisions and seventy-five thousand members. This will be the base from which the future Japanese army will be formed. I need you as my chief of staff, so give up on your idea of Korea."[12]

On July 14, GHQ established the Civil Affairs Staging Area (CASA) in a corner of the main GHQ building, headed by Major General Shepard, with Colonel Kowalski as his chief of staff. Its mission was to create, train, and direct the Police Reserve. Colonel Kowalski was destined never to command a regiment. His first order was to memorize the "Framework for the National Police Reserve," the bible of the Japanese military. Then the colonel, though he was sympathetic to the pacifism of the Japanese constitution, was ordered to organize Japanese rearmament from behind the scenes, which he did faithfully and efficiently, as recorded in his valuable memoirs. The Japanese government could do little but comply.[13] The government created a special section of the National-Rural Police Headquarters and appointed Yozo Kato and Osamu Kaihara to lead the police organization. They deftly laid the groundwork for the creation of the National Police Reserve. GHQ provided the "Framework for the National Police Reserve" to them on July 17, and the Japanese government formally put Governor Masuhara in charge of overseeing the Japanese proposal for organization and composition of the force.

The National Police Reserve formally began life on August 10, 1950. Its fundamental legal and organizational structure had five points:

(1) The Police Reserve shall be a peacekeeping force that deals with civil unrest, public violence, and the like.
(2) The Police Reserve shall have a national command, under which the country will be divided into four regional districts, each with its own regional district division.
(3) The prime minister shall have direct jurisdiction and under him will be a minister of state responsible solely for the Police Reserve.
(4) The prime minister shall appoint a commander of Police Reserve Headquarters who will lead the Police Reserve.
(5) The peacekeeping police units shall have mobility and armaments suitable for their function, namely, pistols and other small arms.

By this point, even those who had thought of the new Police Reserve as a seventy-five-thousand-man increase in personnel could see that it was going to be much more than that. Its structure and character were radically different from the existing police forces, and its mission would clearly evolve with the unfolding of events abroad. It was also easy to see that the four regional district divisions were going to fill the gap left by the four departing American divisions. Masuhara recalled the spirit of those times:

> The reserve started with the creation of four divisions. Within these we deployed the seventy-five-thousand-member force. First, the Americans gave us carbines and light machine guns, then heavier machine guns, then bazookas, and so on. Although the outlines were sketchy, the newspapers instantly began calling the reserve a Japanese rearmament and the formation of a new Japanese army. My feeling is that the newspapers intuitively picked up on what was really going on, and when the Japanese population read the media reports, they agreed. In my view, most Japanese people understood this to mean there would soon be another Japanese military. My friends and others told me to give up this task, that it was too soon after such a devastating defeat to build an army, in particular if it were to be aimed at the Soviet Union. People told me, in all seriousness, to be careful of my life. I received kind advice from many different people. I think the idea of anything like a military arising again generally aroused very visceral feelings.[14]

The government could hardly admit that it was rearming when Article 9 of the constitution renounced war as a "sovereign right of the nation" and pledged that "land, sea, and air forces, as well as other war potential, will never be maintained." Additionally, the Yoshida government worried that the Korean War and the proclamation of a socialist state in China the previous autumn would embolden the domestic Japanese revolutionary movement, especially the Japan Communist Party. The public remained very supportive of the peace constitution. "The disastrous failure of the foreign policy of the military and the terrible suffering of the war years produced a revulsion against military leadership and any form of militarism. The Japanese longed for eternal peace and swung rapidly from seeing themselves as a warrior race to becoming the most passionate of pacificists."[15] The government took a pragmatic approach. It could not in any way promote a policy of rearmament and stay in office, so it never made any attempt to rewrite the constitution to create the option of legal rearmament. The sole remaining option was to bypass the Diet, Japan's bicameral parliament, and to create a police reserve under the authority of GHQ, which, as the supreme legal authority under the provisions of the Potsdam Declaration, outranked the constitution. MacArthur wanted speed. He ordered Yoshida to create the Police Reserve by executive authority. Yoshida became a master in applying the advice given to him by the last wartime premier, Admiral Kantaro Suzuki: "It is important to be a good winner in a war, but it is equally important to be a good loser."[16]

On July 21, Eiichi Nishimura, of the Opposition Socialist Party Japan, proposed to the Foreign Affairs Committee of the lower house of the Diet (the House of Representatives) that the National Police Reserve be established only after debate in the Diet.[17] Yoshida refused to debate the issue: "Because the government is responsible for maintaining the public peace, we want to give this matter complete consideration and are currently studying the matter intensively. The organization and budget of such a group are still the matter of debate. To be perfectly honest, we are not yet ready to present a proposal. Once we do have something to present, we will entertain questions. So while it is a matter of some regret, there is nothing more I can say on this matter at this time." In reality, budgeting, recruitment, and deployment of the National Police Reserve were already underway. The government clearly had no intention of seeking the approval of the people, but was set on presenting its actions as a fait accompli.

On August 10, the government issued the Police Reserve Ordinance, Government Ordinance Number 260 under the Potsdam Declaration, which was implemented the following day. Under the Potsdam Declaration, government ordinances based on GHQ directives were ipso facto law even without Diet approval. No other major act so demonstrates the reach of

Occupation authority. The ordinance stated the purpose of the Police Reserve:

Article 1: The purpose of this ordinance is to establish a police reserve and make stipulations for its organization, etc., in order to maintain peace and order within Japan and to provide supplementary police power for the National-Rural Police and the police forces of local authorities to the extent necessary to protect public welfare.

Its duties were defined as follows:

Article 3: (1) The Police Reserve shall be under the command of the prime minister when there is a special need to protect public security. (2) Actions of the Police Reserve shall be limited to those that fall within the duties of police, and its functions shall not be exercised to infringe upon the rights and freedoms of individuals guaranteed by the constitution of Japan.

Although the words of the ordinance were carefully chosen, those on the inside clearly realized that the nascent organization was an embryonic military force. Colonel Kowalski, chief of staff of the GHQ Civil Affairs Staging Area called it Japan's "big lie:" "America, and myself as an individual as well, were about to initiate Japan's 'big lie.' This lie was to proclaim to the world that the Japanese constitution meant what it said and that troops and small arms and tanks and mortars and rockets and fighter aircraft were not really weapons of war. Japanese and Americans together were desecrating and trampling a national constitution that was one of the greatest achievements in human political history."[18]

GHQ's immense authority as the occupying power and MacArthur's own personal authority eviscerated the pacifist Japan they had worked so hard to construct, and rearmament began. By the time the East-West Cold War hardened with the blockading of West Berlin and the formation of the North Atlantic Treaty Organization (NATO), the "hot war" in Korea had already brought Japan into the conflict. In the months following the outbreak of hostilities along the thirty-eighth parallel in Korea, Japan was transformed into the forward staging base for the United Nations command's operations on the mainland of East Asia. This transformation occurred with the full support, not merely the acquiescence, of the Yoshida government, which was vehemently anticommunist and anti-Soviet. The cabinet secretary told reporters, "If we can make no direct contribution, we, at least, can maintain order here, and act as General MacArthur will want us to act, and free American soldiers from Occupation duty so they can take the field of battle where they are needed."[19]

2

The Inauguration
of the Police Reserve

On October 9, 1950, the top uniformed Police Reserve officer, Keizo Hayashi, addressed the first group of Police Reserve staff. Like Keikichi Masuhara, Hayashi had been a career member of the civilian Ministry of Home Affairs, where he had served as vice chairman to the emperor, and he had never worn an imperial military uniform. Some uniformed officers resented this background; they called him an imperial courtier behind his back. This was Hayashi's first address wearing the uniform of Police Reserve commandant. The staff and assembled American advisors were eager to hear what he would say.

> What are the fundamental concepts behind this new police reserve created by a new Japan? I say the first is patriotism and love for the Japanese people. To put it simply, patriotism is the spirit of caring for our brothers, and working so that our parents, brothers, sisters, wives, and children can live and thrive in peace. The second is to never forget that this reserve is the reserve of the Japanese people. We must flow like life's blood through the national population, pursuing our work aided by their total cooperation. The people will rely on us to act like reserve members in every aspect of our daily lives, and we must both strive for the worthy compassion that will win respect and always conduct ourselves in a manly fashion.

As Hayashi continued, he elaborated the other principles that should define the work of the Police Reserve. The third was to be incorruptible; the fourth, to be modest; the fifth, to defend public institutions vigilantly; the sixth, to cultivate common sense; the seventh, to respect science and technology; and the eighth, to remember the value of teamwork. These ideals were a world apart from those the military had lived by a scant five years before. No longer were conscripts brutalized within their units to make them loyal to the emperor. The old conventional wisdom was that troops were like drums—they sound better when beaten regularly. The new troops were volunteers. They were loyal to the constitution, not to the emperor, and they were not instructed to fight to the death. The Americans in Hayashi's audience stiffened initially at the first principle— patriotism and loving the Japanese people. But as they listened they understood that this was not fanatic emperor worship, but a gentler concept directed at the family and the home. The Japanese replaced the old emphasis on spiritual absolutism and hand-to-hand combat with a focus on ideas like common sense and science and technology. The concept of team work replaced blind devotion to carrying out whatever a superior commanded, and for this term Hayashi used a word of foreign origin emphasizing order and cohesion. There was no mistaking that the Japanese government was attempting to create an army that was radically different in character from the imperial Japanese military.

The new ideas may have been too different, and may have represented too sudden a change. Both in appearance and in substance, the Police Reserve was "Made in Occupied Japan," more American than Japanese. The government's first priorities had originally been to win public recognition and support for rearming, to train the nucleus of an officer corps, and then to start recruiting personnel for the reserve. Because of war developments in Korea, though, GHQ unilaterally dictated the procedures for establishing, recruiting, and deploying the Police Reserve. The order of priorities was therefore reversed. First, members would be recruited, and then officers would be trained and commissioned. In order to accomplish these goals, American models had to be followed.

This rearrangement of priorities resulted in some unusual situations. For example, the military leader of the new uniformed force of seventy-five thousand men was a court official with no military history. His appointment as commandant and his inaugural address were delayed until early October, by which time the deployment of reserve troops was largely complete. For three months after MacArthur issued his memo, GHQ and the Japanese government argued over the character of the new military and its leadership. Finally they agreed on appointing a civilian as commandant, rather than an ex-imperial officer. The selection and appointment of commanders to lead regional district units were even more protracted. These delays did not, however, prevent the recruitment, assembly, movement, and deployment of enlisted men, with the result that units without officers began to appear around Japan.

The announcement for recruitment of enlisted men was posted on August 9, one month after MacArthur's memo. The recruitment began in earnest on August 13, when offices were opened at police stations throughout Japan. The deadline for applying was the 15th, testing was to begin on the 17th, and members were to assemble at regional police academies for training on the 23rd. The GHQ order stated that Japan had to complete assembly of qualified members by October 12. This schedule was coordinated with the transfer of American troops to the front lines in Korea and allowed no time for discussion or delay.

"Peaceful Japan Wants You," the reserve recruitment posters said, with a picture of a flying crane. Conditions for employment were as follows:

(1) Members of the Police Reserve are public servants with a special mission.
(2) Police Reserve members will all be housed in standard housing without charge for training and service.
(3) The monthly allowance is ¥5,000, with incremental raises.
(4) The period of service is two years, at the end of which a severance payment of ¥60,000 shall be paid.
(5) All clothing and meals shall be supplied.
(6) Police Reserve members must be men between the ages of twenty and thirty-five.
(7) Police Reserve members must be at least 156 centimeters in height with uncorrected vision of 0.3 or better.

The monthly pay of ¥5,000 (later reduced to ¥4,500) was twenty percent higher than the salary of a regular police officer, and the addition of clothing and food made it very attractive. The payment of ¥60,000 after only two years of service made the enticement overwhelming for hungry young men. The average monthly pay of a twenty-year-old graduate of one of the old middle schools at that time was around ¥3,000. Seeing a movie at that time cost ¥60, a bowl of noodles cost ¥20, and a glass of beer or sake cost ¥400. One village mayor in Shimane Prefecture even quit his job to apply for the Police Reserve.

Despite the brevity of the announcement and the short three-day application period, 382,003 men applied for the seventy-five thousand positions. The fact that so many young men could be induced to apply in such an extremely short period of time despite the strong social disapproval facing the Police Reserve showed just how attractive the financial inducements were.

The testing of applicants was conducted on August 17 in 183 police stations, police academies, and other sites around the country. The local police chiefs checked the references and background of the successful examinees and posted their names at the test sites that very day. Others were listed as standbys. A total of 74,580 men was selected. The successful applicants were told when and where to assemble and were given the rank of police officer second-class, a new title combining aspects of police and military titles. The Japanese bureaucracy managed to achieve recruitment and assembly of Police Reserve personnel with great efficiency in a period of only eleven days.

Although the new national army had obtained the desired number of enlisted men, it remained without a commandant and could not function as a military organization. The new police troops went to their designated locations and found no platoon or squad leaders from whom to take orders. Out of desperation, the government called in the American army to manage the recruits. *The First Ten Years of the Self-Defense Forces*, published by Japan's Defense Agency, states that, "during this period, American camp commanders were the ones really in charge of some personnel matters and of giving orders for most management and operations. From time to time, some camps experienced a lack of mutual understanding, leading to ambivalence." Even the most conservative accounts refer to early problems of leadership in the SDF.

The absence of officers was due to the fact that GHQ had purged, or barred from public service, most imperial officers.[20] Neither GHQ nor the Japanese government wanted to use men with a record of prior imperial service in the new organization. As a result, a headless Japanese military formed on the American bases and began training under American drill instructors.

The recruits who entered the American camp at Osaka's Shinodayama were surprised at the troop entrance when an American major greeted them with the words, "I'm the camp commander." There were no Japanese officers. Of the twelve hundred Japanese at the camp, all were enlisted men. They were outfitted in the khaki summer uniforms and service caps of the old Imperial Army and American-issue high-top boots. Training drills were all American style—"Don't aim, shoot as

17

you charge." The Americans did not use the familiar phrases of the Imperial Army, such as "attack divided units" and "advance on all fours." The Americans said "eyes right" in English, which they then had translated into archaic Japanese rather than using the standard Japanese equivalent, *kashira migi* (head right). Military courtesies were neither Japanese nor American. "The National Police Reserve looked as though it had been made in the United States. On a visit to one of the training camps, I thought at first I had stumbled into an American base, for everything from guns to fatigues was G.I."[21]

According to Colonel Frank Kowalski, chief of staff for the Civil Affairs Staging Area, the military situation in Korea was the driving force behind the Police Reserve. In his Japanese language memoir, *Nihon Saigunbi*, he recalled the following:

> With Americans being chewed up in the bloody battlefield of Korea, we at least had to put together a military in Japan that could march in formation and display some fighting credibility. Even a single combat unit was a lot more important than the Headquarters in Tokyo. Should the need arise for the Police Reserve to fight, we, the American advisors, could handle the task of commanding them in battle. Lieutenant Colonel Alberghetti was head of the Advisory Group Strategy Section and created a thirteen-week training schedule to start the men on formation and firing drills, even though we were short on boots and hadn't handed out even carbines yet.
>
> The new members of the reserve were of a lot better quality than the average recruit, and that made these officers' work fairly easy. First, the seventy-five thousand were selected from among almost four hundred thousand applicants, and over half of them had experience in the Imperial Army. Many of them had been petty officers and some had actual fighting experience. The average age was twenty-six. I guess it is surprising how well Americans and Japanese got along in this strange early period with its hybrid structure. The Japanese somehow managed to elect sergeants, platoon commanders, and corporals. Battalions were formed and Americans managed these troops like a private army.[22]

When the last American division stationed in Japan was moved to Korea on September 10, the Military Assistance Advisory Group (MAAG) was given strict orders by GHQ to deploy ten thousand Police Reserve troops in Hokkaido. GHQ could not wait for the Japanese to finish their preparations. When the trains transporting the Seventh Division rolled out of Makomanai Camp, Colonel Kowalski arranged for the trains bearing the Police Reserve troops to roll into the camp in perfect synchronization. Drill instructors on the trains taught the recruits while they were in transit how to load and fire the carbines. By September 10, 1950, Colonel Kowalski had stationed ten thousand Police Reserve troops in Hokkaido.

Naturally, both the Japanese and Americans knew their command system was not normal. Moreover, dissatisfaction grew daily among the police officers second-class as they trained on bases flying American flags under American instructors giving orders through interpreters. Some recruits dropped out, purportedly because of humiliation.

Since GHQ and Yoshida had decided not to use former imperial military officers, the Police Reserve aggressively promoted ordinary privates to higher rank. The American troops selected privates at each camp and sent them to the American training facility at Etajima for four-week courses to prepare them to become platoon commanders. The trainees were then promoted to police officers first-class (the equivalent of first lieutenant) or to police aides (the equivalent of petty officer). This program was adequate to create enough platoon commanders and squad leaders, but a shortfall of middle- and high-ranking officers continued to plague the military buildup.

In an attempt to correct this situation, GHQ and Yoshida agreed on a minor revision to the policy banning ex–imperial officers from the Police Reserve. They decided to accept applications from Japanese officers who had served in the one-time Manchuguo Army and from captains and lieutenants of the old

Imperial Army who had not been subject to the Public Official Purge Ordinance. This action provided a middle-rank officer group of eight hundred men, but it still left a shortage. To achieve a radical resolution, before long the decision would be made to introduce top-level imperial officers by rescinding their purges.

The United States had aready set up troop organization, management, supply methods, and the like on the American model, however, and little room remained for Japanese to exercise autonomy and creative capacity. Yet as these new personnel, especially those who had combat experience, entered the Police Reserve, it was slowly de-Americanized.

Although the new Police Reserve was now up and running, postwar Japan lacked the technological or industrial base at that time to support it. American air raids had thoroughly destroyed the munitions factories of the Imperial Army and the Imperial Navy. GHQ orders dissolving the *zaibatsu* (industrial conglomerates) had thrown Mitsubishi Heavy Industries and other large civilian factories into disarray. The remaining factories had turned exclusively to the production of consumer goods like pots and pans. GHQ directives had also outlawed the production of and research on any form of weapon; consequently, Japan could not produce bombs or trucks, let alone tanks and artillery, for the Police Reserve.

GHQ and the Civil Affairs Staging Area were well aware of this problem, and decided that the United States would supply the Police Reserve. *The First Ten Years of the Self-Defense Forces* described the situation: "The primary matériel for starting up the Police Reserve was received on loan from the American forces in Japan. These supplies were not provided under a formal agreement with the United States but were simply loaned from American army weapons stockpiles. The United States government owned all the equipment, and the United States military did the repairs and maintenance."

The Americans called this system the Special Far Eastern Requisitions Plan (SFRP). American military advisors received weapons from American stocks and rapidly supplied the Police Reserve with the equipment it needed for its duties. The Japan–United States Military Support Agreement (MSA) formalized the transfer of weapons to Japan in 1954, when the Self-Defense Forces were launched. Temporary loans to the Police Reserve, requisitioned from American supplies by the military advisors, were accepted practice for four years.

The carbines that were supplied to all the Japanese camps by October 1950 were followed by machine guns, rocket launchers, and howitzers. In the same month, the war in Korea entered a new phase when Chinese troops crossed the border into Korea. Tensions across Asia rose rapidly. The political confrontation between the United States and the Soviet Union escalated, prompting the United States to increase its efforts in arming the Police Reserve. The types of weapons that were available expanded the following year to include 105-millimeter and 155-millimeter artillery, incendiary projectiles, and medium-size tanks. The Police Reserve began to look like and feel like an army.

The United States military was also deeply involved in organizing troops. Mirroring the organization of the United States Army, the Police Reserve was organized into four management district units under a central command in Tokyo. These units were equivalent to United States Army divisions, and were based in Tokyo, Sapporo, Osaka, and Fukuoka. Under the district units were regiments, companies and other smaller units. The Police Reserve was purposely planned as a small carbon copy of the United States military, because the Police Reserve was not really a reserve for the Japanese national police so much as a reserve for the United States forces that were stationed in Japan. The government, the public, and the military were all tacitly aware of the Police Reserve's true function.

They assumed that Japan and the United States would cooperate strategically in the future, and that the two armies therefore needed to have common organization, matériel, supply, and communications systems. Colonel Kowalski of the Military Assistance Advisory Group continually emphasized the advantages of using a common organizational scheme for the United States military and the Japanese Police Reserve, and of making the Reserve "a smaller version of the United States Army."

The aftereffects of the summer and autumn of 1950 would continue to shape Japan long after they had become a memory. The development of the Police Reserve was the third largest organized movement of people and material since the end of the war, exceeded only by the influx of Occupation troops and the return of Japanese from abroad. When the first stage had passed, many Japanese noticed that Japan was an utterly different country.

The government announced the appointment of emperor's vice chairman and former Ministry of Home Affairs official Keizo Hayashi as commandant of the Police Reserve about the same time that the American advisory group assigned the last recruits to units for basic training. Commandant Hayashi's address signaled a complete break with the imperial military and called for a new kind of patriotism, but by his very presence he ironically illustrated just how far the new military was from those ideals. Hayashi himself immediately confronted difficulties in directing the unconstitutional miniature American army that went under the name of Police Reserve. Colonel Kowalski records the following conversation with Commandant Hayashi:

> One day, Commandant Hayashi came into my office with an expression on his face that said he just couldn't take this any more.
> "So what exactly are we forming here, an army or a police force?" he burst out.

"You should know the answer to that," I said respectfully.

"I know. But it's getting impossible! Can you write something as inane as that a police unit is attacking a pillbox with artillery and incendiary rockets? I know we have to replace words like 'pillbox,' and 'artillery,' and 'incendiary rockets' with less military-sounding words, but in Japan we use Chinese characters to form these words and it's extremely difficult because they're based on meaning, not sound. You understand? We're already calling tanks 'special vehicles,' but are we supposed to call artillery 'special instruments'? Are incendiary rockets 'special firing devices'?"

Hayashi was in a state. "Am I supposed to say 'The police encountered the pillbox with special instruments'?"[23]

After that, Kowalski said, they both burst out laughing until tears were rolling down their cheeks, probably as much out of frustration as out of humor.

3

The Return
of Imperial Officers

When Keizo Hayashi became commandant of the Police Reserve, he at first encountered extraordinary personnel problems. A fight continued between ex–military men and Ministry of Home Affairs police officials over the appointment of upper-level officers to posts that were still vacant. Groups of imperial officers tried to insinuate themselves surreptitiously into the nucleus of the new Japanese military. Men from the old national police force linked with men from the old Ministry of Home Affairs, such as Police Reserve director Keikichi Masuhara, strongly opposed the imperial officers. Additionally, the Second Section of GHQ's General Staff Office (G2), which was responsible for Police Reserve recruitment, supported the ex-military group, while the Civil Affairs Section (GS), which was responsible for Police Reserve personnel supported the former Ministry of Home Affairs group. Behind-the-scenes conflicts at GHQ were yet another element in this stew of machinations, all hidden from the public eye. The government did not issue the official announcement of the troop command corps, regulations promulgating unit composition and organization, until December 29, 1950, a full four months after the Police Reserve was created.

The most difficult issues facing the Police Reserve concerned the civilian control of the military, a concept of military management that was completely unfamiliar to the Japanese, and the question of whether to commission purged former Imperial Army and Imperial Navy officers in the officer corps. These issues were also closely related to GHQ's Occupation policies and to the basic attitude of the Yoshida cabinet. Whatever approach the government selected, major political problems were sure to arise in its wake.

For the Americans, the idea that a civilian would hold ultimate authority over the Police Reserve was so natural that there was no debate. For the Japanese, the principle of having an officer in ultimate control of the military had been unchallenged since the creation of the modern army in the early Meiji Period (1868-1912), and they did not take easily to the American idea of civilian control. Director Masuhara was among those who objected to the American plan. He proposed an organization in which there was no distinction between line (military) and staff (civilian) like the organization that the police employed. The Americans wanted a clear separation between line and staff. They saw the head of the Police Reserve as equivalent to the American secretary of defense and instructed the Japanese that a civilian official had to have ultimate authority over the military. Colonel Kowalski described it as being like a seminar in which his superior, Major General Shepard, stubbornly explained the concept of ultimate civilian control to Director Masuhara. He wrote that, "In the West, the principle of civilian rule over a country's military was an inviolable principle. We were bowled over that even those people in Japan who seemed to have the most democratic thinking should find it so hard to understand."[24]

Masuhara recorded his own impression of this discussion in his memoirs:

They said things like, considering all the evil done by Japan's military and militarist parties in the recent war, why not create a Police Reserve organization that uses the American principle of "civilian supremacy." That was the word he used, although actually he was ordering us to do it. We threw ourselves into studying this in a great hurry, questioning, talking it out, reading up, and when we discussed it with Prime Minister Yoshida, he said it was great idea and that we should go with it. But then the [United States military] advisors came up with difficult orders, like they wanted us to limit the civilians to only one hundred people, and that had to include everyone from janitors to drivers. We had to create a staff directly belonging to the Police Reserve with a core of about one hundred people to implement the so-called civilian supremacy. We then had to organize the uniformed troops under the control of that staff.[25]

This staff of one hundred developed into the Defense Agency bureaus. It worked under the director general of the Defense Agency and was often called the defense bureaucracy, or the internal bureaus. Matters of military policy, such as setting policy, planning budgets, and issuing executive orders, that had been the province of the prewar army and navy ministries, which had been completely staffed by officers, were now controlled by civilian bureaucrats. Since defense bureaucrats had also gained the right to stand between the military and the director general and even to oversee orders given by military commands responsible for strategy and operations, the system of civilian supremacy turned out to be stronger in Japan than in the United States itself. This system was then transferred to the Self-Defense Forces when the SDF succeeded the Police Reserve.

The following men headed the first civilian defense bureaucracy:

- Police Bureau secretary: Eizo Ishii (former police official)
- Personnel Bureau secretary: Yozo Kato (former police official)

- Accounting Bureau secretary: Naomitsu Kubotani (former Ministry of Finance official)
- Security Bureau secretary: Masaharu Gotoda (former police official)
- Personnel Section secretary: Nobuyoshi Magari (former police official)
- Weapons Section secretary: Shigeru Aso (former police official)
- Accounting Section secretary: Ippei Kaneko (former Ministry of Finance official)

All these men had also been career bureaucrats in the prewar Ministry of Home Affairs who had worked on police affairs. Civilian supremacy in Japan meant that the police were directing rearmament. This was a useful political gambit, because the government could rightly claim that the new military was, true to its name, a police reserve.

After the Japanese completed their crash study of civilian control, they applied it to the new organization without particular resistance. When it came time to appoint the military's executive staff, however, and in particular someone to command the military, it was not so easy to patch together consensus. Even after the former imperial officers had abandoned hope of setting military policy, they stood firm on the subject of giving military orders and directing troops in the field. Major General Charles A. Willoughby, the head of the information department of the G2 Section, who had participated in the recruitment operations for the Police Reserve, had joined the military personnel operations as a strong supporter of the ex-military men. An officers group represented by Colonel Takushiro Hattori, who had been the strategic operations chief of the Imperial Army general staff and secretary to Army Minister Hideki Tojo, worked frenetically to convince Major General Willoughby to inject the old military traditions into the new military.[26]

Major General Willoughby was one of the Bataan Gang, who had been with MacArthur from Melbourne to Tokyo; MacArthur called him "my beloved fascist." He had been charged by MacArthur with editing his war history as a sideline to his regular work as head of G2 in dismantling Japanese military institutions and demobilizing the troops. Colonel Hattori was Willoughby's Japanese counterpart in organizing Japanese war history materials. As the intensifying confrontation between the United States and the Soviet Union developed into the Cold War, these two men's views of the world situation drew steadily closer. When war broke out in Korea and GHQ decided to create the Police Reserve, Willoughby's G2 Section was already in charge of overseeing the Japanese police structure through the Public Safety Department. G2 was thus able to influence, if not control, recruitment and personnel operations for the Police Reserve. This action was the root of the feud between G2 and GS (which included the Civil Affairs Section and CASA).

As Willoughby envisioned the Police Reserve, the general staff officers group led by Hattori would control the executive staff of the military as heirs of the Japanese Imperial Army. Since GHQ had spared Colonel Hattori and other old soldiers from being purged by garaging them in the military history section of the Demobilization Bureau, their case was stronger. Willoughby ordered Hattori to select four hundred high-ranking officers from the old Imperial Army for the Police Reserve. The new chief of staff, naturally, was to be none other than Takushiro Hattori.

As Keikichi Masuhara and others from the national police staff of the Ministry of Home Affairs engrossed themselves in creating the new Police Reserve, work was also proceeding steadily from another direction, with a different agenda. Masuhara recounts the following exchange with Yozo Kato, the first Personnel Bureau secretary:

Kato: The recruitment of troops had begun and they had started assembling at the end of August; but the executive staff was not yet selected. The Americans had said there would be about four hundred men in the executive staff, so we had informally decided to use former imperial regular officers.

Masuhara: At that moment, seven or eight men suddenly burst into my office. Takushiro Hattori and other imperial officers were among them. "We are going to be working at the Police Reserve," they announced.[27]

Major General Shepard said there was someone he wanted me to meet, and then he introduced Colonel Takushiro Hattori. Shepard had heard from General Headquarters that the military units would be built around this person, so he wanted Hattori to talk to me. I was quite astonished [since that was presumably my role]. According to Colonel Hattori, he had been called by Major General Willoughby, told to work in the Police Reserve, and told to pick former military officers of ability to serve as the core of the executive staff. And today Shepard had brought Hattori to introduce him to me. He was supposed to contact Major General Willoughby over every single detail, like troop composition, but they were told to keep the director (me) in the dark. It was really unexpected for me. But we were both Japanese, Colonel Hattori said, so he had decided to take me into his confidence.[28]

This happened at the beginning of August. Masuhara was very angry to learn that someone elsewhere was planning a structure that he was unaware of. He informed Prime Minister Yoshida of the plot being planned by Willoughby and the Hattori group. Prime Minister Yoshida had opposed the use of ex-imperial officers from the start. He had been incarcerated by the military police as a suspected member of an antimilitary movement during the Tojo administration; consequently, the idea of a man like Hattori, who had been a secretary to Prime Minister Tojo, becoming a member of the executive staff of the Police Reserve probably seemed absurd. Domestic and international concern that a rearmament had begun under militarists from the past was sure to follow. Yoshida turned to the only person he knew who could control Major General Willoughby, and that was MacArthur himself. Through direct negotiations, a decision was reached to eliminate Hattori, and on August 9, the government specifically announced, under the name of Director Masuhara, that the former officers who were being supported by G2, including Hattori, would not be appointed. On the 18th, it was publicly announced that no purged officer would be appointed to the executive staff.

Once this consensus over the executive staff was reached, the name of Keizo Hayashi, a Ministry of Home Affairs bureaucrat was put forward. Hayashi had no military background, and at that time served as the emperor's palace vice chairman. Yoshida gained the approval of the emperor, and the path was cleared for Hayashi to be named the commandant. But Willoughby felt uneasy about this choice of personnel and delayed his approval of the nomination for a month. The result was that, through one scheme or another, the appointment of a commander in chief for the new Police Reserve was delayed a full four months after the reserve was started.

Hayashi was also reluctant. Despite the fact that his father had been a lieutenant general of the army, Hayashi had been a career member of the Ministry of Home Affairs since his Tokyo University days. He was at first resolute in his desire not to abandon his calling, but Prime Minister Yoshida and Hayashi's older colleague Masuhara persuaded him to accept the appointment as first commandant of the Police Reserve. Later as the first chief of staff of the Ground Self-Defense Force, and then as the chairman of the joint staff council, he led the military for its first fourteen years from Police Reserve to Self-Defense Forces. Like Hayashi, the majority of personnel appointed to the military executive staff came from the Ministry of Home Affairs. The commanders of the four regional districts and their previous posts were as follows:

- First Regional District (Tokyo): Chuichi Yoshida (vice governor of Saitama Prefecture)
- Second Regional District (Sapporo): Toshio Nakano (National Police, chief of Sapporo Regional District Headquarters)
- Third Regional District (Osaka): Hiroshi Obayashi (chief of Chiba Prefecture Police Headquarters)
- Fourth Regional District (Fukuoka): Takeo Tsutsui (former colonial governor of Hwanghae Province in Korea)

Despite the strong effort to exclude former members of the imperial military and to break all ties to militarist traditions, that policy quickly failed. Whenever the former officers lost one battle, they began waiting for their next chance. They lobbied the Occupation army to depurge them. The former imperial officers moved step by step to establish themselves in the new military organization, advancing in tempo with the Police Reserve's move from carbine rifles and machine guns to bazookas and tanks.

The permanent exclusion of former imperial officers failed for two reasons. First, the war in Korea had become more intense.* With the entry of communist China into the war, the importance placed by America on its bases in Japan and on Japanese rearmament grew. The Police Reserve became more military than ever. That made it more difficult to ignore the much-needed skills of former military men. GHQ began to soften its attitude toward depurging ex–military men.

Second, though line and staff for the new military were clearly delineated by the use of former Ministry of Home Affairs and police officials, the defense bureaucracy adopted a strongly deferential attitude toward line officers in military

---

*Editor's Note: Ultimately military forces from the United Kingdom, France, Greece, Australia, Canada, and the Philippines fought under United Nations command.

affairs. The police knew nothing about operating tanks and attacking fortifications, and it would be some time before new officers could be trained. The Cold War was not slowing down; the Police Reserve needed fighting ability immediately. With GHQ softening its stance, the idea of commissioning former imperial officers resurfaced at the end of 1950. As recalled by Eizo Ishii, a staff member who was the first Personnel Bureau secretary and who later returned to the police to become director of the Police Agency, GHQ achieved an understanding with the former imperial officers:

> For those reasons, we had gone to extremes over the men who would occupy the ranks at the top, like division commanders, but there was still a problem of what we were going to do about the people at the ranks below that. Many of the men who had been in the military before didn't have any respect for the abilities of men who had been Ministry of Home Affairs and police officials, and they told enlisted men not to obey their orders and to generally look the other way.
>
> The civilian officers responded that they were only temporarily in charge, and that they would put men with military skills in command positions, and let everyone do what he was best at. Units would have competent men in the proper positions to command and so they asked the rank and file for a little patience. Mr. Masuhara and I met with the class secretaries of the Military Academy classes and earnestly laid out all our concerns to them. For the first time, we got them to agree to cooperate. The class secretaries then explained the situation to the Regional District Divisions and told them if they wanted to obey, they could. It was the first time we had gotten them to say this.[29]

With these new circumstances, the government abandoned its guiding plan to not commission former imperial regular officers for at least one year. Prime Minister Yoshida approved this opening of the door, but only with the proviso that every individual be subjected to a thorough investigation.

First, the fifty-eighth class of the Military Academy and the seventy-fourth class of the Naval Academy, who held the rank of second lieutenant or ensign at the end of the war, were depurged in November 1950. Two hundred and forty-five of them, the first crop of officers, were commissioned as reserve officers on June 1, 1951. To reinforce the upper and middle classes of officers of the Police Reserve Headquarters, army colonels and majors and navy captains and commanders with exceptional experience in military affairs, tactics, and leadership began to be admitted in August 1951. Around this time, Director Masuhara and Personnel Bureau secretary Ishii made their appeal for cooperation to the Military Academy class secretaries. As a result, seventeen hundred letters of invitation were issued; nine hundred officers replied. On October 1, a total of 406 qualifiers entered service.

The commissioning of former imperial officers into the officer corps continued thereafter. In 1952, the Police Reserve was opened to colonels, majors, captains, and commanders who had graduated from the Military Academy and the War College. Even some who had been decision makers in directing the war in the Military Affairs Office and General Staff Headquarters of the Army Ministry were accepted for military service upon a special recommendation. This prerogative did not extend as far as admitting men like Colonel Takushiro Hattori, but some members of the Hattori group were commissioned, including Colonel Susumu Nishiura, who was secretary to Army Minister Tojo and chief war historian for the Defense Agency, and Colonel Iwaichi Fujiwara, who was head of the First Division of the Self-Defense Forces. The defense bureaucracy also eventually welcomed Colonel Ichiji Sugita, who was Seventeenth Area army general staff and Fourth Ground SDF chief of staff, and Colonel Kumao Imoto, who was secretary to Army Minister Tojo and the fifth president of the Ground Self-Defense Force Officer's Training School, both of whom had worked in the G2 War History Department under Major General Willoughby.

In the end, more than five thousand regular officers who had graduated from the former imperial military schools entered the military in the Police Reserve and the early Self-Defense Forces years. They continued to have a major impact on the military in Japan for the next thirty-six years, until the last member to come from the former Imperial Army, chairman of the joint staff council Shigehiro Mori, retired in 1987. Mori graduated in the sixtieth, and last, class of the imperial Military Academy, entered the Police Reserve in 1950, and retired in 1987.

One of the men who entered the Police Reserve in 1951, Hiroomi Kurisu, rose to become Ground SDF chief of staff and eventually became chairman of the joint staff council. He was not a Military Academy graduate and the Dutch had delayed his repatriation from Indonesia to Japan until 1949. He remembered this period:

> I heard news that the Police Reserve was starting a special recruitment of Military Academy and Naval Academy graduates. If it was true, the organization was in fact going to become an army [not a police force]. I then surrendered all doubts and joined up. Remembering the treatment I had received [after the war] and the tragic voices of those executed, I knew we had to rebuild a new Japanese military. At the same time, I knew that it couldn't be as it once was, a factor in the fate of the country, directly influencing the direction of politics, but had to be a military in which the common sense of the people held sway.[30]

4

The Constitution
Becomes a Dead Letter

The creation and buildup of the Police Reserve had a unique impact on the Japanese constitution. Occupation alone was not, finally, enough of a justification for creating the Police Reserve. The government had to find a logical position to justify its open defiance of the letter of the constitution. The first attempt occurred in the Diet.

Prime Minister Shigeru Yoshida described the reasons for adopting Article 9 of the constitution in the 1946 constitutional convention:

> This radical article is certainly what stands out most in this proposed revision. Article 9 is a provision rarely seen before in the Constitution of any nation. This measure expresses Japan's desire for eternal peace and entrusts Japan's future security and existence to the fairness and faith of the peoples of all peace-loving nations. The Constitution proclaims this as a high ideal and places Japan at the head of peace-loving countries advancing on a great undertaking and clearly shows our firm resolve in the basic law of the nation.

This starry-eyed regard for Article 9's renunciation of the right to make war, its pledge not to maintain war potential, and its renunciation of the "right of belligerency" met with direct opposition in the Diet from both the right and the left. In the lower house, Representative Tenjiro Hara asked if Japan also had to give up its right to self-defense.

Prime Minister Yoshida replied:

> The provisions renouncing war in the draft of the new constitution do not specifically deny the right of self-defense, but since Article 9, Clause 2, as drafted, does renounce both the maintenance of all forms of war potential and the right of belligerency, it follows that war as a means of self-defense and the right of belligerency in self-defense are also renounced. This provision is desirable because self-defense has been the excuse advanced by both sides in most wars waged in recent years, including Japan in Manchuria and in the East Asian wars. Japan has for that reason come to be widely regarded as a militaristic nation and a threat to world peace, liable to rearm and embark upon a war of retaliation. Our renunciation of war, even in self-defense, is therefore a necessary first step in order to rectify this wrong impression, held by other nations, of our aims and intentions. It should be clearly expressed in our constitution as our contribution to world peace and a model for the peace-loving countries of the world.

Diet member Sanzo Nosaka of the Japan Communist Party stated that wars of defense are just, and said there was no need for Japan to renounce its right to self-defense. Prime Minister Yoshida replied, "To admit the possibility of war in self-defense would, in itself, provide an incentive to embark upon other types of conflict, it being a well known fact that practically every war undertaken in recent years has been undertaken on that plea. If there were an international body, the very fact of a peaceful body recognizing a right of just wars of defense would be ipso facto harmful. Likewise, I believe your argument to be harmful and without merit."

Concerning Prime Minister Yoshida's thoroughness in renouncing war potential and strong demilitarism, Yoshinari Abe of the House of Peers said, "To paraphrase what you're saying, we are going to be completely passive, throw ourselves into the water as though that act itself will summon a good current. The government's position is truly bizarre." Article 9 of the constitution was pushed through more on faith than by logic. That was the Shigeru Yoshida of 1946.

The intensification of the Cold War, the outbreak of the Korean War and the unexpected shift to the right in the Occupation government made Yoshida's 1946 position very difficult to sustain. Having so clearly stated that the constitution renounced even defensive wars, Yoshida could not then openly advocate defensive capabilities and rearmament. His arguments and explications became increasingly convoluted and opaque. In response to a question in the lower house on October 19, 1951, he said, "The country does have the right to self-defense and should war occur upon the use of that right that is unavoidable. I do recall saying that since many wars of aggression have been waged in the name of self-defense, it is not a phrase that we should bandy around."

Yoshida became very vocal in his opposition to communism. He concealed the fact that GHQ was responsible for creating the Police Reserve and stated that what was occurring before everyone's eyes was not rearmament. These three points made up his strategic position. One particular address he delivered at a policy meeting in the extraordinary session of the Diet called on July 14, 1950, soon after the Korean War broke out, demonstrates this point well:

> On June 25, the communist North Korean army crossed the thirty-eighth parallel and invaded South Korea, creating a situation of conflict in our corner of Asia. At the United Nations, the majority of member countries has promptly resolved to confront the aggressor with force of arms and do whatever necessary to restore peace. This situation is not a distant foreign problem; it concerns us intimately. It proves that our country is in imminent danger from the threat of communism. The Korean conflict shows to just what kind of lengths the red aggressors are prepared to go. Japan is already at risk.

These remarks unveiled an aggressive anticommunism that was completely at odds with the sentiments he had expressed during the debates over ratification of the constitution. Prime Minister Yoshida now welcomed the establishment of a Police Reserve to strengthen the police and the maritime safety system, stating that "the goodwill of the supreme commander of the Allied forces has been amply demonstrated, and a Police Reserve would now help to prevent a criminal armed minority from disturbing democracy." In Yoshida's eyes, the Police Reserve was completely unrelated to rearmament. In the upper house on July 30, 1950, he claimed that "the purpose of the Police Reserve is solely to maintain public order. It is not a condition or preparation for joining the United Nations; its purpose is not rearmament. Its purpose is to find the best way to maintain public security in Japan. It is thus not a military."

If the Diet had conducted an investigation into what the government was really doing, Prime Minister Yoshida's argument would have carried no weight. But, as already seen, the government had formed the Police Reserve on the authority of a GHQ directive under the Potsdam Declaration. The Diet was bypassed entirely. The government treated the decision as an order it had no authority to disobey. Minister of Justice Takeo Ohashi described the directive as binding. In remarks to the lower house on July 26, 1950, he noted that "the phrase 'authorize' used in regard to the Japanese government's creation of the Police Reserve, has been generally translated as 'permission being granted.' Since there was no request from the Japanese side, in this context I believe it must be considered a directive from the supreme commander of the Allied forces to the Japanese government."

This statement not only denied the possibility of careful discussion, but warned others that there was a limit to the criticism the government would permit. The minutes record a statement by Legal Bureau secretary, Sato, that criticism of the

Police Reserve was tantamount to resisting the Occupation army and was thus an infraction under Government Ordinance Number 311. The Diet, then, was powerless under Occupation rule.

Hiding behind the immense authority of GHQ, Prime Minister Yoshida outlined a crisis by stating that events in Korea intimately concerned Japan's security, and at the same time lectured a silenced Diet that Japan was "not rearming." He thus completed the foundation for the Police Reserve and for the Safety Boards and Self-Defense Forces that would follow it. The Korean War obviously changed Yoshida's views of the constitution and public security considerably. By playing the roles of both Japanese prime minister and GHQ functionary, he was able to hide this landmark decision from the Japanese people. The constitution had become in some sense a dead letter.

5

The Uninterrupted Navy

Compared to the creation of the Police Reserve, the process of naval rearmament seems almost colorless. This may have been due to the detachment ordinary citizens feel toward ships at sea or to the cosmopolitanism that characterizes navies around the world. Naval rearmament proceeded so unremarkably for three reasons: first, the navy organization was never completely dissolved after the end of the war; second, it participated in the Korean war; third, the American navy provided a friendly source of support outside the General Headquarters (GHQ) system.

Though it now seems surprising, GHQ permitted the Japanese navy to continue functioning in a much diminished way after the Navy Ministry was dismantled on November 30, 1945. The last minister of the navy, Mitsumasa Yonai, said in his parting address, "Our inability to preserve the Imperial Navy is a matter of intense regret and so deeply humiliating as to be unbearable." In fact, the navy retained freedom to operate in at least two areas. First, the navy was charged with bringing back all the soldiers stationed abroad as well as all the colonists in former territories. The navy also performed extensive mine-sweeping to remove all the mines laid around the Japanese archipelago. These tasks were not dramatic, but they kept the

43

navy operating for five years until remnants of the Imperial Navy took part in the Korean War. From there, these remnants developed into the new navy.

The Americans and the Japanese navy itself had planted an estimated one hundred thousand mines, many of them contact mines, in harbor entrances and straits around Japan. If they were not removed, Japan would remain blockaded even though the war was over. The only organization that had the where-withal to accomplish this task was the minesweeping brigade of the Japanese navy. GHQ placed the minesweeping division from the Second Demobilization Ministry under the command of Secretary General Yoshio Yamamoto, who had been the last secretary of the Bureau of Naval Affairs. The minesweeping operation began with 348 small vessels and ten thousand men under the command of Captain Kyuzo Tamura. These men retained the command structure of the navy. Although the rank insignia on the epaulets were removed, the uniforms were otherwise identical to Imperial Navy uniforms and the sailors were allowed to keep weapons necessary for their work, for instance, to blow up the mines dragged up by firing on them. They also retained broad freedom of action.

This situation continued after the Maritime Safety Board was established in 1948. Captain Tamura was appointed chief of the Maritime Safety Board's minesweeping section and was placed in charge of all its sailors and minesweepers. The "hidden navy" was next transferred to a corner of the Ministry of Transport. When the Korean War started, GHQ secretly sent the Japanese naval minesweeping brigade to posts around Korea, where they used their naval capabilities in support of American troops. The government kept the participation of the minesweeping brigade in the Korean War a secret for many years, but it has now been confirmed in Commander James E. Auer's account[31] as well as in *Days of the Call of the Sea*, the memoirs of Takeo Okubo, the first director of the Maritime Safety

Board.[32] The official *Thirty Year History of the Maritime Safety Agency* briefly alludes to the episode as "a special incident under occupation."

In September 1950, General MacArthur made plans to turn the tide of the war with a land attack at Wonsan. United States chief of naval operations Admiral Forrest Sherman, commander of the Naval Forces Far East Vice Admiral C. Turner Joy, deputy chief of staff Rear Admiral Arleigh Burke, and other leaders of the naval command visited the front lines and discussed the strategic requirements of a land attack. After lengthy discussions they concluded that the ocean off Wonsan was an ideal spot for the North Korean navy to lay mines. The problem, then, was that if the communists had mined the surf, the attacking forces would suffer huge losses. "Admiral Burke knew that the United States Navy lacked minesweeping forces capable of handling significant opposition, particularly if the advance into North Korea meant the possibility of encountering sophisticated Soviet influence mines. There was only one expertly trained and large minesweeping force in the world qualified to do the job: the forces of the Maritime Safety Agency, still sweeping the Japanese coastal approaches and Inland Sea area."[33]

On October 2, 1950, Maritime Safety Board Director Okubo received a message from Rear Admiral Burke stating that he urgently wanted to meet with the director. When the director visited Burke at the American Far Eastern Naval Command, Burke showed him the operations center and explained the course of the war on the maps displayed there. "He told me that the United Nations forces were hard pressed and said there was no way out unless the Japanese minesweeping brigade helped. 'I have great faith in Japanese minesweeping skills,' he said. That was what he had called me about."[34]

The need was great and immediate. To get the necessary approval, Director Okubo visited Prime Minister Yoshida at the prime minister's residence. The prime minister determined that the policy of the Japanese government was to support the United Nations forces, and he instructed Director Okubo to dispatch the minesweepers to Korean waters as the Americans had requested. One week later, on October 9, 1950, Director Okubo received formal orders addressed to the Ministry of Transport from Vice Admiral Joy.

(1) The supreme commander of the United Nations forces authorizes and directs the use in Korean waters of twenty minesweepers, one "guinea pig" vessel, and four other vessels belonging to the Security Board. We will issue the necessary directives according to the orders issued by the Naval Forces Far East that the Japanese government assemble these vessels at Moji.

(2) For the task to be performed in Korean waters, these ships shall fly the International Easy (E) flag [a marker indicating special duties] only.

(3) The pay for all personnel serving on these vessels shall be doubled for the period they are performing these duties. The United States Navy shall provide rear support while they are in Korean waters.

Director Okubo described the operation itself in his memoirs:

The Japanese special naval unit, composed of five minesweeping units and the "guinea pig" vessel Taisho-maru, swept mines in and around the ports of Wonsan, Inchon, Kunsan, Chinnampo, and Haeju for about two months from mid-October to early December, when the ferocious counterattack of the communists forced the United Nations troops to start retreating. On December 15, 1950, the unit was disbanded. The sailors on the vessels doing the minesweeping were security officers from the Fairway Safety Office and were accompanied by patrol vessels. Most of them were former members of the Japanese Imperial Navy and were minesweeping experts. The core officers were ninety-two ex–naval officers who had been purged and then specially permitted to serve. The ships were mainly Imperial Navy subchaser and patrol service craft. The ships had seen extensive use after the end of the war and their engines were aging. It was very difficult to keep them operating properly.[35]

In winter, the weather turned bad. The Sea of Japan and the Yellow Sea were very cold, and the sea lanes were subject to dangerous shelling. Conditions were bad for communication, resupply, and everything else. The sailors and officers worked in very difficult circumstances to accomplish their task.

On October 17, ship MS14 struck a contact mine while sweeping the areas for the landing at Yonghugman and sank almost immediately, killing one sailor and injuring eighteen others. Under the command of Captain Tamura, twelve hundred former Imperial Navy personnel, including the ninety-two ex–naval officers, swept 327 kilometers of channels around the Korean peninsula and anchorages extending over 607 square miles. Director Okubo reported to Prime Minister Yoshida almost every day while the minesweeping units were in Korean waters, but the government kept all news of the operation from the Japanese people.

Through this unpublicized history, the chain from the Imperial Navy to the Maritime Security Force, the maritime equivalent of the Police Reserve, to the Maritime Self-Defense Force was unbroken. Unlike the army, the navy was spared total dissolution and disarmament; its organization was permitted to exist in a smaller form in order to perform its minesweeping duties. Its participation in the Korean War also reflected well on the navy and made the process of further rearmament far smoother. The Navy, then, was never fully dissolved after the war. It is perhaps more accurate to say that the Imperial Navy was reincarnated within the United States Navy.

The July 8, 1950 MacArthur memo ordered an increase of eight thousand personnel for the Maritime Safety Board, which was to be modeled after the American Coast Guard. GHQ had limited the board to ten thousand personnel and 125 ships with a total tonnage of fifty thousand tons, and limits of fifteen thousand tons displacement and fifteen knots speed. MacArthur's order increased these numbers to eighteen thousand personnel, two hundred ships and eighty thousand total tons. New personnel were recruited and construction started on thirty new patrol boats and fifteen new patrol craft.

Quite apart from these efforts, the former naval officers group that had been charged with minesweeping and repatriation by the Second Demobilization Bureau had studied the topic of rebuilding a navy even before MacArthur issued his memo. The Korean War and the order to increase Maritime Safety Board personnel gave more life to these efforts and provided an opportunity to be open about them. Just as the Police Reserve created a miniature army separate from the National Police, so too, these men said, should an organization separate from the Maritime Safety Board be considered. As this view gained strength, a group was formed of men who had been spared from purges by the Second Demobilization Bureau, including Rear Admiral Yoshio Yamamoto, Captain Eizo Yoshida, and Captain Ko Nagazawa. Their supporters and advisors included Admiral Kichisaburo Nomura, who had been the peace-preaching ambassador to the United States at the start of the war, and former Naval Affairs Bureau Secretary Vice Admiral Zenshiro Hoshina.

This group became more closely involved with the United States Naval Forces Far East when the Americans dispatched Japanese minesweepers to the Korean war area. Nomura began to meet once a week with Rear Admiral Arleigh Burke, the deputy chief of staff of the Naval Forces Far East under Vice Admiral Joy, to teach Burke about Japanese history and Japan's relations with China and Korea. Gaining the respect of Burke and Joy proved to be a great asset in the rebuilding of the Japanese navy. As the Japanese rebuilt their naval war capability, the group of ex–navy officers repeatedly turned to Joy, Burke, and others in the Naval Forces Far East command for a source of support distinctly separate from that offered by the Occupation army.

Kichisaburo Nomura reviewed the proposal for reestablishing the navy that was prepared by Rear Admiral Yamamoto and forwarded this "research document" to C. Turner Joy in January 1951 for his opinion and response. Because he was the commander of the Naval Forces Far East, GHQ had charged Vice Admiral Joy with matters pertaining to the navy. The policy of the United States Navy was to maintain command of the western Pacific. Admiral Joy's response to the proposal was that the Americans would consider allowing the Japanese to use frigates that were at that time in Yokosuka, near Tokyo. Zenshiro Hoshina, from the Japanese side and Arleigh Burke, from the American side became liaison points, and proposals shuttled back and forth between the two. They arrived at a consensus for the form that the future navy and air force would take.

The memo that Burke sent back to Chief of Naval Operations Sherman in Washington in April 1951 outlined the following three points for the character of the new Japanese navy:

(1) There is a need by the United States for the assistance of Japan in the defense of her own country and in defense of the high seas surrounding the Japanese archipelago. There is an increasing need for a sea patrol around Hokkaido to discourage possible agent landings by the Soviets in Hokkaido;

(2) I personally believe that the solution to this quandary lies in the formation of a small group of United States naval officers to study, plan, and direct the initiation of a small Japanese navy. This Japanese navy need not be called a navy. It can be called a coast guard or a sea police force or anything else. I think that four or five really good officers could handle the job.

(3) I should think it might be desirable to augment this group of United States sailors with about ten Japanese ex–naval officers. This Japanese contingent would become the nucleus of the Japanese Navy Department.[36]

As this historical survey reveals, the progress toward a new Japanese military organization was far easier for the navy than it had been for the army. This was primarily because the important relationship was not between GHQ and the Japanese government but between Japanese and American naval officers on the one side and Washington, D.C., on the other. Although it appears at first glance that the Japanese government was not involved, Kichisaburo Nomura was a member of Prime Minister Yoshida's brain trust, and Yoshio Yamamoto had been the naval attaché to the Japanese embassy in London when he was a captain and Prime Minister Yoshida was ambassador. As with the Japanese minesweeping unit in Korea, all significant information went directly to the prime minister. This naval group operated intelligently and diplomatically.

In August 1951, Admiral Sherman, chief of naval operations in Washington, notified Joy in Japan that the United States had decided to offer Japan eighteen patrol frigates (PFs) returned from the Soviet Union and sitting in Yokosuka, and another fifty large landing ships (LSLs) in the United States, should Japan decide to accept them. At a discussion between General Matthew Ridgway, who then led GHQ, and Prime Minister Yoshida on October 19, Ridgway formally made the offer. If Japan so desired, the United States would make available to Japan a force of sixty-eight naval vessels, including PFs, to be manned by Japanese for security purposes. Yoshida accepted. The basis of the new naval structure, the Maritime Security Force, was established that day.

With this agreement, a new committee, called the Y Commission, was established to handle all preparations, including personnel and organization, for increasing maritime security capabilities. There are two explanations generally given for the name of the commission. The first is that it derived from the first letter of the family names of its chairman, Rear Admiral Yoshio Yamamoto and the second secretary of the Maritime Safety Board, Yonekichi Yanagizawa. The second explanation is that if the letters normally used for the army and navy (A and

B, respectively) were used (e.g., B Commission), the real purpose would be too easily surmised. So they started at the other end of the alphabet, and came up with Y. Not only the work of the commission, but even its very existence, was secret.

The mission that the government gave to the commission was to take possession of weapons, supplies, and vessels from the United States to establish a maintenance system, to draft a proposal for a system to optimize deployment of these capabilities, and to prepare for its implementation. Except for two members, Secretary Yanagizawa and the Maritime Safety Board's emergency rescue deputy director Kazuya Mita, all ten members of the Y Commission were high-ranking former imperial officers (two were rear admirals, five were captains, one was a commander).

Selection of the Y Commission's members was concluded within three days of General Ridgway's offer and they met for the first time at the end of October to discuss the structure of the new Japanese navy. They arrived at the following:

(1) The restrictions on the number of service personnel and numbers of ships for the Maritime Safety Board would be rescinded.
(2) When the peace treaty came into effect, the force would have aircraft suitable for coastal security (the commission anticipated that the Maritime Safety Board would have six helicopters).
(3) A Maritime Security Force would be established as an organization to strengthen maritime security, and its personnel in the 1952 fiscal year would number approximately six thousand.

Internal discussion divided the commission into two factors. The members from the Maritime Safety Board wanted to incorporate the new organization into the Maritime Safety Board, whereas the former imperial officers wanted the new organization to be independent of the Maritime Safety Board and thought that its main function should be to respond to emergencies. When the United States Naval Forces Far East chief of staff Rear Admiral Ralph A. Oftsie indicated that it should be independent and dedicated to emergency response, the Y Commission settled on the creation of a new independent Maritime Security Force, as stated in item (3) of the commission's statement of purpose, and its recommendation was presented to Prime Minister Yoshida.

The Diet enacted the Law Revising Part of the Maritime Safety Board Act in April 1952, thereby creating the Maritime Security Force. The government appointed Kogoro Yamazaki, the deputy director of the Maritime Safety Board, as the force's first commandant. At this stage, the new organization was kept within the Maritime Safety Board; when its time came, it jumped out like a kangaroo from its pouch. While the Maritime Security Force was a part of the Maritime Safety Board, the future commissioned officers of the Maritime Self-Defense Force were selected and trained with the coming separation in mind. Although the rearmament of the Maritime Self-Defense Force was more leisurely than that of the army, its progress was steady and assured. From the point of view of the Japanese people, a Japanese Navy had suddenly appeared again out of nowhere.

The Opening
of the Defense Academy

General Headquarters (GHQ) proceeded with rearmament so quickly, and in many cases so unilaterally, that the Japanese found the process taking place without much control on their part. When they looked for an area in which they could assert some control, the most obvious response was the establishment of a defense university. Education bears its fruit in the future, and the future was the one area to which the power of the Occupation did not extend. Army and naval rearmament were proceeding and the end of the Korean War seemed to be drawing near, with the cease-fire agreement becoming effective in July 1953. Attention was shifting to longer-term concerns, such as the issue of Japan's defense after it concluded a peace treaty and recovered its independence. The creation of a defense university seemed a natural part of that process.

The Defense Academy opened its doors on April 1, 1953. At the opening ceremony, its official name was the "Security University." The government had planned its establishment in the days of the Police Reserve, and when the Police Reserve was renamed the Security Forces, the academy was named the Security University. By the time it graduated its first class in 1957, it had been formally renamed the Defense Academy, the name it still bears.

Two men were instrumental in the creation of the school, Prime Minister Shigeru Yoshida and Tomo Maki, the school's first president. The ideas and personalities of these two men strongly reflected the way the school trained officers for the new national military, and to this day they remain a part of its traditions. They bequeathed to the school not a military spirit, but an attitude of training civic-minded gentlemen. When the Defense Academy first opened, former imperial officers had not yet been accepted for service in the Police Reserve, and the school's new leaders worked hard to free it from the self-righteousness and spiritualism of the old Military Academy and Naval Academy. Yoshida's and Maki's intention was to train officers to be, first and foremost, gentlemen.

The younger officers under Police Reserve Headquarters director Keikichi Masuhara prepared for the opening of the Defense Academy in a way that would embody Yoshida's ideas. Prime Minister Yoshida had given specific orders on the selection of the first university president: "no connections to the former imperial military, no bureaucrats, no graduates of the Tokyo University legal department." Ironically, although the first president, Maki, did meet all Yoshida's conditions, every other president has fallen into at least one of these categories. Maki was a graduate of Keio Gijuku University, where he had lectured in the political science department. He also had managerial experience and had been a student at Oxford University.

The Security University welcomed its first class of four hundred on April 8, 1953. The university had no dormitories, so it housed students in temporary buildings erected at a corner of the Kurihama garrison in Yokosuka City. In his address at the opening ceremony, President Maki told the new students, "First, you all must strive to achieve balance and be free of preconceived bias. Second, you need a firm understanding of the democratic system. In your four-year course of study here, you will be trained as human beings, you will be trained in the basic knowledge and skills you need for engineering and defense, and you will be trained to be leaders."

President Maki was at a remove both in personality and expression from the style of military education that placed loyalty above all else. One man in the audience that day, Kiyoshi Maekawa, recalled in memos that he kept while he was a lieutenant commander, that Maki was an educator who was quite worldly and experienced, and who combined features of both Japan and the West, the ancient and modern.

Among these four hundred new students was Makoto Sakuma, who would eventually become naval chief of staff in September 1989, and would be the first Defense Academy graduate to lead any of the three branches of the Self-Defense Forces. In the second half of the year, future Ground SDF chief of staff Atsushi Shima and future Air SDF chief of staff Akio Suzuki would also enter the academy. Sakuma was born in March 1935, and when he entered the academy he was only 18 years old. He had been ten years old when the war ended. "Our old textbooks were destroyed after the war, and the new textbooks with 'democracy' in them glittered in our eyes. The value system had completely changed, and we wondered what was real." They were a part of what could be called Japan's lost generation. The new students largely shared this outlook. They were criticized for entering the Defense Academy by peers who felt that their actions were antidemocratic and shameful. Newspapers called them "thieves in the public coffers." Standing before these young men, President Maki asked them to become "balanced human beings" and to "understand democracy" so that they could become the leaders of the future.

Before accepting his appointment as university president, Maki visited former Naval Academy president Shigeyoshi Inoue. Against all odds he had tried to educate officers to be gentlemen, even in an age that was unrelentingly militaristic. Kiyoshi Maekawa, a graduate in the Defense Academy's first class, writes in his account of what Inoue said when he went to interview the old admiral while he was a lieutenant commander:

> "Mr. Maki had come to my house," he said, "to ask my opinion of the education about to begin at the new Security University. I asked him, 'Why have you come to listen to this old military fossil talk?' or something like that."

According to Maekawa's account, Inoue gave Maki the following advice:

> "As a former military man, let me make a confession to you. Military men, in all honesty, don't really know very much. And when they think, they tend to have rigid biases. They are themselves unaware of them. . . . Keep that in mind, and try to produce an officer class for this new military that escapes from the mold of the old army and navy. That is my hope, and my chief message for you.
>
> "To which Mr. Maki replied: 'What kind of policy did you follow in educating students at the academy?'
>
> "I said, 'I educated them to be gentlemen.' In other words, I didn't educate them to be soldiers."[37]

Maki must have agreed with everything Inoue had said, since the advice coincided with his own views. It must have given him a great deal of confidence in his approach to hear his own beliefs being advocated by a former admiral who had led the old Naval Academy. Maki's address to the entering class was thus in a sense a continuation of Inoue's ideals.

A newspaper reporter quoted the following comments by Maki in an article published on February 25, 1953:

> We do not intend to train war technicians. We intend to create first-class human beings who can present themselves anywhere in society. With as much freedom as possible, we will train the highest caliber men and give them the highest caliber technical education. If they do not want to serve in the Security Forces or the Police Reserve, our graduates may

work anywhere they want. They will have no duty to join the
forces and we will not force them to repay the expenses of
their education.[38]

There were two other factors that set the Defense Academy
apart from the old military academies. The first was that all officers were educated together for the full four years, regardless of
whether they desired service in the army, navy, or air branches.
The second was that the classes emphasized science, and they
offered an education equivalent to what students would receive
in the engineering department of any ordinary university. Both
these changes were made after an examination of the shortcom-
ings of the old military academies and indicate that there was
no intention to create postwar versions of the old Military Academy and Naval Academy.

The new system eliminated the competition and rivalry that
had existed between the Imperial Army and Imperial Navy.
The people behind the establishment of the new Defense Academy wanted these young high school graduates, who would
enter different branches of service in the future, to have at least
four years of life together, sharing pleasure and pain, to develop
the group cohesion that would lead to interservice cooperation.
The "student troops" that were the center of life at the school
were formed without regard to army, navy or air force, so the primary bonds between students were those of class of entry, not
their eventual branch of service.

The emphasis on science and engineering, too, reflects
reservations about the education provided by the imperial military academies. The imperial schools had emphasized triumph
by virtue of spiritual power and valued the achievement of victory through hand-to-hand combat and the element of surprise.
The Defense Academy wanted to train cadets in a wide range of
fields and develop their powers of rational thinking so that they
would be well-rounded human beings when time came to make

decisions. The academy's science and engineering departments were on par with those at the Tokyo Institute of Technology. General education and military education were supplemented with electrical engineering, mechanical engineering, civil engineering, applied chemistry, applied physics, and aeronautics. Students were required to elect one of these six fields as a major. The proportion of sciences in the educational course was 44.6%, or 2,550 hours over four years, roughly the same as in ordinary universities. This figure was almost four times the 667 hours of science studied in the imperial Military Academy.

In addition to this science course, the Defense Academy also considered it necessary for students to devote 2,074 hours over four years to the study of military affairs in order to "provide an understanding of the work they were to perform as commissioned officers and to provide the qualities and skills needed for their execution." Physical education, in which all the students participated, was also mandatory.

In July 1954, when the first class was in its second year, the Security Forces became the Self-Defense Forces and the Security University became the Defense Academy. The following March, the construction of the main school buildings and facilities in Koharadai in Yokosuka City was completed and the school moved from its temporary quarters in Kurihama. The Defense Academy welcomed cadets for the Air Self-Defense Force in 1954. President Maki earnestly talked each year about "freedom and order," "the individual and the group," and "democracy and the military" as the number of students in each class climbed to 530:

> Order has been described as the habit of reasoned compliance. Your compliance to orders must move as soon as possible from simple passive compliance to cooperation and ultimately to confidence.
>
> You have freedom of opinion. But once something has been decided by the Japanese people, you must conform to

that decision. This is the spirit of democracy and it is the first step in the trust that the Japanese people have placed in you.

To cultivate qualities that are appropriate to group life, there are several rules. The first of these is teamwork. Working with someone else is never a negative thing that operates on ulterior motives, but a positive element of a person.

You have come to Koharadai to study. What we are looking for in you is not that you acquire a simple storehouse of knowledge, but that you gain the understanding and powers of decision that allow you to use that knowledge.[39]

President Tomo Maki's tenure as president of the Defense Academy lasted twelve years, until 1965. Twelve classes, and six thousand students, heard his opening addresses. Twenty-five years later, forty-seven hundred of those students still served with ranks from commander and lieutenant colonel to general and admiral. Over seventy percent of the commanding officers and general staff of the three branches of the Self-Defense Forces come from these classes. Maki's philosophy bore fruit in the Self-Defense Forces of the 1990s, and the true value of his educational philosophy has been proven.

To say, however, that the character of education at the Defense Academy has been shaped exclusively by President Maki would be incorrect. Many others, including former imperial officers from both the Imperial Army and Imperial Navy, have left their mark on the institution, and not a few of their conservative tenets have survived attempts to sever all links between the Self-Defense Forces and the older military. Among the students who first entered the Defense Academy were some who believed that Japan would win the next war.

The man appointed to the post of the director, the most important post at the Security University after the president and vice president, was Makoto Matsudani, a former colonel in the Imperial Army. During the war, Matsudani had been a member of general staff assigned to China and a secretary to Army Minister Rokuzo Sugiyama, and he was no believer in the new philosophy of military education. The ranks of civilian professors also included notorious militarists like Educational Affairs Department chief Yasutaka Fumoto, who rejected the First Gymnasium president Yoshinari Abe during the war as being "uncooperative to the military." Even Momotaro Suzuki, Maki's vice president, was ambivalent about the president's approach. "In his heart of hearts, Suzuki wanted to inculcate the military spirit. Professor Maki's ideas were only superficial. Japan as a national entity has an almost two-thousand-year history. To protect that history, the education at the Defense Academy has to instill this spirit as a basic subject of learning for all students."[40]

Akira Matsuda, who was invited to come to the Security University to teach philosophy, had the following impression of the academy:

> The authorities had announced that the Police Reserve was not a continuation of the older military, but once the Security University opened, it became clear to me as days went by that almost all of the military officers at the Security University had been members of the imperial military. The first officers included Imperial Army colonel Makoto Matsudani, director of security, and police officer first-class Jiro Akabori, from the Imperial Navy, as head of training. And since ship operation required the expertise of naval officers, all the petty officers had been in the Imperial Navy. Even Kenzo Okabe, professor in charge of biochemistry, working in American army laboratory facilities as well as at the Security University, had been a military man, so the Security University (and thus the Public Security Board) was not only a continuation of the imperial Japanese military, it was also undeniably maintaining a deep relationship with the American troops stationed in Japan after the war.[41]

This was the environment in which the first class of students began their trek through the Self-Defense Forces. Although the presence of President Maki certainly had a major effect on the formation of the Defense Academy's character, his was not the only influence. Military science is the systematization of techniques for taking the lives of a fighting enemy and for committing followers to the battlefield. To implement this effectively, patriotism and leadership are more reliable ideals than democracy and freedom.

Shuichiro Ueda, a professor at the Defense Academy, presented a questionnaire to one hundred seniors in the fifteenth class, and asked them what person they most respected. The top responses, published in the December 1970 issue of *Military Affairs Research* were: John F. Kennedy (6 responses); Adolf Hitler (5 responses); Shoin Yoshida[42] (5 responses); and Yukio Mishima[43] (4 responses). Most of the members of that class are now commanders or lieutenant colonels. It appears that Maki's ideals may have been short lived.

However, an interview with Admiral Sakuma, on the occasion of his becoming the first Defense Academy graduate to be named a chief of staff, which was published in *Cho-Un* on September 7, 1989, reveals marked differences between modern military men and the imperial military generation:

> **Q:** What are your feelings on being the first Defense Academy graduate to become a chief of staff?
>
> **A:** In a word, that an age has passed. I left the Defense Academy in 1957. The time is probably close upon us when all branches of the Self-Defense Forces will have someone of our generation as chief of staff. That doesn't mean that they will be Defense Academy graduates.
>
> **Q:** What are your specific plans for leadership?
>
> **A:** It is not my style to try to sum up a leadership direction in a slogan, but I intend to foster the same strong and excellent Maritime Self-Defense Force that my predecessors have shown and thereby faithfully fulfill my duties in protecting the peace and security of the Japanese people.
>
> **Q:** Why did you choose the navy?

A: One reason was that my father was a naval captain. And, very simply, I wanted to ride in ships.

Q: In the near future, the ground and air branches of the Self-Defense Forces will also have Defense Academy graduates as chiefs of staff. What changes can we expect?

A: I don't think we can expect any radical or sudden changes just because Defense Academy graduates are the chiefs of staff. And I don't think there should be. But even though the ground and air branches wear different uniforms, we all went to school together. We're friends. When our opinions differ, we discuss them frankly, and that goes for the classes after us as well. When I was the head of a defense department, the heads of the ground and air defense departments were also from the first class and we got into quite heated arguments. Our ability to have these disputes is something we value for the Defense Agency and the Self-Defense Forces.[44]

The even and leisurely way in which Admiral Sakuma expresses his hopes, sounding almost like an engineer assigned to lead a factory, is typical of that first class of the Defense Academy, those men born in the 1930s, the no-war generation.

7

The Renaming
of the Police Reserve

The new Japanese military that was created after the war went through three incarnations, the Police Reserve, the Security Forces, and the Self-Defense Forces. The changes were not in name alone. After the pace of rearmament had picked up, the driving force behind the military shifted from an emergency response to the Korean War to Japan's fundamental interests within the international power structure shaped by the Cold War.

Changes that influenced Japan's security and defense environment came from two directions. The first was the recovery of national sovereignty, when Japan returned to international society as an independent nation. The second was that Japan had reached a stage where it could set the foundation of its foreign relations in order to assure its external security. Both factors were intimately involved in determining the degree and speed of rearmament. Because Prime Minister Shigeru Yoshida intended Japan to be a member of the free world and an ally of the United States, the Police Reserve began to take on responsibilities vis-à-vis the world outside Japan.

At the time, the Cold War was intensifying. Two large military alliances had formed, the North Atlantic Treaty Organization (NATO) in 1949, and the Warsaw Pact Treaty Organization

63

(WTO) in 1955. The United States decided that it was the Asian region's policeman, while the Soviet Union involved itself behind-the-scenes in struggles of national liberation. Both East and West Germany, the other defeated nation of World War II, began to rearm. At the end of World War II, only the United States had the atomic bomb, but by 1949 the Soviet Union had exploded a nuclear device, and in 1952 Britain announced that it, too, had succeeded. The United States and the Soviet Union, meanwhile, had gone on to the vastly more destructive hydrogen bomb, placing the two countries in the role of clear superpowers. That was the backdrop when Japan's six years as an Allied-occupied nation ended and it became once again a member of international society in 1951.

Throughout this period, Japan had been formally at war with fifty-five nations. Japan wanted a single treaty that would give it peace with all of these nations, but the intensifying Cold War had created a feeling of crisis. The Yoshida cabinet decided to pursue a separate, one-sided peace treaty with the Western bloc first to secure an early end to Occupation. In the Diet session of July 14, 1950, immediately after the Korean War began, Yoshida described his intended policy: "Confronted as we are by the current situation, many argue that we should seek a comprehensive peace treaty or establish perpetual neutrality, but though this may spring from a true patriotism, it is completely divorced from reality. I believe we face a grave danger from the plotting of the Communist Party."

Shigeru Yoshida dismissed as a "band of ivory-tower academics" the scholars led by Tokyo University President Shigeru Nanbara, who called for a comprehensive peace treaty. He launched an unrestrained one-man campaign decrying a comprehensive peace treaty and opposition to rearmament when Kan'ichi Kawakami, of the Japan Communist Party, and others questioned him in the Diet's Disciplinary Committee. Finally he concluded a peace treaty with the forty-eight nations invited to the conference on peace with Japan, which was held in San Francisco on September 8, 1951. President Truman made the opening address on September 4, emphasizing that the peace treaty was one of "reconciliation, which looks to the future, not the past." Yoshida's address was sincere and moving, and he praised the treaty as "unparalleled in history in its fair and generous terms." He declared: "We are determined to take our place among the nations who are dedicated to peace, to justice, to progress and freedom, and we pledge ourselves that Japan shall play its full part in striving towards these ends."[45]

Although representatives of the Soviet Union, Czechoslovakia, and Poland attended the conference, they refused to sign the treaty, calling it "a treaty for a new war." India, Burma, and Yugoslavia were invited, but did not attend. Since the Chinese government had split between Taiwan and the mainland, the inability to determine whom to invite led to neither being invited. The same happened with the Koreas. So although Yoshida obtained his early end to Occupation, the matter of a peace treaty signed by all the belligerents was not closed.

Although the peace treaty had been signed, negotiations continued with the United States over defense policies and long-term goals for external security. As for the American government, its conflicts in the Far East with the Soviet Union and China worsened. Furthermore, because the two countries had signed the Chinese-Soviet Friendship Pact in 1950, the Americans were even less willing to give Japan unconditional independence and autonomy in its national security policy. The national security arrangements made after the end of Occupation had to fit into the United States' strategy for Asia, and, indeed, for the world. That meant, inevitably, that Japan had to sign a treaty of military alliance with the United States, and this created a blatant opportunity for East-West confrontation.

Prime Minister Yoshida had no objection to Japan's retaining allegiance to the West after the recovery of independence, but he resisted American requests that Japan embark on a full-fledged rearmament. Yoshida gave his reasons to John Foster Dulles, then advisor to the State Department in charge of the peace treaty with Japan, and later secretary of state. Yoshida explained to Dulles why Japan was not enthusiastic about rearmament. "Rearmament will prevent Japan from establishing an independent economy and will also arouse the fears of its neighbors. Domestically, it may lead to the resurrection of military cliques. Nevertheless, though rearmament is a problem, within the wider conflict of confrontation between two worlds, we would like America to consider Japan, in the broad sense, part of the American circle."[46]

Yoshida had never linked his opposition to rearmament to demilitarization. Rather, he favored a gradual approach in building up Japan's defensive strength. There was another factor for the Americans that argued against an overt rearmament of Japan. Many of America's allies in Asia and the Pacific, such as Australia, New Zealand, the Philippines, and South Korea, had been the object of Japanese aggression before and they were strongly opposed to Japan's development of any offensive capabilities. At the second Japan–United States negotiations, Dulles advanced an idea for a Japan–United States arrangement to assure mutual security. This initiative became the basis of the United States–Japan Security Treaty.

The result was managed rearmament. When the security treaty formalized the stationing of American troops in Japan, Japan did not have to embark on a full-scale public rearmament. The other countries of Asia and the Pacific could also accept this smaller Japanese rearmament because the Americans were monitoring it. But within that framework, Japan had to make a contribution to building up its defensive strength and regional security. In the words of Dulles, "Although countries that have the ability to contribute to security must not take a 'free ride,' Japan should not again develop military power that presents an offensive threat." While this is certainly different from open rearmament, it is also different from no rearmament at all.

On the same day that Japan signed the peace treaty, it also signed the United States–Japan Security Treaty. Those who had hoped for a comprehensive peace that included China and the Soviet Union and would entrust national security after the recovery of independence to the peace constitution were doubly disappointed. Even though Occupation had ended, American troops remained in Japan, only now they were called "stationed troops." Since no bases changed hands, the absence of change was pronounced. Okinawa and the Amami islands remained under American military rule. The Japan Socialist Party split over whether to accept both the peace treaty and the security treaty. Thereafter, the Security Treaty with the U.S. became the single largest issue in Japan's international relations.

The two treaties had an immediate effect on Japan's defenses. The security treaty called specifically for Japan to bear a gradually increasing responsibility for its own defense against aggression, both direct and indirect. On May 10, 1952, twelve days after the security treaty came into force, the government presented the Security Board Bill to the lower house. The government proposed to integrate the Police Reserve and the Maritime Security Force; to increase security capabilities on both land and sea; and to provide for the defense of Japan, an independent country, against both direct and indirect aggression. The government arrived at the following interpretation of Article 9 of the constitution: "'War potential' refers to a deployment of armaments sufficient to effectively pursue modern warfare. The armament of the Police Reserve and Security Forces does not have such potential in either scale or power."

The phrase *senryoku naki guntai* (military without war potential) became a popular expression at the time. The Diet passed the Security Board Bill on July 31, 1952, and it went into force at the Security Force establishment ceremony held on the

Meiji Shrine Garden Arena on October 15, 1952. Prime Minister Yoshida served as the Security Board's first Director, and he described the purpose of the Board: "We must particularly remember the purpose of establishing the Security Board and its duties. Though not an army, the Security Forces have substantial power to maintain peace and security in Japan. They must always be an institution for the public good that faithfully pursues the political goals set forth by Japanese public opinion. The Security Forces must truly be of the people, for the people, and by the people in order to be trusted by the Japanese nation and to receive its respect and affection."

Yoshida's addition of naval power to the Security Forces raised concern among other Asian countries. When Japan regained its independence, the United States formed pacts with other countries to allay fears of Japan, such as ANZUS, the treaty between America, Australia, and New Zealand, and the United States–Philippines Mutual Defense Treaty. Aware of these developments, Yoshida gave voice to his past reservations:

> We must not forget the understanding friendship and goodwill that we have received from the democracies. In the past, Japan was in such a rush to build itself up that it forgot to work with other nations and permitted an exclusivist militarism to dominate it, earning Japan the enmity of the world and leading to this painful defeat. We must take the still-fresh lesson of this history to heart so the Japanese people absolutely never again commit these crimes. Japan cannot develop without world peace. Japan's development cannot occur without cooperation with the democracies.[47]

Yoshida was expressing an awareness held by other countries of Asia and the Pacific that had been absent during the creation of the Police Reserve. Nevertheless, the government still concealed the new nature of the Security Forces.

The duties and purposes of the Security Forces were not identical to those of the Police Reserve. The addition of the maritime department to the Defense Forces signaled an end to the former objective of 'supplementing police capabilities' and clarified the military character of the forces. It also increased the maritime department's weapons and armaments. The main changes that came about with the establishment of the Security Forces were:

(1) Total personnel was increased to 110,000.
(2) With the increase in personnel, the executive staff ratio was increased to ten percent.
(3) The increased troop strength was stationed primarily in Hokkaido.
(4) The United States military system was to be used in education and training.
(5) The instructors needed were to be trained according to the American model.

The armaments of the Police Reserve were expanded from light weapons such as pistols, small arms, and machine guns, to heavy weapons such as artillery and tanks. By August 1952, Japan had received on loan forty 105-millimeter and 155-millimeter howitzers and forty M-4 tanks, twenty-ton vehicles. By October of the same year, the Security Forces had also received their first aircraft, forty L-16 and L-20 liaison aircraft, paving the way for the developing air branch of the forces.

The signing of the Japan–United States Ship Lending Agreement resulted in the loan of eighteen Tacoma-class patrol frigates (PFs), with 1450 tons displacement and fifty large landing ships (LSLs), with 300 tons displacement. The PFs were respectable coastal patrol ships constructed in large numbers during World War II; they carried three 3-inch guns and depth charge throwers for antisubmarine warfare. Ironically, the United States had lent them to the Soviet Union during the war and was now lending them to Japan for use in an anti-Soviet strategy. PFs were active as the mainstay of the maritime defenses until Japan was able to make its own destroyers in the 1960s.

The first ships that the new Maritime Security Force got were six of the eighteen patrol frigates and four of the fifty LSLs. The PFs were named after trees: Kashi, Matsu, Momi, Sugi, Kusu, and Nara. The LSLs were named after plants: Yuri, Kiku, Hagi, and Ran. The new ships formed the First Fleet, with four PFs, the Second Fleet, with two PFs, and the Eleventh Fleet, with four LSLs. On January 14, 1953, at a ceremony for the transfer of these ships, held at the American base in Yokosuka, Security Board director Admiral Tokutaro Kimura gave the following address to commemorate the event:

> With the enactment of the peace treaty, it is only natural that the Japanese government set out a complete strategy to autonomously ensure the domestic peace and security of Japan as an independent country. Japan is an island nation surrounded by seas on all sides, with ninety thousand miles of coastline. At present, the police boats are far from being able to adequately protect this huge territory.
>
> However, the recovery of national vigor after the recent defeat is distant, and we still lack the capability to quickly produce the new ships needed for this task. Given this situation, the congress of the United States has responded to the request of the Japanese government by granting the United States president the authority to lend to Japan eighteen patrol frigates and fifty landing support ships for its security. As the first part of this day's agreement, we today take possession of six patrol frigates and four landing support ships. These lay the cornerstone for our maritime defense of Japan's security. This demonstrates the profound understanding and kind trust that the United States government has in the reconstruction of Japan, and we are truly grateful.
>
> To enable these vessels to execute their duties in the Security Forces, I believe it is our responsibility to use them in the most effective way possible. I also believe this is the best way to respond to the goodwill of the United States. In conclusion, I would like to express my sincerest appreciation to his excellency [Vice Admiral R. P. Prescow of the United

States Far Eastern Naval Command] for his tireless efforts to make the loan become a reality and to the American government authorities, and to express my hope for continuing friendship and support in the future.

As the United States transferred more powerful and more numerous weapons to Japan, the free-form supply of weapons from the American forces in Japan outlived its usefulness. The United States government proposed in 1953 to switch to a military assistance system based on the Mutual Security Assurance (MSA) Act. The MSA Act was an economic and military assistance law that the United States Congress passed in 1951 to strengthen liberal democracies. In return for financial and in-kind assistance, the United States expected recipient countries to contribute to the individual and collective defense of the free world. Countries accepting MSA assistance were obliged to increase defense spending. For Japan, accepting the MSA meant reorganization of the Self-Defense Forces. Negotiations with the United State began in July 1953. The Americans strongly requested that the Security Forces be increased in strength, using MSA aid as a lever. The Japanese could not fund this increase by itself. Consensus between the two sides was difficult to achieve.

These efforts climaxed at the October 1953 Ikeda-Robertson talks in Washington. Hayato Ikeda, the Liberal Party's Policy Research Committee chairman, and later, the prime minister, was sent by Yoshida to open the negotiations and became involved in a heated debate with the assistant secretary of state for Asian affairs, Walter Robertson. The question of rearmament entered a whole new dimension. When the talks ended, the negotiators had reached a plan to rename and reorganize the Security Board and Security Forces into the Defense Agency and Self-Defense Forces.

At the third meeting between Ikeda and Robertson on October 12, the United States Department of Defense presented the American proposal to increase Japan's defenses. Its targets were:

- land units: ten divisions with 325,000 troops
- maritime units: eighteen destroyers with 13,500 personnel
- air units: eight hundred fighting aircraft with 30,000 personnel

The Japanese considered this to be a completely unrealistic proposal in terms of the capabilities of the Security Forces, since Japan did not have the requisite funds. Ikeda responded by outlining the legal, political, social, and even economic and physical restrictions on Japan's rearmament. He stated flatly that Japan could not rearm at the level suggested by the United States. In his account of the talks, Keiichi Miyazawa, who was a member of parliament at the time and was later foreign minister and prime minister, and who was translating for the meeting, described Ikeda's response:[48]

(1) The legal restriction is that Article 9 of the constitution is extremely clear, and the procedures for its revision are difficult and, in the near term, impossible.

(2) The political and social restrictions are that the Occupation army has thoroughly indoctrinated the Japanese people regarding the benefits of peace. Japanese are widely of the opinion that they should not take up arms. The young people trained to this idea are now of age.

(3) The economic restriction hardly needs describing. People who have lost their fathers and sons in a losing war are still struggling just to get by on their own. The first step of defense really must begin with providing these people with sufficient social protection, and this requires considerable money.

(4) The physical restriction is that even if we were to draft and adopt a plan, we lack the manpower to implement it. The troops entrusted with Japan's defense cannot accept just anybody without qualification or condition. As a result of the peace education that I mentioned, only a limited number of young people are willing and able to enter

the Security Forces. We cannot try conscription because the constitution expressly forbids it.

Miyazawa described the exchange between Ikeda and Robertson over the Constitution:

> Robertson: "You believe that you can't implement a full-fledged rearmament unless the Constitution is revised?"
> Ikeda: "Revising the Constitution is not something that can be lightly accomplished."
> Robertson: "How many years would it take to revise it?"
> Ikeda: "It can't be done easily. It has to be done gradually."

Miyazawa recalled that at the meeting, "they were ready for us to say that Japan wanted to embark on a rapid military buildup, but that is not what we did. Behind our backs they were bad-mouthing us—all this talk about peace and constitution meant that we weren't serious. They hoped for as much [rearmament] as they could get, so when we said we couldn't do it, their counter-arguments were furious."[49]

Although Ikeda wielded the constitution as a weapon against the American request for a defense buildup, he did not at heart have any belief in the demilitarization enshrined in the constitution. For Ikeda, the constitutional restriction meant that Japan could not become a military power, but that gradual increases in defense capabilities were permissible. He countered the American proposal with his own personal proposal in an attempt to reach a compromise.

- land units: 180,000 troops
- maritime units: 16,550 personnel
- air units: 558 fighting aircraft with 7,600 personnel plus 13,100 radar personnel

Miyazawa stated, "There was nothing that made 180,000

acceptable when 320,000 was not. It was a political judgment on our part. The constitution certainly did not say that 180,000 was okay. We thought that, with everything taken together, 180,000 was probably a reasonable figure. We had to make a decision of some sort."

Ikeda and Miyazawa's constitution defense thus led to their compromise proposal for a force of 180,000. In the joint communiqué issued at the end of the talks, on October 30, the understanding on defense issues that had been reached between Japan and the United States became clear:

> Representatives of the congresses of both countries have come to a consensus that Japan needs to strengthen its defensive capabilities to protect itself from the threat of invasion and to reduce the burden on the United States for the defense of Japan. Nevertheless, in Japan's current condition, constitutional, economic, and budgetary considerations and other limiting factors do not permit an immediate strengthening of Japan's defensive capabilities sufficient to meet this task. The Japanese side will undertake to accelerate its defense buildup in the future, with due consideration to restricting factors. In response, the United States, with the approval of Congress, will provide required items needed to supply Japan's land, sea, and air troops and shall aid in their organization.
>
> The representatives also reached a consensus that as Japanese troops gain in capacity to meet Japan's defense needs, they shall replace American troops stationed in Japan.

Parallel to the Mutual Security Assurance Act negotiations between Japan and the United States, there were a flurry of policy proposals and deliberations concerning the "security of an independent country" in domestic politics. At that time, the faction most in favor of strengthening Japan's autonomous defense capability was the Progressive Party, led by Mamoru Shigemitsu, of which Yasuhiro Nakasone was a member. The Progressive Party's policy, broadly, was that the strength of a democratic self-defense force must reflect national strength and that the Japan–United States Security Treaty needed to be converted to a mutual defense pact quickly so that Japan could join in collective security arrangements. In September 1953, Prime Minister Yoshida and Progressive Party chairman Shigemitsu held a conference. They agreed to change the Security Forces into the Self-Defense Forces and to strengthen its ability to directly meet any invasion.

On the basis of this understanding, the Liberal Party, the Progressive Party, and the Japan Liberal Party, all conservative parties, continued their policy deliberations and set a course toward establishing the Self-Defense Forces. In January 1954, in an administrative policy speech in the regular Diet session, Prime Minister Yoshida announced the decision to reorganize the Security Forces into the Self-Defense Forces:

> There is no change in our basic policy that as Japan becomes stronger we must gradually do more for our own defenses. This is not just one individual's request based on the Japan–United States Security Treaty. To the degree that our national strength permits, we must by our own hand establish a system that enables us to defend our own country as soon as we can, because it is our natural duty to contribute to the establishment of a common defensive system with other free countries. For that reason we will soon enter into a mutual assistance agreement with the United States.
>
> The government has considered these circumstances and at this time will adopt the necessary revisions in the Security Board Act and other related laws. The Security Force and Maritime Security Force will be changed to the Self-Defense Forces, an Air Self-Defense Force will be established, and the provisions necessary for the Self-Defense Forces to take up their duties dealing with direct aggression will be enacted.

The government brought before the Diet two defense bills, the Law Establishing the Defense Agency and the Self-Defense Forces Act, and with the support of the three conservative parties these two bills passed the lower house on June 2. An Air

Self-Defense Force was established and a joint staff council was created as a consultative institution to bring together the chiefs of staff of the Ground, Maritime, and Air branches. Following the practices of the Ground and Maritime Self-Defense Forces, the government appointed General Kentaro Murakami, who was originally a civilian bureaucrat, as head of the Air Self-Defense Force. The first chairman of the joint staff council was Keizo Hayashi. The personnel levels of the three services were set as follows:

- Ground Self-Defense Force: 150,000
- Maritime Self-Defense Force: 15,808
- Air Self-Defense Force: 6,287
- joint staff council: 20
- secretariat, etc.: 12,424

On July 1, 1954, the Defense Agency was inaugurated, only four years after the creation of the Police Reserve under MacArthur's memo and nine years after the atomic bomb destroyed Hiroshima and Nagasaki. Postwar Japan had completed its rearmament on the installment plan.

WHAT IS "WAR POTENTIAL"?

Article 9 of the Japanese constitution clearly states that "Land, sea, and air forces, as well as other war potential, will never be maintained. War is not recognized as a sovereign right of the nation." There has been much debate

over the past forty years over what the term "war potential" means.

The arguments can be divided into three groups. When
it was creating the Police Reserve, the government's position was that the constitutional provision concerning war
potential did not apply to the Police Reserve. It argued that
the Police Reserve existed to "supplement the policing
capabilities of the National-Rural Police force and the
police forces of local authorities," and defined it as an organization that existed to maintain public security. When
"special vehicles" (tanks) and artillery were added to the
Self-Defense Forces arsenal, however, this interpretation
became impossible to sustain. The next interpretation of
war potential suggested that it was "the capacity to pursue
modern warfare." Tokutaro Kimura, director of the Security
Board, explained the new reasoning to the lower house
Budget Committee in February 1952: "'War potential' as I
understand it, refers to troop strength that is effective and
sufficient to pursue war. In our age, what is this kind of
capability to wage war? It is the ability to fight with sufficient equipment as military units. The Police Reserve of
Japan as it is presently composed does not possess any
such ability. It only has the power sufficient to maintain
public security in Japan, so it is not in violation of Article
9 of the constitution."

At the same time, the Cabinet Legislation Bureau
defined a military unit as "an organization that is able to
fight an external enemy given common sense assumptions
and conditions." Strangely, they were unable to deny the
existence of the Police Reserve as a military unit. The
common phrase of the period, "military without war
potential," shows the back-and-forth of this debate over

whether the Police Reserve and its successors constituted a military. The government was trying to claim that the reserve lacked war potential and at the same time to call it a ground, sea, and air military, which is inherently contradictory.

In December 1954, the government revised its position to create a consistent definition of 'war potential.' Under the new interpretation, the government no longer considered the ability to wage a modern war to be part of the definition of war potential. The new idea was that war potential was anything beyond the minimum required for self-defense. The relationship between the constitution and war potential has ever since been discussed in this context. According to the government, the maintenance of military forces within that limit was not in contravention of the constitution. Director Yoshikuni of the Cabinet Legislation Bureau gave a comprehensive explanation of this concept at a November 1972 meeting of the upper house Budget Committee:

> "War potential" in its broadest sense is, just as the words say, the potential to make war. Going from the definition of the words, any kind of organization has some capability of exerting power, but the war potential prohibited in Article 9, paragraph 2, of the constitution is only that war potential covered in the literal definition of the words that exceeds the minimum required for self-defense. For some years now the government has taken the interpretation that Article 9, paragraph 2, does not prohibit the maintenance of any power below that level.

Thus the government achieved a compromise between the meaning of "war potential" and the constitution.

This, of course, was the position to which all Liberal Democratic Party administrations adhered.

Since this compromise did not specify just what the minimum required for self-defense was, an inevitable conflict arose as years passed, and in the 1980s the inherent contradictions in Japan's defense posture became obvious to many. Was the world's third largest military budget really the minimum required for self-defense? This led to a loss of credibility for Japan in the international community, as other countries were treated to the spectacle of a nation whose constitution pledged the country not to maintain war potential continuing to renounce war while at the same time increasing its defense budget year after year and maintaining Self-Defense Forces with considerable war potential.

8

Life in the Base Town Sasebo

Japan's incremental rearmament had the strongest impact on the municipalities in which military facilities were located. Those communities were a microcosm of defeated Japan as a country, and their fortunes were directly linked to the economies of the bases. The small towns had no choice but to follow orders from the Occupation troops, and when the threat of war abroad intensified, plans for the future were put on hold while civic life returned to wartime routines. The military port city of Sasebo, in Nagasaki Prefecture, is a representative example of these communities.

Ever since the Japanese Imperial Navy established the Third Naval District Naval Station in Sasebo over a century ago, in 1889, the fortunes of the town have been tied to the fortunes of the navy. The greatest event during that period was, of course, the Japanese defeat in World War II. Six weeks after B-29 bombing raids had burned the entire city to the ground, Japan surrendered unconditionally to the Allied forces. The United States marines who came to occupy the country in September ordered the fortieth, and last, Naval Station commander, Vice Admiral Rokuzo Sugiyama, to provide housing facilities for three hundred officers and fifty thousand soldiers, and to provide three hundred thousand square feet of hospital facilities, thirty passenger cars, and eighty cargo trucks. This was Sasebo's first order under Occupation.

Under Occupation rule, the people of Sasebo wanted to convert their town to a civilian port. It was believed that the appropriate manner for a "war crimes city" to make its way in the new Japan was to take its good port and Imperial Navy factories and convert them to a trading port for peaceful purposes. In January 1950, the City Council unanimously adopted a declaration of peace:

> The naval port, which required vast national expenditure and sixty years of labor to construct, has been dedicated solely to the pursuit of war. Our nation constructed enormous munitions factories in Sasebo and the port developed into a military city with a population of three hundred thousand. Now, the recent great war has brought Japan to the brink of utter destruction. The civilian populace, which has set down roots here for generations, has nowhere to live, no ancestral villages to return to, and passes its days in unemployed misery. As we look on the mountains of scrap from ship dismantling and the piles of rubble from half-destroyed buildings, we sense the enormous cruelty and futility of war.
>
> As all Japan and all the world now know, Japan has adopted a Constitution that proclaims it to be a demilitarized nation.
>
> Sasebo hereby pledges this day of January 13, 1950, to undertake a 180-degree turn, dedicating what imperial military assets remain to an eternal future of prosperity for humanity so that it may become quickly a city of peaceful industry and a port of international trade.

Elections to enact the Imperial Naval Port Conversion Act that would convert former military facilities to civilian uses in not only Sasebo, but in the other military ports of Yokosuka, Kure, and Maizuru as well, were held on June 4. In Sasebo, the measure passed, with 97.31% of the population voting to convert to a peaceful industrial port city. Three weeks later, war broke out in Korea, on the other side of the Goto and Tsushima Straits.

Sasebo's plans for derequisitioning its military facilities came to an immediate halt when the town became the point of shipment for troops and matériel to Korea. United Nations troop trains arrived at Sasebo National Railway Station twice daily, in the morning and in the evening. To prevent enemy submarines from entering the harbor, the United States Navy strung submarine nets across its nine-hundred-meter mouth. Ships were not permitted to enter without special permission; consequently, trade and fishing activities ceased. On the night before the Inchon landing, the battleship Missouri, carrying United Nations commander General MacArthur, secretly set sail from Sasebo.

The repaired imperial naval factories became the hub of round-the-clock activity as workers replaced naval gun barrels burnt and blistered from naval shelling. Oilers of ten thousand tons anchored at the oil storage facility. The dream of a peaceful port city seemed increasingly distant. Changes within the city were even more extreme. *The City History of Sasebo* describes the period: "At this time an event occurred that completely transformed Sasebo—the June 1950 outbreak of the Korean War. Sasebo, which had just begun its transition to a city of peaceful industry, became a base for United Nations troops. Ships, men, and war material jammed the port. On the commercial strip from Matsuura-cho down the main street, new curio stores, cafés, cabarets, and dance halls sprouted like mushrooms after a rain to entertain and serve the United Nations troops. Pedicabs jammed the streets."[50]

The United Nations troops spent in excess of ¥600 million each month, and people from around Japan poured into Sasebo to get their share of the wealth as the town recovered rapidly amid exploding prosperity. A modern city arose from the ashes, where seven years earlier not even a shadow could be seen.

Cabaret owners made so much money that they filled orange crates to overflowing with ¥100 bills. Sasebo's economic boom has been referred to as a blood-soaked gold rush. Over ten thousand prostitutes rushed in from around Japan to fill Sasebo's 597 brothels. Sasebo's bars and liquor stores sold more beer than those in any other city in Japan.

After the war had breathed economic life back into Sasebo, the Police Reserve entered. In the seven days between September 2 and 10, 1950, eight detachments totaling 1,116 troops arrived at the American camp that had been the old Hario marine base. Their main duty was to guard the American base and the port facilities. Later this battalion moved to the Ainoura District, which would become the initial training ground for recruits to the Ground Self-Defense Force.

The Sasebo City Council continued to petition throughout the Occupation and the Korean War for derequisition of its port facilities and conversion to a commercial port. When Japan signed the peace treaty and the United States–Japan Security Treaty, their hopes for a purely civilian port were shattered. The government announced its intention to continue to make Sasebo's moorings, docks, and repair facilities available to the American military and set aside the majority of the port waters for the United States Navy. The port would remain out of the hands of townspeople. Sasebo had to revise its long-term plan of becoming a port for international trade.

The one section of the former Imperial Navy facilities that was kept from the American navy was the Kurashima District, where the city began to build a fishing industry base with the assistance of the Ministry of Transport's Ports and Harbors Bureau. Although the city officials had devoted their full energies to this construction, they were informed by the national government that the Maritime Security Force was considering locating its headquarters there. The Sasebo authorities were not enthusiastic about this plan, since the Kurashima District was the only section of the port that could be converted to peaceful, commercial purposes. The townspeople were ambivalent about the plan as well. Some felt that they should welcome the Maritime Security Force, but should attempt at the same time to proceed with the original plan for a commercial port. Others felt that Sasebo's geographic location and the presence of an American base meant that there was little or no hope for Sasebo's development as a trade port, and so it would be in the town's interest to welcome Maritime Security Force. Many of the townspeople felt a certain nostalgia for the bustling days of the naval port of the past, and so decided to bet their futures on the new navy.

In the end, the town welcomed the new headquarters:

> The people of Sasebo express their full approval of the siting of the headquarters of the Maritime Security Force at Sasebo, and having asked for favors many times in the past, we now ask again that the headquarters be sited here.
>
> As the base of the old Imperial Navy, Sasebo is in both name and reality the best port in the Orient and has been the object of enormous investments on the part of the Japanese nation. Sasebo has an excellent sea wall that Maritime Security Force ships can use for anchorage, as well as older fortifications, including buildings, that the Maritime Security Force would naturally desire to use.
>
> For that reason, the Sasebo City Council considers it fitting that should the Maritime Security Force build a base in Sasebo, it would make use of these fortifications, and we would welcome it to do so. Having reached this conclusion, the entire city hereby strongly requests that the Security Force headquarters be located here.

The City Council's pledge "to renew itself as an international trade port" was replaced by the more servile language, "having asked for favors many times," and its request was successful. The Sasebo Fairway Safety Office opened as part of the Security Board's Security Force on August 1, 1952. In September of the next year, the office was upgraded to a Regional District Headquarters. Its first commander was Security Force director (later admiral and Maritime Self-Defense Force chief of staff) Sadayoshi Nakayama, a former staff member of the Naval Academy.

When the Maritime Self-Defense Force was launched in 1954, it home ported its Second Escort Flotilla at Sasebo and assigned the patrol frigates Momi, Tsuge, Kaede, and Buna, (all 1,450 tons displacement) to the flotilla. The Maritime Self-Defense Force decided to use the same naval ensign flag that once flew over the imperial Grand Fleet. The sight of the old imperial flag flying over ships received from the Americans aroused a variety of feelings in the citizenry of the town.

Ichizo Tsuji, who was at that time chairman of the Sasebo City Council, and became mayor of Sasebo during the 1960s and 1970s, recalled the era in *The Silent Port:*

> Eighty years previously, Sasebo had been chosen as a naval port as part of national policy, and most of the town's folk had welcomed it happily. After the end of the war, the citizens chose to have a peaceful commercial port, but this was not permitted. Instead, again through a national decision, a base for the Americans, and then for the Maritime Self-Defense Force, was established so that now Sasebo is a mix of military and commercial ports. The period from its birth as a military port to today has lasted for over eighty years. If they wanted to make Sasebo a home port for nuclear submarines and nuclear aircraft carriers, they should not have been surprised that this aroused anguish in many people. It is hard to avoid the feeling that this is Sasebo's fate.[51]

The real power that convulsed Sasebo was the Cold War. Within that context, if Shigeru Yoshida was unable to resist a partial peace treaty or the United States–Japan Security Treaty, how could Tsuji, a single local politician, be expected to sail against the wind? With the Cold War and national policy behind it, the port city of Sasebo could not resist again becoming a naval town.

ARE THE SELF-DEFENSE FORCES UNCONSTITUTIONAL?

Many cases have been brought to court concerning the constitutionality of the Self-Defense Forces under Article 9 of the Japanese constitution. With suits over the constitutionality of the United States–Japan Security Treaty and trials seeking the reversion of bases and compensation for damages, these cases represent an important chapter in Japan's postwar legal history.

The suits brought against the Self-Defense Forces can be generally placed into one of several categories: base suits; suits relating to violation of religious conscience by the Self-Defense Forces; suits of conscientious objection to military expenditure; and suits relating to antiwar Self-Defense officers and their civil rights. The following cases are typical of these categories.

(1) The Police Reserve constitutionality suit, March 1952: Chairman Mosaburo Suzuki, representing the Japan Socialist Party, was the original plaintiff in this case and brought a direct suit to the Supreme Court seeking confirmation that the creation of the Police Reserve and all its actions were unconstitutional and invalid. The plaintiff sought a judicial review and recision from the Supreme Court in its role as constitutional court. In October, the suit was unanimously dismissed. The basis of the dismissal was that "some specific complaint must be present before the powers of jurisdiction can go into effect. We find that there is no such specific complaint and we cannot exercise rights every time a symbolic case is brought regarding a constitutional issue that may arise in the future."

(2) The Eniwa Incident, 1962: Brothers who operated a farm in the Eniwa district of Hokkaido cut a field operations telephone line in protest over the continuing damage sustained by milk cows during gunnery practice. The defendants were accused of breaking the Self-Defense Forces Act. They alleged that the Self-Defense Forces and the Self-Defense Forces Act were unconstitutional. In a 1967 decision of the Sapporo District Court, the brothers were found not guilty, but the reason given was that the communications line was not an item provided for the purpose of defense under the Self-Defense Forces Act, so no constitutional review was conducted. The court returned a not-guilty verdict and the prosecution did not appeal.

(3) The Hyakuri base suit: In the construction of an Air Self-Defense Force base in Ibaragi Prefecture, a trial between the state and the residents was held contesting ownership of the base site. The residents brought suit in 1958 and went through thirty-one years of litigation before a decision was reached by the Supreme Court in 1989. The core argument of the suit centered on the dispute over land ownership. From there the suit developed into a conflict over Article 9 of the constitution. The Supreme Court ruled that "Article 9 of the constitution does not directly apply to matters of civil law, such as the current action," and dismissed the residents' final appeal without rendering a constitutional decision.

(4) The Konishi antimilitary suit: During the 1970 United States–Japan Security Treaty riots, Staff Sergeant Makoto Konishi of the Sado Branch Station of the Air Self-Defense Force pasted up a handbill on the base calling for Self-Defense Forces members to reject demonstration sup-

pression training and was arrested for breaking the Self-Defense Forces Act. Because the Defense Agency did not comply with the order to submit documents on the current state of its "special security training," no examination of evidence could be conducted, so the defendant was found not guilty. When remanded for further processing in a public trial after the appeal, a verdict of not guilty was again upheld.

(5) Naganuma Nike suit: A suit questioning the constitutionality of the Self-Defense Forces was brought by farmers opposed to the installation of a Nike surface-to-air missile base in Naganuma-cho, Hokkaido. In the September 1973 decision of Justice Fukushima, the Sapporo District Court conducted a fact-finding investigation of the Self-Defense Forces and issued a declaration that the Self-Defense Forces were unconstitutional from the viewpoint of the people's right to live a peaceful existence. This verdict shocked the government. A higher court, however, did not find a right of peaceful existence, leading to a defeat for the plaintiff. A Supreme Court decision in September 1982 eventually dismissed the case on final appeal without a finding on constitutionality.

Overall, the stance of the Supreme Court regarding the constitutionality of the Self-Defense Forces has tended toward the act-of-state theory that "questions of the constitutionality or unconstitutionality of the Self-Defense Forces are a fundamental problem of national administration that has the highest political character, so is not a subject for our legal review." The court has been strongly criticized for discarding its role as the guardian of the constitution.[52]

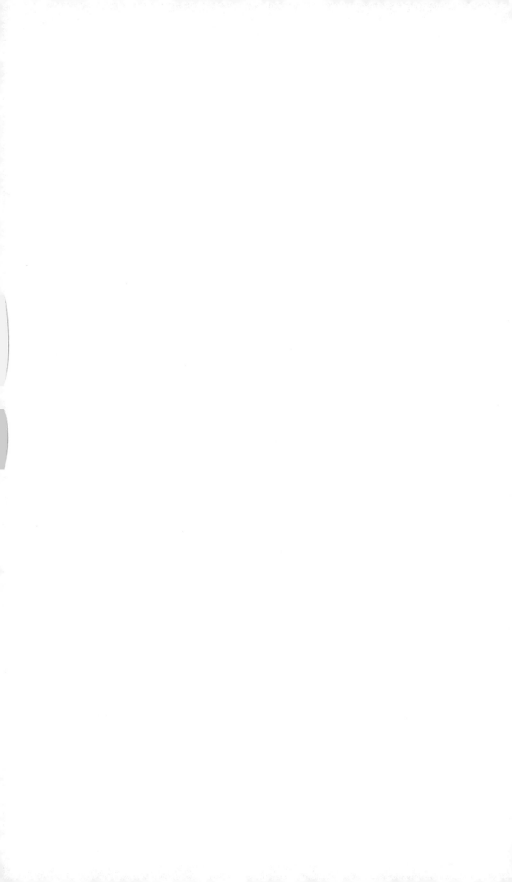

PART **II**

The Development of the Self-Defense Forces, 1955–1974

9

The Basic National Defense Policy

Japan rearmed steadily, if haphazardly, during the Korean War. Yet the government never publicly acknowledged the process, because re-establishing a military was not part of the government's overt agenda. The Japanese people were largely unaware that the government was rebuilding Japan's ground, sea, and air fighting forces. The government made no move in the Diet, however, to create more than a vague awareness of the legal status of rearmament under the country's basic law, the constitution.

Clearly, an armed organization could not exist in Japan indefinitely without a clear understanding of why the country was rearming and whether the new military was intended to fight. When the Self-Defense Forces leadership became aware that it had no justification, it came to demand one.* With the transition from Police Reserve (1950) to Security Forces (1952) and finally to Ground, Maritime, and Air Self-Defense Forces (1954), the belated need to formulate a basic policy for Japan's defense grew. In the mid-1950s, the government yielded: it

---

*Editor's Note: On July 20, 1994, Tomiichi Murayama, the socialist prime minister, declared before the Diet that the Japanese Self-Defense Forces were legal.

established a basic national defense policy, set goals for building defense capabilities for the future, and clarified the justification for the Self-Defense Forces through a series of four Defense Buildup Programs.

From the latter half of the 1950s to the 1960s, four features defined the Self-Defense Forces. The first was the feeling of kinship with the American military, which was becoming Asia's military policeman from Korea to Indochina. Forced to accept a cease-fire in Korea, the American government saw the ties among China, the Soviet Union, and North Korea as a large Asian plot to export revolution to the other countries of Asia. Many Asians believed that the domino effect would work from Northeast to Southeast Asia. After the cease-fire in Korea, America supported Taiwan against mainland China, intervened in the Laotian civil war, and took France's place in Vietnam.

The Japanese archipelago, from the Sea of Okhotsk to the Taiwan Strait, was an important strategic area. Japan could not help being part of America's Asian strategy, which encompassed not just the main islands, but also Okinawa. The powerful force of anticommunism created an irresistible influence on the character and direction of the Self-Defense Forces.

The Japanese economy's dramatic recovery comprised the second factor influencing the development of the Self-Defense Forces. An early economic White Paper, an annual report by the Japanese government, declared that the postwar period had ended in 1956, the second year after the creation of the Self-Defense Forces. That same year, Japan joined the United Nations and returned as a respected member of international society. With its transition from coal to petroleum as a primary energy source, Japan embarked on several years of high growth.

This high-growth economy was extremely fortunate for the growing Self-Defense Forces. Economic vigor was not only an assumption of the Defense Buildup Program, it also played a role in masking the SDF's increasing growth. The fast pace of economic growth let defense spending double during each of the four Defense Buildup Programs. The ever-increasing costs went unchecked, and the government argued that Japan's armament budgets were still quite low given the country's increasing wealth and international norms. The prosperity of the golden sixties continued unbroken until the 1974 oil crisis.

The third factor shaping the Self-Defense Forces was domestic political stability. In 1955, the merger of the Liberal Party and the Japan Democratic Party created the Liberal Democratic Party. Conservative rule became entrenched. At about the same time, the Japan Socialist Party, which had split into left and right wings, coalesced. Thus began a long period of political stasis. Conservatives ruled, but the revolutionary and proconstitutional parties maintained at least one-third of the seats in both houses of the Diet and served as a check on excessive rearmament. This equilibrium of right and left set the tone of domestic politics. The Liberal Democratic Party (LDP) was the party of "reality" in its reliance on the United States under the United States–Japan Security Treaty, while the Japan Socialist Party (JSP) was the party of "legality" in its fealty to the constitution of Japan.

Prime Minister Nobusuke Kishi, who led the mainstream conservatives after Shigeru Yoshida retired, tried to manage a transition from Occupation politics to a new age of United States–Japan relations based on equality. The question of revising the United States–Japan Security Treaty gave rise to the 1960 security treaty riots that toppled the Kishi cabinet. But this struggle did not change the equilibrium between right and left. As a result, the security treaty crisis never developed into anything that could call Japan's defense policies into question.

The fourth, and final, factor affecting the development of Japan's military was the changing of generations within the Self-Defense Forces as graduates of the Defense Academy climbed in rank. After spending one year in officer candidate schools following graduation from the Defense Academy, the 6,377 members of the first fifteen classes began service as junior officers. The early years of future Maritime SDF chief of staff Makoto Sakuma are instructive:

March 1957:	entered Maritime Self-Defense Force, petty officer (age 22)
April 1958:	officer candidate school, ensign (age 23)
February 1960:	lieutenant junior-grade (age 24)
June 1964:	chief navigator of the destroyer Ayamina, lieutenant (age 29)
March 1966:	chief navigator of the destroyer Yamagumo, lieutenant (age 31)
December 1970:	Kure Regional District Headquarters, Defense Department, lieutenant commander (age 35)
July 1972:	central communications unit general staff, commander (age 37)

The basic national defense policy that mapped out the process of growth from the First Defense Buildup Program, begun in 1958, to the Third Defense Buildup Program, which was completed in 1971, grew out of questions posed in the lower house by a Japan Socialist Party member. The questioner was a thirty-three-year-old junior Diet member named Masashi Ishibashi. After being demobilized, Ishibashi had worked in Sasebo for the Occupation troops and helped form the Sasebo chapter of the National Stationed Troops Labor Union Federation. He became a career union leader, his party's expert on defense matters, and, eventually, the Japan Socialist Party's ninth chairman. If Sasebo had succeeded in becoming the peaceful industrial port city it had planned to be, he might never have had a platform from which to spring into national politics.

Ishibashi said to Prime Minister Kishi, "Several years have passed since the inauguration of the Self-Defense Forces. While it is obvious that their minimum duty is to defend Japan, in point of fact, Japan has no basic national defense policy. Japan also has no defense plans. With this ridiculous state of affairs, there is no point going to America, since no substantive talks can be held."[1]

Kishi had just become prime minister in February and was slated to visit the United States in June, so this was an important issue for him. "I will come up with a defense plan quickly and it shall be complete before I visit the United States," he replied, but Ishibashi then continued by asking him how the government conceived of Japan's basic defense needs. Defense Agency director general Akira Kotaki answered on behalf of Kishi:

> Our basic approach to Japan's defense has been our expectation that the United Nations, of which we are now a member, would develop an institution for collective security. Simultaneously, we are pursuing peaceful foreign relations with a view to improving the total picture for our national defense. Since the United Nations has yet to create such a collective security organization, we ultimately must rely on a joint defense between Japan and the United States under the current United States–Japan Security Treaty. Our basic stance is to field a defensive capability that is the minimum required to the extent our national capabilities permit, to which aim a gradual buildup is underway. As it proceeds, our defense relationship with the United States must gradually change. This is an abstract picture of our general approach to Japan's basic defense through the Self-Defense Forces.

This dull summation, of course, hardly satisfied Ishibashi. He pressed the government to formalize this statement in the National Defense Council and obtained a commitment from the government to write a basic national defense policy. The National Defense Council was organized under the Defense Agency Establishment Act with the prime minister as its chairman and the ministers of foreign affairs and the treasury and the director generals of the defense and economic planning agencies as its members. They were charged with "deliberating on important matters of national defense." On May 2, the National Defense Council set a discussion of basic policies of national defense as its agenda and settled on the following four-point policy:

Basic National Defense Policy

The objective of national defense is to prevent direct and indi-rect aggression, and, once invaded, to repel such aggression, thereby preserving the independence and peace of Japan, founded upon democratic principles. To achieve this purpose, the government of Japan hereby establishes the following principles:

(1) To support the activities of the United Nations and pro-mote international cooperation, thereby contributing to the realization of world peace.

(2) To stabilize the public welfare and enhance the people's love for their country, thereby establishing the sound basis essential to Japan's security.

(3) To develop progressively the effective defensive capabili-ties necessary for self-defense, with due regard to the nation's resources and the prevailing domestic situation.

(4) To deal with external aggression on the basis of the United States–Japan security arrangements, pending more effec-tive functioning of the United Nations in future in deter-ring and repelling aggression.

These principles have guided the organization and opera-tion of the Self-Defense Forces ever since. All defense policies, programs, and planning have developed under this constitution of the Self-Defense Forces. It seemed to many to be an unex-pectedly moderate policy, since the first two goals were com-pletely nonmilitary—international cooperation and pacifism, and stable living standards. The role of the Self-Defense Forces is relegated to the third article, and the United States–Japan Security Treaty is only mentioned in the fourth, and even then it is considered to be a temporary resource until such time as the United Nations can implement collective security arrangements. There is no sense in the text of any desire to expand the Self-Defense Forces. It is far easier to read the document as an expression of the limits and structures placed on the defense establishment.

In practice, however, the third and fourth principles of the national defense policy have lent themselves to a flexible application that has created the framework for the Self-Defense Forces and has led to the SDF's expansion, to the point that by the early 1990s Japan had the world's second largest defense budget.

How were defense officials able to apply these principles so selectively? The abstractness of the policy's language certainly gave the government a margin for interpretation. The unmistakable intention of the defense bureaucrats was to make the principles as vague as possible to allow themselves latitude for later reinterpretation. There were other factors as well. The revolutionary and progressive parties latched onto the phrase "national defense" and ignored and passed over the basic policy itself, giving the government the opportunity to interpret the policy's intentions broadly and implement it flexibly. Although the Japan Socialist Party had sought a basic approach to national defense, once the government had enunciated the policy's principles, the socialists returned to their stubborn opposition to dealing with any principles other than Article 9 of the constitution. They did not try to clarify the vagueness and abstraction of the government's policy or fully to exploit the opportunity to pursue a nonmilitary approach to security based on the first and second principles.

Partly because of these developments, the basic national defense policy did not become widely known to the Japanese public, despite its potential for developing a nonmilitary approach to national security. The policy attracted the interest of policy analysts only and came to be be applied on a discretionary basis. The progressive parties' rigidly mechanical response and failure to exploit an opportunity was repeated in the 1970s, when the government presented its peacetime defense strength guidelines during the period of détente and the oil crisis. No momentum developed to reduce the scope of the military. The four Defense Buildup Programs were implemented under an equilibrium of inaction created by the government's submission to the status quo and the opposition's flight from reality.

The month after it formalized the basic national defense policy, the National Defense Council took up deliberations and handed down a decision on another important matter, targets for the defense buildup. The First Defense Buildup Program was described as "setting a defense buildup plan for the three years from fiscal 1958 to fiscal 1960, to reach defense strength commensurate with the minimum levels required for defense based on national resources and economic health." If the basic national defense policy was the car, the first buildup program provided the gas to take the Self-Defense Forces as far as they wanted to go. The goals of the buildup plans expanded steadily throughout the first four plans, and the total defense budget doubled each time.

CONSCRIPTION

The Self-Defense Forces are staffed by volunteers selected from a pool of applicants. In recent years, there has been a shortage of applicants, especially of enlisted men, and the supply of qualified individuals has become erratic. Since the SDF's inception, calls to study the possibility of conscription have been made many times. When the Soviet Union invaded Afghanistan in 1980, defense policy was a hot topic in Japan. Of the many policy proposals made at that time, the revival of conscription proposed by Kansai Economic League chairman Hosai Hinata was the most innovative. "We need to research the possibility of conscription in times of emergency," he stated, setting off a furious debate. An opinion poll conducted by the Youth Conference Center at that time revealed that 33.1% of the Japanese were in in favor of conscription, and 40.9% were opposed to it.

The government, oddly enough, has consistently supported the position that conscription is unconstitutional. The government has defined conscription as "a universal conscription system forcing a duty to obey military orders on the national population." Under the government's interpretation, conscription cannot be permitted, regardless of the peacetime or emergency status of the country, because it contradicts several articles of the constitution, including Article 13's right to liberty and the pursuit of happiness and Article 18's prohibition of involuntary servitude and hard labor.

Air Self-Defense Force general Goro Takeda, who was then chairman of the joint staff council, asked, "Does that then mean that Self-Defense Force officers are being subjected to involuntary servitude and hard labor? Defending the country is a mission of high honor that is the exact opposite of slavery and cruel treatment. These government assertions will only increase our difficulty in recruiting. If there were to be a war and soldiers deserted, what recourse would we have?"

The government has also stated, however, that though conscription is unconstitutional, the commandeering of civilians and requisitioning of assets in time of emergency are not unconstitutional. Should the Self-Defense Forces go into action, it has stated, orders to provide services such as medical care, construction, and transport are covered by other laws and are, in fact, constitutional.

10

Establishing the Defense Industry

The military-industrial sector, like the rest of the Japan's military establishment, discarded its old name, the munitions industry, after the war in favor of a more modern title, the defense industry. It began to operate in earnest during the First Defense Buildup Program of 1958–1960.

By the late 1950s, the wartime prosperity brought by meeting the demands of the Korean War was a fading memory, and many of the smaller new companies went bankrupt. The Defense Agency became the prime purchaser of military goods, and the United States supplied almost all military goods for the Police Reserve and the Security Forces. When the Self-Defense Forces were formed, they started to place domestic orders, but the SDF did not buy from as many sources as the United States had during the Korean War. Instead, the SDF's orders went to the postwar reincarnations of the old *zaibatsu* (industrial conglomerates). The list of defense industry suppliers was almost identical to the list of munitions industry stalwarts under the prewar regime.[2]

While it required the purging of career military men, the Potsdam Declaration also dissolved industries that could be used for rearmament.[3] The Occupation regime had initially carried out this mandate. After it dissolved the imperial military, GHQ made efforts to break up the *zaibatsu* "war criminal corporations" like Mitsubishi and Mitsui. These restrictions were first relaxed during the Korean War, and little by little production resumed in the same piecemeal way that the imperial military men had been readmitted to service.

The Korean War brought work to the factories. Industrial production progressed as the war went on, from ordnance manufacture to vehicle and ship repair, and then to aircraft maintenance. Despite the prohibition against production of weapons and aircraft, the United States military began to place orders in Japan to meet its emergency needs. In October, 1951, the Japan Technological Cooperation Council, which would later change its name to the Japan Weapons Industry Association, was formed to meet this demand. In August of the next year, the center of the financial community, the Keidanren, the Federation of Economic Organizations, set up the Defense Production Committee, further legitimizing the organizational infrastructure behind the growing defense industry.[4]

In March 1952, GHQ issued an order rescinding the prohibition on Japanese production of weapons and aircraft. The Japanese government drafted and enacted the Law for Production of Weapons in 1953 and the Aircraft Production Enterprises Act in 1954. Japan's desire for a defense industry had always been present; now the industrial organization and legal structure for such an industry were in place.

No sooner had the defense industry reappeared publicly than the Keidanren's Defense Production Committee announced its proposal for a defense buildup in February 1953. In this proposal, the Japanese financial community mapped out its plans for a full-fledged rearmament after Japan recovered its sovereignty. This document was very revealing of the importance placed on the defense industry. It was clear that military demand had been crucial to the national economic resurgence during the Korean War, and the Keidanren foresaw high levels of rearmament in the future. The proposal was intended to be implemented over the six-year period from 1953 to 1958 and called for the following levels of strength:

- army strength: fifteen divisions with supplies for thirty divisions and other troops and three hundred thousand men
- naval strength: 290,000 tons of ships and seventy thousand sailors
- air strength: 3,750 planes and 130,000 personnel

This program was expected to cost a total of ¥2,894.2 billion. Japan could hardly achieve this enormous addition to its armed forces on its own. According to the Keidanren proposal, "Given forecasts for the Japanese economy, its financial resources, military production capabilities, technological development and ability to handle orders, we estimate that Japan can only handle fifty-six percent of this figure on its own. The remaining forty-four percent will have to come from the United States in the form of financial or in-kind assistance." They expected ¥1,270 billion in assistance from the United States government, and calculated that the proportion of national income that Japan would need to devote to defense was roughly equivalent to what Italy, Belgium, Holland, and other European countries were allocating.

The plan called for construction of three six-thousand-ton-class patrol ships, noting that "we have excess building capacity and hope to receive orders for ships from other democracies," and the acquisition of 1,330 F-86Ds, the most advanced fighter jets of that time. It estimated annual personnel costs per man at only ¥40,000, since most of these men would be conscripts. The strong desire to replace the exceptional demand of the Korean War with domestic defense needs seems to have prevented a close economic analysis.

In many ways, the Keidanren proposal bears a strong resemblance to the proposal developed by the Hattori group before the Police Reserve was created. Both assume an open and publicly acknowledged rearmament and a return to prewar military modes. Both proposal also relied even more than the government did on an American contribution, probably assuming that anticommunism would be rationale enough for the United States. Just as the ex–imperial staff officer Takushiro Hattori joined hands with Major General Willoughby, the financiers of the Japanese economy looked to past models in their plans to rebuild the defense industry after independence.

The Keidanren proposal was presented to the United States Department of Defense through the American embassy in Japan, and it undoubtedly contributed to the tenor of the talks in Washington between Ikeda and Robertson in October of that year. The initial American proposal of 320,000 troops on the ground certainly seems to have relied heavily on the Keidanren proposal. But both proposals were the product of a fundamental miscalculation of the age and a blind exaggeration of economic capabilities. The plan's fanciful logic could not persuade economic rationalists such as Ikeda and Miyazawa, and it eventually died.

The Diet adopted the first buildup program in June 1957, under Nobusuke Kishi as speaker, one month after the government presented its basic national defense policy. The goals of the buildup were as follows: "Under this plan, Ground Self-Defense Force personnel are to reach 180,000, Maritime Self-Defense Force ship displacement is to reach 120,000 tons, and Air Self-Defense Force capabilities are to reach 1,300 aircraft." The plan had two major aims. The first was to increase ground fighting strength to the 180,000-troop level pledged by Japan in the Ikeda-Robertson talks, so that the United States could withdraw troops from Japan as soon as possible.[5] This required an increase of 130,000 in the number of Ground Self-Defense Force troops. It also required expansion of the defense industry. Documents from the National Defense Council emphasize this point repeatedly:

> Research and development must be devoted to all types of new weapons within the limits required for self-defense, and gradual improvement of frontline equipment must be planned for.
>
> Scientific and technological development must be promoted, development of new weapons must be accelerated, and organizational techniques and equipment must be updated to provide a qualitative improvement in defense strength.
>
> The buildup of defense strength also requires measures to build up the defense industry.

Despite efforts at disguise, a mutuality of interest between government and the financial community emerged. This alliance created a plethora of Defense Agency orders to compensate for the dwindling of Korean War demand. Though the government was not as brazenly self-promoting as the Keidanren's Defense Production Committee, it was in agreement on the broader goal of nurturing and strengthening the defense industries. The most obvious differences between the two were that the financial community urged rapid political action, financial aggressiveness, and pro-American anticommunism, whereas the government emphasized political moderation without constitutional revision, fiscal health to control inflation, and pro-American cooperation. The government had to consider public opinion and elections, which the financial community did not. Both industry and government pushed the lofty-sounding goal of domestic production of Self-Defense Forces equipment, and both placed special importance on the precariousness of demand for defense industry products compared to those of ordinary industry.

Although 1957 was the year before the start of the First Defense Buildup Program, orders from the Defense Agency were already in excess of orders from the United States military.

The many new or smaller companies that had profited from wartime demand were largely ignored in favor of the giant suppliers like Mitsubishi. In terms of weapons, vehicles, aircraft, and electronic equipment ordered, the turnaround in defense demand is clear. While United States military orders shrank from ¥12.5 billion in fiscal year 1955 to ¥5.3 billion in fiscal year 1958, Defense Agency orders grew from ¥7.6 billion to ¥32.7 billion.

The First Defense Buildup Program was the engine for enormous growth in domestic spending, and the companies that reaped the greatest benefits were the old *zaibatsu* firms. The Korean War provided a major boost to these firms, which five or six years earlier had teetered on the brink of extinction. Many of the major manufacturers of the imperial era began to merge in the 1960s, during the first two Defense Buildup Programs. In 1964, three Mitsubishi heavy industry companies merged and returned to their previous name of Mitsubishi Heavy Industries; in 1969, three Kawasaki group companies merged into Kawasaki Heavy Industries (1969); in 1960, Ishikawajima Heavy Industries and Harima Heavy Industries merged to form Ishikawajima-Harima Heavy Industries; and another two mergers in 1962 and 1967 created Mitsui Shipbuilding. The companies all began to assume the forms they had taken before GHQ broke up the *zaibatsu*.

It is, of course, too simple to ascribe the resurrection of these Imperial military industry giants solely to the Defense Buildup Programs. Japan's economic prosperity had created a shipbuilding export boom that encouraged mergers, and many large corporations were not primarily dependent on Defense Agency orders. Nevertheless, reliable government-guaranteed purchase contracts extending for a period of five years for warships, or ten years for aircraft and tanks, were among the most valuable for these corporations, and the government's investment in research and development had important ripple effects on the rest of the products produced by these corporations. A widely cited example is the use in the bullet train braking system of the disc brakes developed for the production, under license, of the F-104 fighter in the early 1960s. These companies also were better able to advertise their wares abroad based on the prestige they gained from manufacturing complex products like warships and aircraft.

The importance of eighteen years of weapons spending under the Defense Buildup Programs from the late 1950s through the early 1970s should not be underestimated. Although not as sexy or ambitious as the American and Soviet space exploration efforts, the Japanese government's defense program was surely just as important in terms of national planning. The phrase "income doubling," which was coined in the 1960s to describe Japanese economic growth, applies perfectly to the defense industry. The greatest effect of the Defense Buildup Programs was the development of domestic production and research capabilities. Companies moved from the assembly of imported knockdown sets, to domestic manufacturing under license, and finally to production of domestically developed products. Just as the Police Reserve and the Maritime Security Force were transformed into the Self-Defense Forces, the Japanese defense industry transformed itself step by step from producing goods that were "Made in Occupied Japan" to those that were industry's "Made in Japan." When the First Defense Buildup Program started, barely half the defense orders were placed domestically; by the late 1960s, over ninety percent of orders were domestic. American grants and loans were rapidly phased out.

Domestic production advanced first in destroyers, submarines, and other naval fighting equipment, then in tanks and other equipment for the ground forces, and finally, in air force fighters. Fighting ships and tanks were the easiest to develop, since they were developed from World War II models. Aircraft technology had greatly advanced since the war, however, and

Japan lagged behind other countries in the design and manufacture of jet engines.

Prior to the First Defense Buildup Program, the destroyers Harukaze and Yukikaze were commissioned as ships Number 101 and Number 102. Their standard displacement was seventeen hundred tons, and they were each equipped with three 5.38-inch single-mount dual-purpose guns and antisubmarine depth-charge throwers. They drew attention as the first large Japanese warships constructed for the Maritime Self-Defense Force. They were very reminiscent of American destroyers, but were designed and constructed in Japan. The Harukaze class was followed in the first program by the Ayamina class, which was composed of seven 1,700-ton ships of the same configuration, and the Murasame class, composed of three 1,800-ton ships. Planning was also started for the Amatsukaze class, which included 3,050-ton ships equipped with Tartar anti-aircraft missiles constructed during the second program. Submarines were also constructed under the second program, with the typical Self-Defense Forces designation of underwater high-speed target vessel. These included the 1,600-ton Ooshio-class submarines, two 750-ton Hayashio-class vessels, and two 790-ton Natsushio-class ships.

Japan also constructed tanks. In keeping with the government's position that the Self-Defense Forces had no war potential, tanks were referred to publicly as "medium-sized special vehicles." These tanks, which were described as carrying one 90-millimeter gun because of the smaller body size of Japanese and smaller roads in Japan, were constructed by Mitsubishi Heavy Industries and Nippon Works on a prototype basis during the first program. The prototypes were approved in 1961 and the tanks entered mass production in 1962 during the second program. Five hundred and sixty of these vehicles were constructed and were used by the Ground Self-Defense Force until the Model 74 tank superseded them in 1974.

Because the Air Self-Defense Force required newer technologies that Japan lacked, and because it was the last of the three SDF branches to be established, its transition from foreign purchasing to domestic production has been slower and less certain, although the government promoted its technological development quite vigorously.

Unlike the ground and maritime forces, the Air Self-Defense Force started with complete support for domestic assembly production derived from the United States government's military assistance program. At first, the Air Self-Defense Force had planes like the T-34 reciprocating-engine trainer, the T-33A jet trainer, and the C-46 medium transport plane. When the United States began in 1956 to supply the SDF with the North American F-86F, the workhorse of the Korean War, the Japanese and American governments started a jet assembly operation under the Mutual Security Assurance (MSA) agreement. The goal was for Japan to become self-sufficient in aircraft production. The new Mitsubishi Heavy Industries was the chief contractor overseeing F-86F production. The United States supplied the engines, Kawasaki Heavy Industries handled preparation and parts production, and later Ishikawajima Heavy Industries handled repairs and some additional parts production. Each F-86F cost ¥109.8 million, with additional yearly maintenance costs of ¥2.2 million, a very high cost for Japan at that time. The United States provided financial assistance to Mitsubishi and the other firms under the MSA agreement, with ¥1.5 billion going to Mitsubishi alone, in addition to salaries for workers and production parts under the Military Assistance Program. This allowed Japanese firms to learn jet aircraft manufacture.

Mitsubishi Heavy Industries, which was headquartered in Nagoya, had changed its name to Central Japan Heavy Industries after GHQ broke up the *zaibatsu*, then to New Mitsubishi Heavy Industries, and finally to Mitsubishi Heavy Industries. The company had been receiving orders for aircraft repair from the United States Air Command Far East since 1953. In 1954, the company began to repair F-86F fuselages. For the first few dozen aircraft, Mitsubishi had to assemble aircraft fuselage parts sent from America using tools provided by the United States. The company worked with plans written in English, with yards and pounds for measurements and tools graduated in inches. At the start of production, Shinzo Fujii the president of Mishubishi, described his hope that the company's workers and engineers would learn the new technology quickly:

> The F-86F was a near-supersonic aircraft and was structurally and technologically in another league from what the line had itself produced in the past. The technological gap was very hard to leap. Since we were fortunate enough to have a technology link with North America, which had the world's most advanced aircraft technology, we were able to get hold of this technology quickly and cheaply. We tried to absorb and digest it in the shortest period of time. Everyone gave up on the idea of developing our own technology. Aircraft technology was developing so fast, and it was important not only for military applications but for peacetime applications as well, and was becoming even more so. The current and future challenges might be formidable, but we were dreamers. We worked very hard and hoped for a day when we would be developing things ourselves.[6]

The assembly factory for the F-86F was located in the Ooe area. The plant had been burned to the ground in the B-29 bombing raids during the war and had been disused for many years. Mitsubishi rebuilt the factory and completed the first order for seventy aircraft in September 1956. It then completed a second order for 110 planes and a third order for 120 during the first program, for a total of three hundred F-86Fs delivered to the Air Self-Defense Force. In November 1959, while the F-86F production line was still running, the Diet adopted a resolution to use the Lockheed F-104 as Japan's next main fighter. Mitsubishi was the prime contractor for this plane as well. The

Nagoya Aircraft Works, onetime manufacturer of the Zero fighter, was renamed Meiko (Nagoya Aircraft) and transformed itself into the main supplier of Air Self-Defense Force jets.

The First Defense Buildup Program had set domestic manufacture of weapons as a goal. The second and third programs, from 1962 to 1971, accelerated this effort. The first completely Japanese-produced weapons under the second program were tanks, armored cars, machine guns, rifles, and naval vessels. The introduction of new technologies under license allowed domestic production to expand from the F-104 into new areas such as the Base Air Defense Ground Environment (BADGE) system, an early warning radar aircraft-detection system, and the P-2V antisubmarine patrol plane. In the third program, Japan selected McDonnell Douglas's F-4EJ Phantom as its primary fighter, and Mitsubishi Heavy Industries produced the plane under license. Mitsubishi, NEC, and Toshiba produced the Nike surface-to-air missile and McDonnell Douglas's Hawk surface-to-air missile. Roughly ¥1.2 trillion of the total five-year defense budget of ¥2.34 trillion was devoted to upgrading and purchasing new equipment. Japanese companies received ¥920 billion of this amount. Since the comparable figures for the second program had been ¥474.6 billion of a total of ¥1.37 trillion, it is clear that the defense sector of Japan's economy was growing fast.

Because the Japanese designed and produced more of their own weaponry themselves, it is easy to assume that the Self-Defense Forces were becoming more self-directed in the use and operation of these weapons. This was not the case at all. As the 1960s progressed, the Self-Defense Forces faithfully followed the direction of their friendly ally, the United States military, just as they had done in the days of the Police Reserve.

THE GRUMMAN-LOCKHEED FIGHT

When it came time for Japan to select its primary fighter plane for the 1960s, the Defense Agency selected the Grumman F-11F-1F and the Lockheed F-104C as its candidates and sent a survey team to the United States to evaluate their respective technologies. In April 1958, after the team had returned, Defense Agency director general Naka Aichi announced that he had reached an informal decision to select the Grumman F-11F-1F as the Air Self-Defense Force's next primary fighter.

In August of that year, however, the chairman of the Budget Committee of the lower house, Shoji Tanaka, asserted that there had been irregularities in the fighter's selection and summoned Prime Minister Nobusuke Kishi and others as witnesses against the Defense Agency. These accusations had been brought to Tanaka by a prominent member of the right wing, Yoshio Kodama.[7] He had led the Kodama Machine during World War II, supplying war matériel to the Imperial Army. After the war, he forged deep ties to conservative administrations and was known for his political acumen and his influence behind the scenes.

Under pressure from Tanaka and Kodama, the Defense Agency delayed its decision on which plane to buy. It overturned the informal decision in favor of the Grumman plane and ordered Air SDF general Minoru Genda to return with a second survey team to the United States. This time the fifty-four-year-old Genda personally flew the supersonic aircraft to compare their performance, and after his return issued the Genda Report. He favored the F-104C, made by Lockheed. On the basis of this report, in November 1959, the Diet formally selected Lockheed to supply the next generation of fighter aircraft.

Although Japanese domestic production increased dramatically throughout the 1960s, all of the primary fighter aircraft, the F-86F, the F-104C, and the F-4EJ, were American products, as were the Tartar anti-aircraft missiles and the Asroc antisubmarine rockets aboard Japanese-made warships. Though "creation of a defense industry base" was their stated goal, Defense Buildup Programs expanded the introduction of American-made weapons, designed by the American military, in Japanese factories. While the F-104J fighters rolled out of Mitsubishi's Nagoya factory had Japanese red circles on their sides, and were flown by SDF pilots, all two hundred thousand parts, down to the screws and rivets, had to be made to exacting United States military specifications. All inspection methods and quality control procedures for the factory itself were also to United States military specifications. The domestication of equipment that the companies boasted of was no more than domestic production of United States military equipment. The United States–Japan Security Treaty system did not permit any changes in United States military specifications; on the contrary, the introduction of high-performance American-made weapons into all three branches of the Self-Defense Forces only increased the scope and depth of cooperation between the United States and Japanese militaries.

THE LIMITS OF DEFENSE

The expression "the minimum fighting power necessary for self-defense" in Japan's national defense policy posed serious problems of interpretation. New factors had beguiled the government time and again as it tried to define this minimum quantity. Does it include nuclear weapons? Is there a difference between offensive and defensive weapons? Can technological advances be ignored? How much does the minimum that is necessary depend on the fighting strength of a hypothetical enemy? The task of interpreting this phrase was made more difficult by the fact that a variety of factors converged to push Japan toward expanding its military.

In its first defense White Paper, published in 1970 and entitled "The Defense of Japan," the Japanese government proposed guidelines for determining the appropriate limit for ordinary defensive capabilities. "Since our military power is intended for self-defense, its size and scale must be that which is proper and necessary. What degree of defense power this means in concrete terms cannot be described categorically because of various conditions, such as the progress and development of science and technology at a given time; but in any case Japan cannot possess weapons that will pose a threat of aggression to other nations, such as long-range bombers like B-52s, nuclear attack aircraft carriers, and intercontinental ballistic missiles (ICBMs)."

This White Paper, also called the Nakasone White Paper, allowed a margin for change in circumstances and technology and set broad standards, drawing a line at weapons that "pose a threat of aggression to other nations."

After the fourth White Paper was published in 1978, however, the phrase "pose a threat of aggression to other nations" was changed to "cause mass destruction to the territory of neighboring nations," which in effect dramatically raised the upper ceiling of the weaponry permitted under the constitution. The 1989 defense White Paper presents the following guidelines: "For individual weapons, the possession of any kind of offensive weapon whose performance permits its use solely for purposes of mass destruction to the territory of neighboring nations is not permitted in any circumstances, since such weapons obviously exceed the minimum level necessary for self-defense; for example, ICBMs, long-range strategic bombers, and offensive aircraft carriers may not be possessed by the Self-Defense Forces."

By 1989, the standard had been changed from the psychological principle of making other countries feel a threat of aggression to the physical principle of being able to cause mass destruction to the territory of another country. This meant that, rather than exercising self-restraint in consideration of the feelings of its neighbors, Japan would base its standard of necessary weaponry on its own situation. Although there was no change in the weapons given as examples, there was a profound change in the impression created by the guidelines.

The reasons behind the change in guidelines most probably rested in Japan's changing defense situation. By the mid-1970s, Japan's most likely enemy had become the Soviet Union rather than China and North Korea. The Defense Agency probably considered the psychological considerations of the Soviet Union largely irrelevant, since it was a military superpower and had never been invaded by Japan. Because Japan's strategic response to the Soviet Union assumed close cooperation with the United States, there was also a need to revise the concept of the defensive limit.

This revision, however, effectively removed the barriers to a larger force structure. When Japan selected the F-4 Phantom as its primary fighter in 1968, the Air Self-Defense Force removed the Phantom's bombing sights and mid-air refueling equipment before placing it in service, since these could be considered conducive to a "threat of aggression." When the Phantom was replaced by the F-15, no such move was even considered. When development of the F-1 ground support fighter began in 1972, the SDF shortened its range to prevent it from making a round trip to Pyongyang, so that North Korea would not consider the plane an aggressive threat. By contrast, in 1989 the Defense Agency's final design for the FSX, the next generation of ground support fighter, gave that plane the ability to reach any spot on the entire Korean peninsula. And though offensive aircraft carriers are still considered banned, there is no such prohibition on antisubmarine aircraft carriers.

11

The New Security Treaty System

On January 19, 1960, Prime Minister Nobusuke Kishi signed the Mutual Cooperation and Security Treaty Between Japan and the United States of America in Washington, D.C. Before leaving Japan, Prime Minister Kishi had described his aspirations: "The new treaty I am going to sign will bring to fruition a new era in relations between Japan and the United States based on the principle of common interest and cooperation set forth after my meeting in 1957 with American president Eisenhower." The signing of the new United States–Japan Security Treaty established that the status of American troops who had been stationed in Japan since September 1945 had been changed from temporary and provisional to something more long-term and continuing.

In the nine years since Japan's recovery of sovereignty, the United States military in Japan had made no move to withdraw from its sprawling bases. Dissatisfaction arose among local residents, and the signing of the new United States–Japan Security Treaty only served to increase their discontent. The domestic political disturbances that ensued within Japan after the signing called for an immediate and massive change in Self-Defense Forces policy.

The government cited two major reasons for revising the security treaty. First, the old treaty seemed one-sided, because the United States had no clear obligation to come to the defense of Japan. This omission needed clarification. Second, under the old treaty the United States also had the power to help put down "domestic disturbances," a clear infringement on Japanese sovereignty that demanded to be removed. The Liberal Democratic Party (LDP) claimed in policy statements that the Self-Defense Forces had achieved sufficient strength and competence and that they were able, in cooperation with the police and other institutions for keeping the public peace, to handle civil disturbances. The new United States–Japan Security Treaty, which made suppression of civil unrest solely Japan's concern, placed the Self-Defense Forces at a crossroads, forcing the government to decide whether they should take a role in keeping the public peace.

The first article of the old security treaty, which was signed along with the peace treaty in San Francisco in 1952, specifically included the suppression of major civil unrest and riots in Japan as a purpose of the American troops stationed in Japan. These were more than mere words. When the government signed the new security treaty, the left wing held May Day demonstrations in front of the emperor's palace, renaming the area "People's Square." About one thousand people gathered, but the crowd quickly grew to over 6,000 when workers joined the group after a clash with police. A pitched battle broke out between the placard-waving crowd and five thousand policemen. The police broke up the demonstration with tear gas and pistols, leaving two demonstrators dead and fifteen hundred injured. The commander of American forces in Japan, General Ridgeway, was ready to send troops into action. As he described the situation in his memoirs, "I watched with the greatest attention. Violence had broken out several times in the past and I had no intention of condoning it. I had tanks carrying armed American soldiers stationed out of sight in several locations with instructions not to do anything except on my personal direct orders. Our troops were well trained in controlling violence."[8]

The Self-Defense Forces paid close attention as well. One original purpose of the Police Reserve had been to maintain domestic order. In addition to their role as a defensive force, the Security Forces were charged with performing public peace-keeping actions, should there be an act of indirect aggression or other emergency. This provision had been reserved for the Self-Defense Forces. With the disappearance of the old security treaty's civil disturbances clause, the Self-Defense Forces were now the first line of defense.

When Japan signed the new security treaty, opposition parties and the government hotly debated Japan's new military obligations under the treaty, particularly the definition of "Far East" and the bringing of nuclear weapons into Japan. A People's Congress Against the Security Treaty was convened outside the Diet, and student protesters from the National Federation of Students' Self-Government Association surrounded the Diet building with a human wall. Some members of the government were in favor of calling out the Self-Defense Forces. Prime Minister Kishi was planning for President Dwight Eisenhower's arrival in Japan for the ceremony exchanging instruments of ratification. Calm had to prevail around the Diet building and the imperial palace. The demonstrators had to be cleared.

The director general of the Defense Agency at that time was Munenori Akagi; the chairman of the joint staff council was Keizo Hayashi; and Ichiji Sugita was the Ground SDF chief of staff. Sugita, who accepted the British surrender at Singapore and was present for the Japanese capitulation on the Missouri, believed he was seeing the prelude to a full-blown revolution.[9] Opposition to the security treaty and to Prime Minister Kishi became more violent daily. On April 1, Sugita ordered a "police exercise." For the two days of April 20 and 21, Ground SDF deputy chief of staff Hiroshi Hosoda led a national-scale public security command post exercise, and he invited Director General Akagi to the Ground SDF staff operations room. Meanwhile, actual troop movements were well underway throughout the Tokyo area. Sandbags and barbed wire were secretly shipped in from Hokkaido and other locations for the exercises. The SDF stayed in close communication with police authorities. Although several officials questioned the purpose of the exercise, the chief of staff was not swayed from his task:

> It had been my experience on the battlefield that the confident way to deal with a crisis is not to hope that what you fear does not happen but to prepare for what you fear might. That is why I accelerated public security preparations after taking my post and why I emphasized preparing for an indirect aggression. There were some in the staff and below me who were concerned that the public security mobilization was happening too quickly, but I was keenly aware how important these mobilizations were for Japan and so I tried to prepare for anything that might be required, however unlikely.[10]

What worried Sugita's critics most was the possible use of weapons by the Self-Defense Forces. If he deployed the Self-Defense Forces instead of the police, the action might not stop at arresting demonstrators and breaking up demonstrations but could extend to major bloodshed. Guns might be fired and people killed. The Self-Defense Forces Act stated that weapons could be used [to maintain public order] to the extent judged reasonably necessary given the prevailing circumstances. This statement left some ambiguity regarding specific standards and whether the Self-Defense Forces members were obliged to follow the orders of their superiors in such cases. While Sugita stated that firing on Japanese countrymen should be avoided, he relied on the restraint of troops who had undergone only regular military education and training. He sent live ammunition to the troops and waited for the prime minister's directions.

On May 19, 1960, the Liberal Democratic Party strong-armed ratification of the new security treaty and agreement through the lower house of the Diet. Violent demonstrations swept Tokyo. On June 15, the Labor Federation marched on the Diet to oppose the security treaty but were attacked by a crowd of anticonstitution rightists organized by Yoshio Kodama. The police did not interfere. The student league *zengakuren* then mobilized eight thousand students, who stormed the Diet building and occupied the Diet courtyard. That night the police moved in with tear gas and clubs. Forty-three were seriously injured, 182 arrested, and one woman, Michiko Kanba, was killed. The doctor who conducted the autopsy said that she was strangled and trampled. Charges of police brutality were aired. Tensions became extreme between the LDP government and antitreaty forces led by the opposition parties. The noisy prelude to revolution that Sugita had foreseen seemed to blanket the capital.

At the height of this unrest, Eisenhower set out for Japan and the Far East, and Kishi remained fully determined to have the American president visit Tokyo. He decided to call out the Self-Defense Forces. Defense Agency director general Munetoku Akagi strongly opposed even considering deployment of the Self-Defense Forces, the central part of the prime minister's strategy. He worried that deployment of the SDF would introduce a chasm between the Self-Defense Forces and the Japanese people that would be difficult to repair. After the death in front of the Diet building on June 15, Kishi summoned Akagi to the prime minister's residence at Minamihiradai and questioned him about the use of the Self-Defense Forces. The minister of finance Eisaku Sato and minister of international trade and industry Hayato Ikeda were both present. Sato pressed Akagi to send in the SDF, and Akagi responded to Kishi by stating his opposition. "If we send them in, they have to be armed, probably with machine guns. They may end up having to use them. If that does happen, many people will die."[11]

The prime minister of Japan has the power to dismiss cabinet officers who deny his authority, but Kishi backed down. He called a special cabinet meeting the day after Michiko Kanba was killed. The cabinet decided to ask President Eisenhower to postpone his visit. The president had already arrived in Okinawa, which was then under American administration, but though he had entered Japan, he had to end his trip without visiting Tokyo. "I could not help but be disappointed," Eisenhower said in his memoirs. "No matter how you looked at it, this was a victory for communism."* Ground SDF chief of staff Sugita also felt that "the success in holding off the visit was in fact a victory for the communist camp," but he also said that "for the Self-Defense Forces this huge uproar was actually a very good training opportunity. It lent our training exercises a seriousness of purpose and made the Ground Self-Defense Force keenly aware that they had a real mission and role in the Cold War conflict."

The possibility that the Self-Defense Forces might be deployed against a civil disturbance soon became less thinkable after the riots stemming from the 1960 security treaty. In November of that year, a draft of the *Public Security Mobilization Guidebook* was prepared under Sugita and distributed to the troops. Many people, both inside and outside of the government were outraged. Under pressure from the Diet, the manual was discarded and no more training materials for action in quelling public disturbances were prepared. A precedent had been established. In the 1968 Diet session, Defense Agency director general Kaneshichi Masuda described the developments as follows:

---

*Editor's Note: Almost certainly this turmoil resulted from the shooting down of Francis Gary Powers' U2 and his subsequent capture.

The Self-Defense Forces will not be deployed except in the most exceptional of circumstances. In such cases we must have the consent of all of you, and it is my duty even then to try strongly to dissuade you from such actions. If the riot police, whose primary function is to handle these situations, cannot manage to restore public order, it is not reasonable to expect us to do any better. Because I believe it to be in my authority, I have strictly ordered the director of the Education Bureau and the chiefs of staff not to study the suppression of riots, since public security is not our mission.[12]

On the occasion of the 1970 renewal of the security treaty, the police riot troops had available the personnel and the equipment of a small army, thus avoiding any need for the Self-Defense Forces to become involved. By this time the civilian population had come to think of itself as overwhelmingly middle class and stable, and no longer preferred public demonstrations as a reaction to defense policy.

The signing of the new security treaty resulted in a smaller role for the Self-Defense Forces in civil disturbances and public security. In other strategic fields, the opposite was true. The new United States–Japan Security Treaty made a prominent feature of "mutual cooperation" and Article 5 called for common Japanese and United States responses to common dangers. This change in the treaty implicitly expanded coverage by the armed forces of areas far from Japan and its periphery. For the strength of the Japanese military, 1960 was thus a watershed year. Japan was becoming tightly bound to America's Asian-Pacific strategy and increasingly saw the three socialist nations of northeast Asia, the Soviet Union, China, and North Korea, as its hypothetical enemy, despite the absence of any actual threat from the Soviet Union and the inability of either China or North Korea to launch offensive actions against Japan.

THE THREE NOES INCIDENT

In December 1961, Tokyo's Metropolitan Police Office discovered a plan for a coup d'état. The plotters were right-wing activists and graduates of the old imperial Military Academy. They had aggressively recruited the support of the Self-Defense Forces, and the plot is sometimes referred to as the Self-Defense Forces Plot. Toyosaku Kawanami, a former president of Kawanami Industrial Works Corporation, was the spiritual guide of the plotters.

Kawanami believed that leftists were plotting a communist revolution and that the only way to resist this revolution was to replace the political world through a coup d'état that implemented his Three Noes philosophy: no war, no taxes, no unemployment. Takashi Mikami was a leader of the group that was planning the coup, which also included a band of graduates of the fifty-ninth and sixtieth classes of the imperial Military Academy, who called themselves the National History Society. They planned to attack and occupy the Diet when it convened on December 9, and to imprison or kill all the Diet and cabinet members. They would then proclaim a national emergency.

The National History Society set about enticing and persuading members of the Self-Defense Forces to join them. According to the indictments, from early October to late November, they contacted and sought out commissioned officers of the Ground SDF at the Defense Agency and at the SDF bases in Nerima, Narashino, Ichigaya, and other locations around Tokyo to entice them to join in the plot. They even used Ground Self-Defense Force firing ranges for shooting practice.

The Metropolitan Police Office followed the National History Society, though, and discovered the coup d'état plot. Information indicated that the plotters had approached Ground SDF chief of staff Ichiji Sugita, and the police pursued the contact to discover the identity of the plotters. Eight of the leaders were arrested before the coup could be executed. In his memoirs, Sugita hints that not all of the officers who had been contacted reported it to the police, but, in the end, the plotters received no help from the Self-Defense Forces.

The Asian-Pacific scope of the United States–Japan Security Treaty soon came into play. Beginning in the mid-1960s, the government allowed the United States to use its bases in Japan to pursue its deepening involvement in the Vietnam War. Although no Japanese-American operations were carried out before the 1970s, several strategic plans that were exposed during the 1960s indicated that Japan and the United States had agreed to cooperate should a second Korean War break out or if there were another Taiwan Strait crisis. The two most famous examples of this were the Mitsuya exercises and the Bull Run strategy.

The Mitsuya exercises were formally referred to by the Defense Agency as the "Fiscal 1963 Comprehensive Defense Map Problem." These were exercises that extended for a full five months from February 1, 1963, with the participation of eighty-four officers of the Ground, Maritime, and Air Self-Defense Forces and staff from Section 1 of the Defense Agency, under the command of General Yoshio Tanaka, the chairman of the joint staff council. The main purpose of the exercises was to determine what defensive measures would be required, including deployment of forces and enactment of emergency legislation, to defend Japan should an armed conflict break out on the Korean peninsula and extend into Japan. In February 1965, Diet member Haruo Okada, of the Japan Socialist Party, presented the Budget Committee of the lower house with part of a document he had obtained and demanded to know who was responsible for it. The document envisioned seven military scenarios in great detail and described the stages of war activity and the operations that the Self-Defense Forces would pursue in each of these scenarios. A major political uproar ensued.

For example, one of the scenarios describes a hypothetical military situation during the month of July. On July 19, North Korea and China together cross the thirty-eighth parallel and invade South Korea. On July 21, the United States–Japan Security Treaty Security Consultative Committee convenes in Tokyo, the government calls an extraordinary cabinet meeting, and the prime minister goes on national television to state that Japan is in a crisis of direct aggression from the communists and that the Japanese people must rise to action. The country then shifts to wartime policies. This is typical of scenarios envisioned in Okada's document.

Prime Minister Eisaku Sato was at first stunned by the suddenness of this explosive disclosure: "I would absolutely never allow the kind of actions just described. It is very alarming that this kind of situation is even being contemplated without the knowledge of the government." The prime minister appeared to have absolutely no idea of what was going open and was genuinely angered.

Such frankness was shown by the government on only this one occasion. Several days later, the prime minister exhibited an entirely different attitude. "It is absolutely natural for a defense authority to conduct the type of exercise being performed. I am more concerned that top secret documents have been leaked." The focus of the incident changed into an investigation of the breach in security, and Deputy Director Yoshio Miwa and others below him were punished for lack of attention to security. The government viewed the Mitsuya exercises as a study, not as an actual contingency plan.

But the Mitsuya exercises had more significant implications than would be expected of a mere study. The words of United States Assistant Secretary of Defense Roswell Gilpatric on his return from a visit to Japan in January 1963, immediately prior to the start of the research, indicate the importance of the exercises:

> The United States wants Japan to take up a far greater share of the defense burden on the western side of the Pacific than it has been doing. To this end, we expect Japan to be able to back up the defense efforts of the Philippines and Australia, as well as the Ryukyu Islands defense. The United States also expects that Japan may in future have sufficient military surveillance capability and defensive strength, not offensive strength, to defend part of the Korean Peninsula. This would mean that in the event of an outbreak of hostilities in the Koreas, a response might be possible without requiring a reinforcement of American divisions.

Given American expectations and the fact that Japan and South Korea were negotiating over normalization of diplomatic relations as a prelude to the signing of the Basic Treaty between Japan and Korea in June 1965, the Mitsuya exercises can be seen as an exploration of ways for Japan–United States defense cooperation might operate after normalization of Japanese relations with South Korea. It was far from a simple academic exercise. It seems more realistic to consider it a contingency plan.

In the scenario involving an invasion of South Korea; "In the evening of July 19, 196X, North Korean bomber divisions, probably including the backup from the communist Chinese Air Force, suddenly launch a surprise attack on major South Korean air bases and cities and by midnight the North Korean army has crossed the entire length of the demilitarized zone and begun an invasion." Under these conditions, the topics to be investigated were: (1) collaboration between relevant government agencies during emergencies; (2) criteria for armed actions; and (3) collaboration with the command of American forces in Japan. Measures to be taken under the hypothetical situation were considered in two categories, guidelines for national policies to be taken in emergencies, and measures to be taken by the Self-Defense Forces. The research produced a book of 1,419 pages, parts of which were stamped "Top Secret."

The problems posed by the Mitsuya exercises were multifaceted. For example, the document's guidelines for national policies to be taken in emergencies extend to economic and informational controls, and especially to control over the distribution of goods. The consideration of Japan's defense policies examined the problem of the power of command in the Self-Defense Forces and the possible use of nuclear weapons.

The examination of the command structure of the Self-Defense Forces foresaw that a Japan–United States joint strategy coordination office would be established in the event of an emergency and that a supreme command would direct the military operation. The study clearly stated that its operation "would be directed by the American forces in Japan, except in special cases when the defense of Japan itself was directly involved, since the authority of the commander of the American forces in Japan is already recognized for necessary preparatory strategies for the defense of Japan, such as patrols, reconnaissance, lookouts, strategic preparations, and the like." The study thus envisioned the Self-Defense Forces fighting under American command.

There were three areas of activity for the strategic coordination office: (1) coordination of the American Pacific Command and the Defense Agency; (2) coordination of the command of the American forces in Japan and the joint staff council of the Self-Defense Forces; and (3) coordination of the individual branches of the American forces in Japan and the staffs of the individual Self-Defense Forces. At each stage, command was to be left to the Americans after coordinating operations. The forces of several different nations were to be consolidated and were to operate as a single force under the command of a single individual as was done with the United Nations forces during the Korean War.

From a military standpoint, this was all unexceptional. But the session of the Diet had just endured debates on the United States–Japan Security Treaty, and these exact points had been the subject of contention. Because the government had so pointedly emphasized the independence of the Self-Defense Forces in response to questioning from opposition Diet members over the military's relationship to the American military, the idea of a strategic coordination office was enough to arouse suspicion in the Japanese people that presentation and reality were not consistent and that the government was lying.

The Mitsuya exercises also aroused cautionary feelings because they mapped out an aggressive policy of bringing nuclear weapons into Japan and using them. Because it was assumed that the Soviet Union would enter a second Korean War and that Japan could face full-scale air and sea assaults as well as a land invasion in northern Japan, the problem of nuclear weapons was raised as part of a joint Japan–United States strategy for the direct defense of Japan. Understandably, fears of an expansion of war into a full-scale conflict between the United States and the Soviet Union led to a negative attitude about the strategic use of nuclear weapons. For tactical uses of nuclear weapons, however, the study stated that if "in the initial period when [the Soviet Union] invaded [Japan] by land, nuclear offenses against advantageous enemy targets, or, if unavoidable, in a war of attrition, can be undertaken to supplement Japanese infantry power. If use is absolutely limited to artillery warfare, an expansion to full-scale war should be avoidable." The implication of bringing nuclear weapons to Japan and of their possible use was clear.

The entry of nuclear weapons into Japanese territory had been a prime focus of the debate over the United States–Japan Security Treaty. The government had bowed to the strong anti-nuclear sentiment of the Japanese people and appended a "prior agreement" clause to the ancillary documents of the treaty. This clause established that prior consent would be required for the United States military to bring nuclear weapons into Japan. In the past, the Japanese government had made it clear it would refuse such permission in all instances. The Mitsuya exercises brought this agreement into question as well.

Finally, the Mitsuya exercises demonstrated that the major founding principle of the Self-Defense Forces, civilian control, was not working cleanly. The Japan Socialist Party and other opposition parties demanded that the results of the Mitsuya exercises be released in full to the Diet, but they were not able to investigate the Defense Agency's statement that "the Mitsuya exercises are nothing more than a map problem worked by the military general staff. They are not formal research of the Defense Agency." The conflict ended with only a promise to strengthen civilian control over the military.

The Bull Run strategy was a Far East emergency plan, drafted in 1966, that went beyond the hypotheses of the Mitsuya exercises. It was said to have been created jointly by the United States Pacific Command and the Defense Agency. Although it was widely publicized by the weekly magazine *Shukan Gendai*, the government and Defense Agency remained secretive about its strategic details and about the status of Japanese-American cooperation. No debate of any substance ever developed.

The Bull Run plan began by stating that "the purpose of this plan is to create a strategy to contain and decide in the Korean peninsula any conflict the united communist armies of communist China and North Korea should extend to other regions [indicating the Korean peninsula]." Bull Run set its sights on China as the predominant threat in Asia and thus represented a broadening of the Mitsuya exercises. Since the plan did not foresee any invasion of Japan itself, it concerned itself largely with the Maritime and Air Self-Defense Forces as units likely to be mobilized under American command. A crossing of the thirty-eighth parallel by the North Koreans was again the perceived start of the crisis, but this strategy also considered a more important simultaneous Chinese move against Taiwan by concentrations of troops at the Taiwan Strait and set forth countermeasures to contain such actions.

How were the Self-Defense Forces expected to be involved? According to the plan, (1) the air and naval power of the Self-Defense Forces would play a supporting role, supplying the United States military in other regions; and (2) Self-Defense Forces ground troops would not take up positions against an enemy until there was a clear offensive against Japanese territory. In other words, cooperation under the United States–Japan Security Treaty would already have begun even without any "clear offensive against Japanese territory."

The deployment of the Self-Defense Forces was to be as follows:

> The Air Self-Defense Force shall concentrate four-fifths of its total strength in the Chugoku and Kyushu areas, with the remaining one-fifth in Hokkaido and along the Japan Sea coast.
> Naval forces of the Self-Defense Forces shall assemble in the Inland Sea region. The ocean area north of Kyushu would be divided into ten sectors to be patrolled by Maritime Self-Defense Force warships and by the Air Self-Defense Force. Areas to the south of Kyushu would be under the control of the American Seventh Fleet.
> Three-fifths of the total ground forces of the Self-Defense Forces would assemble on the coasts facing the Korean Strait and American Marine divisions would be used as support forces.

Once war had begun:

> The supreme commands of Japan and the United States would jointly determine strategy thereafter, but the Americans would have the power of command and control over operations.
> Even if the Self-Defense Forces should join an offensive system, the battle area would not extend beyond the bounds set by the right of self-defense [although those bounds are not defined].

The Bull Run strategy again showed graphically that the structure of the United States–Japan Security Treaty made the Self-Defense Forces part of the American Far Eastern strategy and would pull Japan into war should any crisis erupt in Asia. The enormous gulf between the government's policy statements in the Diet and in solemn Japan–United States exchanges of official documents and the Mitsuya and Bull Run war plans was mirrored by the United States–Japan Security Treaty.

Most of the contradictions emanating from the security treaty in the 1960s, however, existed only on paper in the strategy plans. These ideas were not yet taken to the point of being tested in comprehensive exercises and multinational maneuvers. Exercises with troops had to wait until the latter half of the 1970s.

12

Nakasone as Director General of the Defense Agency

Throughout the 1960s, the Self-Defense Forces remained a military without a face. Although the government drafted a basic national defense policy seven years after the establishment of the Police Reserve, extremely few Japanese knew that the government's real intent was to establish a military. The Self-Defense Forces had to choose between gradually becoming involved in the American strategy for Asia and the Pacific or being disregarded. The United States–Japan Security Treaty provided the Self-Defense Forces with strategic criteria for action. The SDF became better equipped under the Defense Buildup Programs, but they were isolated from the Japanese people and did not develop significant operational skills. They functioned mechanically, without character.

When fifty-two-year-old Yasuhiro Nakasone came to the Defense Agency as its director general in January 1970, crisis and change were swirling through northeast Asia and the Pacific and around the Self-Defense Forces. An end to the Vietnam War seemed to be in sight under the new American president Richard M. Nixon. Détente between the United States and the Soviet Union was creating a new international environment. Nixon's Guam Doctrine pledged that the United States would not intervene in ground wars in Asia and called on allied countries to be self-reliant. The role of Japan under the United States–Japan Security Treaty would change. It was at this crucial time that Nakasone become the director general of Japan's Defense Agency.

Known as the Young Officer from his early days as a member of the Democratic Progressive Party, Nakasone was a leader in calling for constitutional revision and an autonomous defense policy. Referring perhaps to his own strong political convictions as a nationalist, Nakasone spit out a daring address at his swearing-in that demonstrated his extraordinary will. He said, "Prime Minister Sato shows considerable courage in appointing someone like me as director general of the Defense Agency." Only one week after he took office, he rode in a jet trainer to inspect Chitose Base in Hokkaido, leaving an impression of youth and vitality that Japan had never seen before in a director general. His flamboyant gestures also brought defense issues and the Self-Defense Forces to the forefront of public attention. The Self-Defense Forces finally had a face.

In his year and a half as director general, Nakasone succeeded in reversing the perception that his post was one for time-serving ministers and lightweights. Other events highlighted the actions of the Defense Agency as well. The Vietnam War and negotiations over the reversion of Okinawa to Japanese administration were both winding down. Japan needed to change course in its security policy. As a vocal nationalist, director general Nakasone tried to win for Japan the ability to chart its defense policy autonomously.[13] His views on defense were not hard to know. They suffused his Defense Agency White Paper, the debate over revision of the basic national defense policy and the drafting of the fourth defense program.

Counterpressures to Nakasone's reforms were also building. Amid the throes of the Cultural Revolution, Chinese leadership was increasingly critical of Japanese militarism. Also during

Nakasone's tenure, the famous author Yukio Mishima aroused an intense national reaction by entering the Self-Defense Forces grounds and committing *seppuku* (ritual suicide by disembowelment). These events derailed the bold aims of Nakasone's White Paper, and forced him to table his plans for over a decade until he rose to the position of prime minister.

Nakasone's strong advocacy of revising the constitution was remarkable even among fellow conservatives. His breed of nationalists was quite distinct from the pro-American conservative mainstream represented by Shigeru Yoshida. Even after the conservative party merger of 1955, Nakasone made no attempt to alter his public views on matters of defense and security policy from the opinions he espoused during his days in the Progressive Party. He was a passionate young politician, and in his early career he was never seen without his trademark black necktie, which he wore to symbolize the death of the nation under Allied occupation. In 1956, he wrote the lyrics for a "Constitutional Revision Song" which sounded very dated even in that day and age:

Constitutional Revision Song

Destroyed by war,
occupied by enemy troops
under the name of peaceful democracy,
an Occupation constitution is forced,
the fatherland's dismantling contemplated,
a mere six months after the war.

Occupation troops command,
"If you don't use this Constitution
the Emperor will go."
The population swallow their tears,
and despairing of their future
they accept MacArthur's constitution.

As long as this constitution survives
the unconditional surrender continues.
Defending the constitution
makes you MacArthur's lackey.
Those who would set the nation's future
must decide to rebuild the country.

Nakasone held these sentiments deeply and his support for the mainstream conservative security policy and for the Self-Defense Forces was tepid at best. At one time he proposed that Japan develop its own nuclear weapons. Because of his critical attitude toward the United States–Japan Security Treaty, he absented himself from his chair and abstained when the lower house voted to ratify the treaty. His political views clearly marked him as being outside the mainstream. In *My Private Life*, the English-language version of his memoir, he described how he felt at this time:

> Even under Occupation I believed that Japan would be soonest able to achieve independence if it governed itself and controlled its own defense, and contributed in some form to the security and welfare of other nations. I wanted the constitution to be revised with the return of independence and for Japan to create an independent defense structure under civilian control. I still believe these opinions to have been entirely correct, but my fervent nationalism so alarmed the Americans that they considered me a dangerous person.[14]

It is difficult to understand why Eisaku Sato, as mainstream a conservative as there was, would appoint such a radical proponent of rapid rearmament to the post of director general of the Defense Agency. He may have thought that giving Nakasone the post was necessary, since he needed the cooperation of Nakasone's faction to function effectively. Sato was renowned for his expertise in personnel affairs; perhaps he felt that he was giving Nakasone the rope to hang himself.

Nakasone's first order of business was the defense White Paper. Most agencies of the Japanese government publish a yearly White Paper, but the Defense Agency never had. Drafting a White Paper had been on the agency's agenda since the basic national defense policy was drafted in 1957, and a draft had been completed under Nakasone's predecessor, director general Arita. Nakasone had this draft completely revised to reflect strongly his own personal views. For that reason it was called the Nakasone White Paper. The Arita proposal had explained and justified the government's defense policies, but Nakasone placed primary emphasis on presenting basic issues of defense before the nation with phrases like "the importance of the impulse to defend the country" and "non-nuclear middle-ranked nation." It did not try to explain the existence of the Self-Defense Forces, but attempted to persuade others of its necessity.

The first section of Nakasone's White Paper dealt with the nature of defense in a modern society. The second section discussed Japan's approach to defense, and the third discussed the current state of the Self-Defense Forces and their various problems. Nakasone's influence on the content of the paper is clear throughout:

> Defense today is different from what we used to call "national defense" before and during the war. That concept focused on a single country, Japan, and that single country's military strategy. Today's concept of defense has evolved from the worldwide spread of humanitarian compassion. Now defense must be a "defense of the community on Japanese soil" and it must be guided by a comprehensive political strategy.
>
> Starting from this viewpoint, we advocate a defense model of Japan as a "non-nuclear middle-ranked nation." In the past we have operated on Western Europe's received wisdom that an economic power must also be a military power. We want to challenge that way of thinking so that the Japanese people can become a great people by developing a culture that nurtures world peace and a spiritual order for a new age by becoming an economic power that is not a military power.

By this time, Japan's gross national product had become the world's third largest, and many Asians were growing fearful of the revival of a strong Japan. Meanwhile, the Japanese were achieving a basic level of physical comfort and were starting to devote attention to new issues. Yet past debates over defense issues had made the idea of constitutional reform unpalatable to many Japanese; revision seemed to require acceptance of backward-looking conceptions of national security. Nakasone caught the spirit of the times and avoided emotionally loaded, regressive phrases like "independent nuclear forces," or "constitutional revision" in favor of less charged terminology like "defense of the Japanese community," "non-nuclear middle-ranked nation" and "a nonmilitary power." His defense White Paper signaled a new Nakasone and provided an opportunity for him to articulate a new approach to defense.

Nakasone also showed an impressive ability to adapt to the times by recasting the terms of the debate so that autonomous defense was no longer considered equivalent to an independent Japanese defense nor was the United States–Japan Security Treaty considered synonymous with a common United States–Japanese defense:

> In today's world, autonomous defense is not always synony-
> mous with independent defense. Even the strongest nations,
> the superpowers of the United States and the Soviet Union,
> handle their defense within organizations for collective
> security. A system of collective security can also be a mode of
> autonomous defense if it works to protect the national inter-
> ests and is directed with autonomy. We will clarify the respon-
> sibilities and limits of Japan–United States cooperation for
> mutual security assurance and establish a defense system
> unique to Japan as we efficiently pursue mutual cooperation
> and flexibly implement the United States–Japan Security
> Treaty to accelerate the management and consolidation of
> American bases in Japan.

By prominently pushing for the establishment of a defense system unique to Japan, Nakasone maintained his position as a proponent of an autonomous defense policy. He seemed to forget that he had ever criticized the United States–Japan Security Treaty. He treated defense cooperation under the treaty as a supplementary tool for implementing an autonomous defense policy, making the treaty not Japan's master but its servant. This was the core of Nakasone's new position.

This view also colored the Fourth Defense Buildup Program, which the Defense Agency was preparing at the same time. Nakasone did not believe that the fourth program was simply an extension of the third program. He retitled it the New Defense Capabilities Buildup Program to emphasize that the next ten years would see a new model. In March 1970, the degree of his enthusiasm for the fourth program became apparent in his testimony before the Liberal Democratic Party's Security Treaty Survey Group:

> The United States–Japan Security Treaty concluded in 1960 represents progress from the old treaty, but we must go further. Japan itself must create its own Japanese strategy for defense so that we are sharing both burden and capabilities with the United States. Fortunately, America is now in a period of retrenchment, even as Japanese are beginning to feel a desire to be more active. We must set aside our old vague expectations of America and our unprincipled dependence in order to clarify the division of responsibilities and work toward establishing true equality in our relationship. A vague expectation that support will come from America is not a sufficient defense policy for Japan.
>
> The Self-Defense Forces already can field considerable strength. To a certain degree, the SDF is able to repel an attack from abroad in a local war even without American assistance. For offensive capabilities, we will still rely on the United States in the future, but we must study in the direction of such an autonomous defense under the Fourth Defense Buildup Program.

The growth of Japan's economy made the ideas of equality with the United States and an autonomous defense real possibilities. But while the defense White Paper raised the possibility of an economic power that is not a military power, the defense policies that it was proposing meant that the SDF would have to expand its fighting potential in order to gain the ability to repel an attack outside of Japan and its surroundings without American assistance. Asian countries began sounding the alarm, but Nakasone remained confident.

When he announced the fourth defense proposal, Nakasone proclaimed that "the control of seas surrounding Japan, including the area to the southwest islands that contains Okinotori-shima and Minamitori-shima, by the submarines of other nations will not be tolerated." His basic policy was that "for limited direct aggression, Japanese defensive capabilities will be the first line of defense; air and naval supremacy will be maintained to the degree necessary to control the periphery of Japan and to provide early warning and to counter and contain damage or aggression." At that time, many of the southwestern islands, including Okinawa, were not under Japanese administration, and Japan's sovereignty had not yet been extended to twelve nautical miles, or its economic zone to two hundred nautical miles. Thus, the idea of exercising control as far as the southwest islands, including the distant rocks of Okinotori-shima and Minamitori-shima, was highly ambitious.

Nakasone's plan set the following targets:

(1) The Ground Self-Defense Force, while roughly maintaining its status, would make qualitative improvements and increase endurance. Its buildup goals were five district armies, thirteen divisions, 180,000 men, approximately 990 tanks, and approximately 480 aircraft.
(2) The Maritime Self-Defense Force would increase its peripheral ocean defense capacity. Its buildup goals were the

introduction of antiship missiles, an increase to approximately 530 aircraft, and about two hundred ships, including construction of two large destroyers capable of carrying helicopters, with total tonnage of approximately 247,000 tons.

(3) The Air Self-Defense Force would make a moderate increase in strength and would modernize its capabilities. Its buildup goals were to increase the number of F-4EJ Phantom fighters, to reach a total force of approximately 920 aircraft.

The total estimated expenditure for Nakasone's plan was ¥5.8 trillion, roughly 2.2 times the amount spent during the Third Defense Buildup Program.

The Maritime Self-Defense Force was slated to receive the lion's share of the buildup efforts. The Nakasone plan's most striking feature was the proposal to add two helicopter-carrying large destroyers (DLHs) to form the nucleus of hunter-killer antisubmarine fleets. The DLHs were to displace eighty-seven hundred tons, carry six antisubmarine helicopters, and be equipped with Tartar ship-defense anti-aircraft missiles. They were to have 120,000 horsepower turbine engines for high speed and long range. These were the weapons that Nakasone had in mind when he stated that control of the sea by submarines of other nations such as the Soviet Union, would not be tolerated. Nakasone served in the navy during World War II; he and some officers retained a nostalgia for the Imperial Navy and longed for the glories of the Imperial Grand Fleet. Helicopter-bearing carriers could gain local naval supremacy, ensure the safety of the merchant marine, and provide for both military and civilian emergencies.

Along with the ambitious proposals of the Fourth Defense Buildup Program, Nakasone devoted great efforts to revising the basic national defense policy. He tried to recast it to clarify the importance of autonomous defense and to build a true military. Immediately after taking up his post, he presented what he considered to be the five basic principles of autonomous defense at a conference of the highest-ranking officers of the Self-Defense Forces as guidelines around which they should construct the new defense buildup plan. Nakasone's five principles were:

(1) Protect the constitution and defend Japanese territory.
(2) Maintain coordination between defense policy and foreign relations, attempt to integrate them, and maintain an equilibrium between diverse national policies.
(3) Consolidate civilian control.
(4) Support the three non-nuclear principles.
(5) Supplement Japanese defense capabilities with the United States–Japan Security Treaty system.

Principle 5 was the heart of Nakasone's proposal. Although he had transformed himself into a supporter of the security treaty upon taking his post as director general, as a nationalist he still objected to the idea that the United States–Japan Security Treaty dictated Japan's policies and that autonomous defense capabilities were subservient to it. The fourth item of the basic national defense policy was, after all, "to deal with external aggression on the basis of the Japan–United States security arrangements, pending more effective functioning of the United Nations in future in deterring and repelling aggression." The United Nations represented the ideal future security arrangement, and the United States–Japan Security Treaty represented the current stance toward external aggression. Nakasone felt that the security treaty should be subsidiary to Japan's defense efforts. When he presented his draft for the fourth program to the security treaty survey meeting of the Liberal Democratic Party, he expanded on this point: "The fourth article [of the basic national defense policy] is particularly thick with dependence on America. I believe we should revise this article to read that Japan should first throw all of its national abilities into repulsing any aggression and then, if necessary, seek the cooperation of the United States."

Nakasone included inflammatory statements in his draft: "The trend for the Japanese people to see the Self-Defense Forces as pawns of the Americans cannot be eradicated," and "Remove the cross borne by the Self-Defense Forces." His speech emphasized the importance of backing up the hardware provided under the Fourth Defense Buildup Program with the cultivation of human capital by adopting a basic defense policy that put autonomy of defense first. On the basis of this declaration, in late March 1970, Nakasone directed the Defense Agency bureaucracy to propose a revision to the basic policy that incorporated the five principles of autonomous defense he had announced earlier and to make autonomous defense primary and the United States–Japan Security Treaty subordinate to that.

Things, however, did not go as Nakasone had planned. Waves of fierce criticism came from three directions, forcing him to backtrack. Hardware and personnel levels were scaled down. What remained in the end was simply a continuation of the existing model centered on the United States–Japan Security Treaty.

The first source of resistance was the pro-American factions of the Liberal Democratic Party (LDP). Foreign Minister Kiichi Aichi, LDP secretary general Shigeru Hori, and other mainstream conservative groups close to Prime Minister Sato viewed the Nakasone proposal as a provocation that scorned the United States–Japan Security Treaty. Party notable Deputy Prime Minister Shojiro Kawashima and other party figures were also cautious about advocating autonomous defense so prominently. In party debates, Nakasone said with his customary eloquence, "I want to bring autonomous defense into the basic national defense policy in order to give the Self-Defense Forces a 'soul' so they can defend the country." But Foreign Minister Aichi and others countered that though autonomous defense was impor-tant, it did not come close to overriding the valuable role of the United States–Japan Security Treaty. Nakasone was not able to rebut this, and Secretary General Hori sent the matter for study, which effectively shelved it. The conservative mainstream was painfully aware of how firmly committed they were to follow-ing America's path.

Nakasone's second miscalculation was to underestimate the alarm that other Asian countries would feel. The most extreme criticism of his plan came from China, which railed against the idea that Japan would become a military power. The Nixon Doctrine affected American policy in Asia and the Pacific, and it was Nakasone's misfortune that some members of the finan-cial community had responded to the doctrine with a call for Japan to make the Malacca Strait safe for the transport of oil. China saw Nakasone's advocacy of autonomous defense and the new Defense Buildup Program as a disguised first step toward exerting military power in the Malacca Strait. When the Defense Agency announced the Fourth Defense Buildup Pro-gram, the *People's Daily* immediately denounced it: "These two counterrevolutionary documents [the defense White Paper and Fourth Defense Buildup Program] are a new challenge by reac-tionaries among the Japanese people to the peoples of the nations of Asia and the Pacific. With words like "our goal is peace" and "we will not become a military power," they hope to drown out violent intentions with a veil of extreme peace. They are trying to get the people to lower their guard against Japan-ese militarism."[15]

In April 1970, Chinese premier Zhou En Lai visited North Korea and the two countries issued a communiqué denouncing the revival of Japanese militarism. China under the Cultural Revolution denounced Nakasone's proposal for a military buildup in Japan, saying that it is "a delusion that it can put Asia under its rule again as a lieutenant of the American emperor," and calling the proposal "Japanese militarism vigorously search-ing for an excuse to send troops overseas."[16] The attacks became more virulent daily. Other Asian countries reacted with alarm at the defense White Paper that "in legal and theoretical senses, possession of small nuclear weapons, falling within the mini-mum requirement for capacity necessary for self-defense and not posing a threat of aggression to other countries, would be permissible." In combination with Nakasone's earlier declara-tions, this proposition seemed very threatening.

Government officials began to make it known that direct discussion of increased power of the Self-Defense Forces and of autonomous defense would not lead to any substantive changes and would only aggravate China, the Soviet Union, and the countries of Southeast Asia. They rebuffed Nakasone for his approach not only because it affected Japan–United States rela-tions, but for reasons of Asian diplomacy as well. Nakasone had failed to predict this.

The debate over the Nakasone plan was shortly overshad-owed by the death of the author Yukio Mishima.[17] With four members of his paramilitary club, the Shield Society, behind him, Mishima entered the headquarters of the Eastern Com-mand of the Ground Self-Defense Force on November 25, 1970, took the commandant prisoner, and gave an address to the members of the SDF, asking them, "Why do you defend a consti-tution that denies you?" Seeing that the troops did not heed him, he committed suicide by *seppuku* (ritual disembowelment).

Nakasone's first reaction was to deny the political implica-tions of Mishima's act by stating, "It was not a coup d'état but an action of personal conviction using the Self-Defense Forces as a stage." But the intense impact on both the Self-Defense Forces and on Nakasone personally could not be hidden.

Mishima began his manifesto by saying that "the SDF has nurtured the Shield Society; the SDF is our father, our brother," and continued, "I have been welcomed by the troops as a reserve officer for four years, and by the students for three years." Mishima and his dandyish Shield Society, though given to wearing Pierre Cardin–designed uniforms for their drills, had nevertheless maintained a close relationship with the Self-Defense Forces. While the members of the Self-Defense Forces did not respond to Mishima's call to action, the Mishima incident provided a dramatic demonstration of the hidden desires within the Self-Defense Forces to restore a true military. The incident occurred barely a month after the Defense Agency published the Nakasone White Paper on October 20. The imagery in the defense White Paper of the officers of the SDF as citizens clashed intensely with Mishima's imagery of true Japan and true Japanese. Mishima himself contradicted the Nakasone White Paper, and his suicide remains the most celebrated public death in postwar Japan. Its implications resonate through the political mythology of every Japanese leader.

Nakasone himself had a difficult time responding to the Mishima incident as well. As director general, Nakasone applauded the young cadets at Ichigaya, where the incident took place, for "not fanning the novelist's flames." He described Mishima's use of the Self-Defense Forces as being "a great inconvenience." Nevertheless, the incident forced Nakasone to acknowledge his nationalist feelings publicly. He noted the deep historical and ideological roots that connected the incident with the nineteenth-century imperial loyalist Shoin Yoshida, a member of a group called the Kamikaze League: "Just as the Kamikaze League dramatically opposed the Meiji enlightenment, so too did Mishima go to his death resisting the postwar civilization. I regret the sudden death of this novelist, contemporary Japan's proud gift to the world. The weight of this action, for which he placed his life on the line, painfully illustrates the lightness of our words. Though I can understand the purity of those ideas, I cannot condone such direct actions."[18]

Regardless, the Mishima incident left deep scars on the Self-

Defense Forces. First, the ideological ramifications of Mishima's act slowly began to appear in the forces. More important, however, it fomented criticism from China and other Asian countries of the revival of Japanese militarism. A domestic backlash grew against the fourth buildup program, whose total budget of ¥5.8 trillion was more than double the budget for the third buildup program. Nakasone's defense buildup met with a chilling upsurge of opposition both domestically and abroad. When the cabinet was reformed in July 1971, Nakasone was not kept on as director general. The succeeding director general abandoned the attempt to revise the buildup program and the basic national defense policy. Only traces of these plans remained when the new director general, Masami Ezaki, addressed the Diet on the subject of the fourth buildup program. "The basic national defense policy and the Nakasone proposal, which was drafted on the assumption that the basic policy would be changed, are completely different from the current fourth defense program, which will be based on the 1957 proposal."[19]

Nakasone left the Defense Agency wrapped in defeat, but he certainly intended to return. He was still the leader of a Diet faction and one of the movers and shakers of the Liberal Democratic Party. It was entirely likely that he would one day have a position of greater authority in which he could confront the question of the Self-Defense Forces. Eleven years later, he achieved that post. Yasuhiro Nakasone would return, not as the director general of the Defense Agency, but as prime minister, the commander in chief of the Self-Defense Force.

YUKIO MISHIMA AND THE
SELF-DEFENSE FORCES

On November 25, 1970, famous author Yukio Mishima
marched into the commandant's office at the Eastern
Command of the Ground Self-Defense Force, in the Ichigaya district of Tokyo, with four of his supporters. They
were all dressed in uniform and threatened to kill the
commandant if SDF troops were not brought out to hear
Mishima speak. The troops were assembled under the bal-
cony of the commandant's office and Mishima exhorted
them to action. It was the last speech Mishima gave, and
in it he declared that he was severing his ties to the Self-
Defense Forces.

> What does the principle of becoming a true army mean
> to the Self-Defense Forces? It means defending Japan!
> And what does defending Japan mean? Defending
> Japan means defending the history, culture, and tradi-
> tions whose source is the emperor!
>   Listen well! Listen, listen listen! Listen quietly! I
> am just one man up here, risking my life to talk to you!
> Do you understand? Do you hear me? If I do not rise
> up, if you Japanese do not rise up with me, if the Self-
> Defense Forces do not rise up, the constitution will
> never be changed. You will forever be nothing more
> than American mercenaries! Aren't you warriors? How
> can warriors defend a constitution that disowns them?
> You are cringing and cowering before a constitution
> that disowns you!
>   Isn't there even one among you who will stand
> with me? There isn't even one, is there? Then I will
> die. It is now absolutely clear that you will not rise up
> to revise the constitution. I have no more dreams for
> the Self-Defense Forces.

I cry out, Long live the emperor! Long live the emperor! Banzai! Banzai!

The uniformed cadets assembled in the courtyard below Mishima jeered at him ferociously. Comments such as "Get down!" "Drag him down here!" "You're crazy!" and "Shoot him!" are audible in the recordings of Mishima's speech. Reports that he had imprisoned the commandant had infuriated them, and the bond between Mishima and the SDF was dramatically transformed from an intimate one to a nonexistent one.

Mishima had undergone his first induction into the Self-Defense Forces three years earlier, in April 1967. On the recommendation of the Defense Agency's administrative vice minister at the time, Yoshio Miwa, the SDF permitted him to undergo a long and exceptionally grueling forty-six days of boot camp, first at the Ground SDF Officer Training School at Kurume, and then at Camp Fuji, with its expansive training grounds at the foot of Mount Fuji. Finally, he underwent training with the First Airborne Division at Narashino. For reasons of anonymity, he entered the force under the name of Kimitake Hiraoka, which was his true name; Mishima was a pen name. He was especially proud of the fact that during ranger training he was called Ranger Hiraoka. At last he was experiencing for himself the world he had described in earlier works. A character in his play, "My Friend Hitler," which is set in a regiment of Nazi storm troopers, says, "The army is a man's paradise. Nothing brings out the beauty of men's faces like the army."[20] The play describes Mishima's political and military views in a male-only setting that is thick with homoeroticism.

Mishima's fascination with the army is reflected in his record of his own military experience:

> I was immediately captivated by the lyricism of the national flag full of the sun's last rays as it was lowered in the courtyard, and by lights-out at ten o'clock. [In the ranger exercises] I was first taught how to make my shoes shine brilliantly by rubbing them with paper and spit. I rubbed the spit on with my finger, then licked my finger in apology. It had a remarkable taste.
>
> The Airborne Division was a community of sailors riding on a huge, invisible boat, alive with danger. Their vitality, health, cohesion, and foul mouths were those of a classical group of sailors. They were obsessed with their parachutes. The glorious freedom gained by giving their bodies over to its seduction gave them a strength found nowhere else in the Ground Self-Defense Force, though they were quite mannerly. They had little of that stink of bureaucracy of modern militaries, probably because their officers had come up from within the ranks and had been through the same jumps.[21]

For Mishima, lyricism, a world in which stoicism was a virtue and not an eccentric habit, was alive in the Self-Defense Forces. Stoicism was present throughout the day's tasks and the troop training. He mesmerized the teenage troops with his tender words: "All we need is food and bath. We are content that women simply admire us from afar." Mishima had honed himself into good physical shape and was quite taken with the Ground SDF, where the body was the focus of attention. The military accentuated his own disposition and interests.

Mishima's advocacy of autonomous defense played a large role in his deepening involvement with the Ground

Self-Defense Force, particularly in his last three years:

> My interest in the Ground Self-Defense Force springs
> from the fact that since the constitution prohibits any
> dispatch of military forces abroad, the only thinkable
> possibility of war would be one waged on Japanese soil,
> and the most probable scenarios of indirect aggression
> all involve the Ground Self-Defense Force as the princi-
> pal agent in the response. Although most experts
> believe that the probability of indirect aggression is
> extremely low in industrialized nations, it doesn't take
> any special foresight to see in the May revolution in
> Paris that the formulations of these experts are no
> longer valid.

This concern drove Mishima. He believed the real
threat to Japan was not the military might of China or the
Soviet Union, but class struggle within Japan and ideological war. Many Japanese continue to agree. The scenario
Mishima hoped for was that Japan would see a student
protest (zengakuren) movement like the Paris May Revolution of 1968. The movement would take fire and lead to
another swell of antigovernment unrest like the 1960 riots
over the United States–Japan Security Treaty. When
unrest peaked, it would be put down by the Self-Defense
Forces. This repression would show the need to revise the
constitution. More important, it would provide a sense of
purpose to the Self-Defense Forces and restore honor to
the Japanese military.

For its part, the Self-Defense Forces were increasingly
thrilled to have the attention of the famous author Yukio
Mishima. They seem to have been virtually blind to Mishima's militaristic ideals and the purposes of the Shield Society. The Ground SDF chief of staff gave not only Mishima

but all the members of the Shield Society special permission to join in long-term basic training and worked with Mishima at Camp Fuji, which Mishima called his mother school, to create a training course for the members of the Shield Society. Thirty society members trained at a time, for a period of one month, and training focused on tactical education, a special course for officer training. Mishima himself went back to Camp Fuji the next year, this time with the young men of the Shield Society:

> In March 1968, I worked secretly for about two weeks with the students, running around every day, walking, breathing, and sometimes straggling. We were comrades. Their attitude became far more grounded than it was when they began basic training and they achieved a close relationship with the drill instructors and aides. When they left the training, the students all shook hands with each individual instructor, crying as they did so. Outside of movies and plays, it was the first time I had seen real men's tears since the end of the war.

The Shield Society regularly participated in Camp Fuji's basic training, with one special exception leading to another, so that by June 1970 the society was holding regular training exercises quite openly on the Ichigaya garrison grounds. On the fateful day of November 25, 1970, the guards allowed Mishima and four members of the Shield Society to enter the Ichigaya grounds wearing special uniforms with illegal and deadly Japanese swords. The sentries waving them through the front gates didn't even ask them to sign their names. The rest is history.

Although the Mishima incident undeniably had a major impact on the Self-Defense Forces at the time, twenty years later that impact now looks transitory. The incident had no lasting effect on the Self-Defense Forces or on the attitudes of SDF members. Mishima's image of the SDF members was too idealized to stand up to reality and Japan was too rich to bother with an austere military romanticism. Today few members agree with Mishima's autonomous defense theory. Still, the Mishima incident added a chapter to the history of the SDF, and the traces of that chapter have not entirely disappeared. Since the Mishima incident, the idea of autonomous defense has retreated from all fronts. Cooperation between Japan and the United States has grown stronger than ever.*

---

*Editor's Note: Mishima's speeches and reports of his suicide appear at great length in: *Sunday Mainichi*, special edition, December 23, 1970; *Shukan Asahi*, December 18, 1970; *Shukan Gendai*, special edition, December 12, 1970; *Shukan Post*, December 11, 1970.

13

Sasebo Revisited

When Japan's Security Force was formed in 1952, only five minesweepers were stationed at the port town of Sasebo, with a complement of 247 seamen and 37 administrators. Two years later, in 1954, the Security Force had become the Maritime Self-Defense Force. The Second Escort Flotilla, part of the self-defense fleet, was home-ported at Sasebo so that it could patrol the Tsushima Strait and the ocean areas northwest of Kyushu along with four patrol frigates lent by the United States; the Momi, Tsuge, Kaede, and the Buna. New ship construction from Japanese yards in the 1960s under the Second and Third Defense Buildup Programs placed increasing numbers of ships and personnel at Sasebo. By 1966, Sasebo was a true naval port, with over three thousand Self-Defense Forces personnel stationed there alongside the American naval base.

By the end of 1966, all fleet escort forces were composed of Japanese-built vessels. This marked the end of the Maritime Self-Defense Force's reliance on American-built patrol frigates and large landing support ships. The fleet at that time consisted entirely of new ships: the Second Escort Flotilla flagship Harukaze, the first domestically constructed warship, and its sister ships Yamagumo and Asagumo. The Yamagumo class was the mainstay of the fleet, built under the Second Defense Buildup Program and displacing 2,150 tons. These ships were designed primarily for antisubmarine warfare; they carried weapons and electronic equipment that were quite different from those found on the old Imperial Navy destroyers.

Sasebo, however, was still very unsettled. During the Korean War the old imperial factories were put in service to repair United States warships. A massive petroleum facility was built and the city became a United States Navy liberty port, similar in many respects to Long Beach and Norfolk. United Nations troops spent six hundred million yen in Sasebo each month. Even after the uproar of the Korean War had subsided, two divisive national policies had buffeted Sasebo: the United States–Japan Security Treaty and the defense buildup. The small western Kyushu port was divided and thrown into turmoil.

In January 1963, American ambassador Edwin O. Reischauer sounded out the opinions of the Japanese government on the idea of nuclear-powered submarines calling on Japanese ports. These were ordinary submarines that simply used nuclear power as a motive force, not Polaris submarines armed with nuclear missiles. They needed to visit Japanese ports to resupply and to provide shore leave for the crews. Defense secretariat director general Hideyuke Kurogane and the Ministry of Foreign Affairs decided that there would be no objection to port calls. The government would not tolerate such a contentious issue near the capital, but Sasebo was far out of the public eye. The name of Sasebo made the rounds. Sasebo's fate as a liberty port for American nuclear submarines was decided by a word from a government official.

At that time, submarine-launched ballistic missiles (SLBMs) were just being developed as the third leg of the strategic triad of nuclear weapons, alongside intercontinental ballistic missiles (ICBMs) and long-range bombers (B-52s). America was devoting great efforts to their development as a sea-based deterrent to

Soviet nuclear weapons. Forty-one Polaris A-3 ballistic missile–carrying attack nuclear submarines were planned during the 1960s, and they required double that number of attack nuclear submarines for their defense. These submarines required ports of call for shore leave and resupply in order to carry out their strategic function on the world's oceans. Rota in Spain and Holy Loch in Britain were to be part of this network, with Subic Bay in the Philippines, and Sasebo, Yokosuka, and Okinawa in Japan. The United States could use Okinawa freely, since it was still under American administration, but needed the Japanese government's permission for the other bases. Ambassador Reischauer sounded out the Japanese government, and it volunteered Sasebo.

THE ACCIDENT AT SHIZUKUISHI

At 2:02:39 P.M. on July 30, 1971, an F-86F fighter jet of the First Airborne Division out of Matsushima banked forward and clipped the left horizontal tail of a Boeing 727 passenger plane. The aircraft was operated by All Nippon Air (ANA) en route from Chitose to Haneda, and was eighty-five hundred meters above Iwate Prefecture. The ANA plane broke up in mid-air and crashed, killing all of the 162 passengers and crew members on board. The pilot of the F-86F, however, Technical Sergeant Yoshimi Ichikawa, parachuted to safety. Ichikawa was under the command of squadron instructor Captain Tamotsu Kuma and was flying a formation training exercise under visual flight rules. The accident was the greatest loss of life in Self-Defense Forces history.

Captain Kuma and Technical Sergeant Ichikawa were charged with involuntary manslaughter caused by occupational negligence, violations of the Aviation Act, and other violations. The District Court, High Court, and Supreme Court all found that the responsibility for the accident lay with the Self-Defense Forces' plane for entering the J11L jet route (a government-assigned airway) after deviating from training air space into the ANA plane, which was flying on its scheduled route on time. They found that the SDF plane had failed in its responsibility to keep watch; however, since Technical Sergeant Ichikawa was flying under the direction of his instructor, and since he had no knowledge of the flight plan of the ANA jet, two courts found him not guilty.

The SDF alleged that the ANA pilot also was negligent in his duty to watch for other planes, and the so-called Shizukuishi Accident trial dragged on for twelve years. In September 1983, the Supreme Court sentenced defendant Kuma to three years in prison with a three-year suspended sentence. The decision read, "The defendant is an instructor and as such must properly exercise his duty to watch and should have been able to see the All Nippon Airways jet and the training jet and then direct trainee Ichikawa so that the collision could be avoided." It also indicated that the Self-Defense Forces authorities bore some responsibility: "By filing and executing a slipshod training plan, the Air Self-Defense Force authorities, particularly the Matsushima squadron officers, have a major responsibility. To overlook their negligence would be unthinkable."

On November 12, 1964, the first American nuclear-powered submarine, the Sea Dragon, arrived in Sasebo. The citizens of the town had misgivings about the safety of the nuclear reactor and their new involvement in American nuclear strategy. Debates on technology and international politics raged throughout Sasebo with surprising sophistication for such a backwater city. The Sea Dragon arrived in Sasebo guarded by a phalanx of riot police. Countless demonstrations erupted, attended by up to 140,000 people, but the submarine came anyway. The cabinet passed a resolution approving the port call, and Foreign Minister Etsusaburo Shiina asked Sasebo mayor Ichizo Tsuji for cooperation. The mayor made a half-hearted appeal to the citizens of Sasebo: "The power to decide whether to permit the port call of nuclear submarines resides with the national government. Its safety has been ascertained under the United States–Japan Security Treaty and on the government's authority its porting here has been approved. We have no say in the matter."

Between the 1950s and the 1960s, Sasebo experienced numerous crises that all related in some way to the Cold War. Although this is to some extent the fate of any military port, the town was undeniably treated by Tokyo as a convenient dumping ground for its problems. Mayor Tsuji describes this tumultuous period in his book *The Silent Port*:[22]

> I was constantly the object of protests and was castigated by many people who saw me as the government over issues from the peace constitution, the United States–Japan Security Treaty, the right of self-defense, the safety of radioactivity, bringing nuclear power and weapons into Japan, and so on. I often felt like giving up. The central government was never in close communication, and we did not know what was going to happen, or how to respond, or what we should do, and were often unable to respond with any confidence as local authorities. We often felt we were fighting alone and being whittled away.

Behind this turmoil, the Maritime Self-Defense Force expanded steadily. Whatever Sasebo's political and social problems, it had become an extremely prosperous city and a school for future leaders of both navies.

ANTIWAR SDF OFFICERS

The Konishi incident sparked a democracy movement within the Self-Defense Forces. On several occasions so-called antiwar Self-Defense Forces officers have declared they would not fire on fellow citizens. A minority of people of an ideological standpoint diametrically opposite to that of Yukio Mishima have tried to reform the Self-Defense Forces from within. While no soldiers' union like those found in western Europe has developed, this is attributable to the fact that the SDF is not a conscript force but is an open organization that members can leave of their free will.

One of the reasons that activists are so common in the SDF is that the SDF lacks a penal code and a military secrets act. It also lacks military prisons and military courts with the capacity for courts-martial, so officers must be tried in civilian courts, where they have access to the press and outside legal assistance.

In April 1972, five uniformed officers read ten demands directed toward their superior officer at the front gate of the Defense Agency. They demanded no SDF deployment in Okinawa, no firing on workers and farmers, and complete freedom of speech for themselves. Okinawa was only then reverting to full Japanese sovereignty, and plans were underway to start deploying the SDF there. This deployment was strongly opposed by Okinawans.

The authorities of the Defense Agency charged the men with actions not befitting SDF members under Article 46 of the Self-Defense Forces. In 1987, the Tokyo District Court found that: "the rights and freedoms of Self-Defense Forces officers are not protected to the same degree as for general civilians. Officers have joined of their own free will, so the restriction of their rights and freedoms to the extent necessary to perform duties is not an infringement of the constitution." The antiwar officers lost their case.

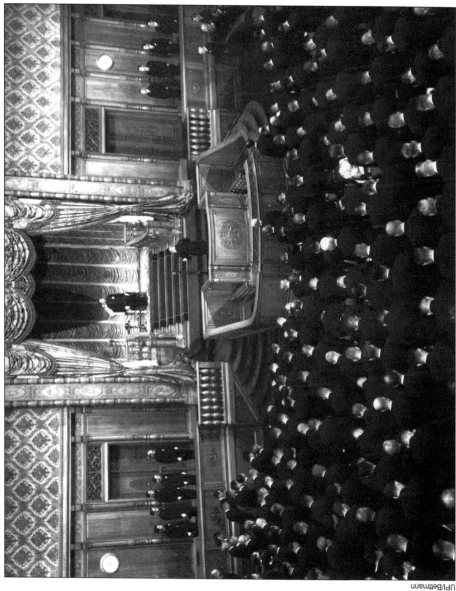

In the chamber of Peers on November 3, 1946, Emperor Hirohito and Prime Minister Shigeru Yoshida read the new constitution drafted by the American Occupation Forces. The document became famous for its Article 9, which forbade war in any form under any pretext; it renounced forever the maintenance of an armed force in Japan.

Japanese soldiers grudgingly clean their weapons (1951).

Prime Minister Shigeru Yoshida, along with General
Douglas MacArthur, shaped modern Japan (1951).

The Self-Defense Force was organized so hastily it was forced to wear American uniforms and use American equipment (1952).

The shortage of officers in the SDF's early days is revealed by this company officer's unusual salute and the odd positioning of his personal gear (1950).

Werner Bischof/Magnum Photos, Inc.

Japanese Ground Forces spent much time in the field to attain modern standards. The officer's Japanese cap worn with an American jacket testifies to the speed with which the new army was fitted out (1952).

President Eisenhower and Prime Minister Nobusuke Kishi sign the United States–Japan Treaty of Mutual Cooperation and Security on January 19, 1960.

Japanese destroyer forces can now patrol the sea lanes as far south as the Straits of Molocca and out to the Aleutians with superbly equipped anti-submarine squadrons.

The SDF is a weapon-intensive force compensating for its small size with the great amount of firepower it can bring to bear.

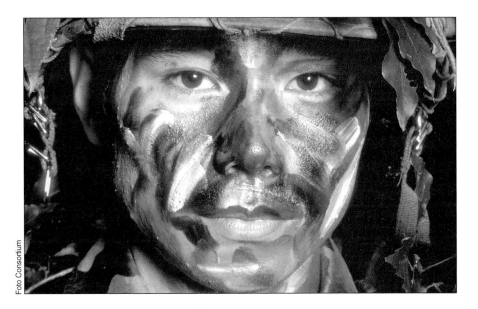

An SDF soldier prepared for night patrol exercises.

Flame-throwers were used against Japanese positions in World War II. These weapons from the SDF retain their usefulness even in the nuclear age.

Although never a sworn member of the SDF, Yukio Mishima remains the most remembered military figure of the postwar era. A brilliant writer, he lived according to the ancient Japanese military code in his private life. He committed suicide a few minutes after this picture was taken (1970).

Not so mannerly
Tokyo protesters
confront Japanese
police in June 1971
over the U.S. presence
in Okinawa.

Bruno Barbey/Magnum Photos, Inc.

Japanese fighter-interceptors patrolled constantly against a well-manned Soviet threat, principally in the North where Japan has restated its claim to the still-Russian–occupied Sakhalin Island (1985).

Japanese aircraft are maintained and flown in an unusually effective manner. Their performance equals that of any other air force.

Helicopters and tanks in a coordinated attack during the annual maneuvers held near Mt. Fuji (1986).

Japanese heavy weapons units exercise. The flag, which is red, means the weapon is in the firing mode.

Japan's destroyer fleet, meant principally as an anti-submarine force, consists of about sixty first-class units (1987).

A formal dress inspection of SDF troops by Prime Minister Toshiki Kaifu, on October 29, 1989, showed a gradual growth in politicians' respect for the military.

SDF academy graduates toss their hats in the air after graduation much as their American counterparts.

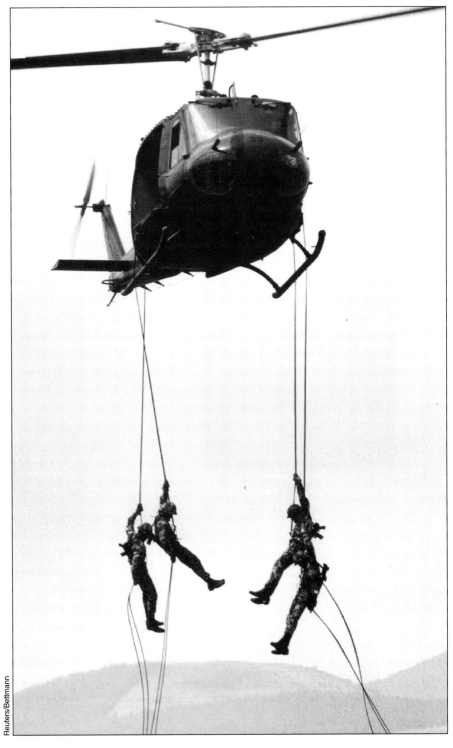

SDF soldiers rappell from a helicopter, a fine example of the mobility required in modern war (1992).

Japan has developed its own defense industry. Its equipment, including armor, is second to none. These Type 74 tanks are soon to be replaced by the world-class Type 90 heavy tank (1992).

SDF soldiers on parade in their Sunday best, with the addition of weapons and helmets (1992).

Not all Japanese favored the deployment of Japanese troops to Cambodia to keep the peace and to supervise local elections. The troops went anyway (1992).

PART III

The Self-Defense
Forces from 1975
to the Present

14

Did the Doves Win?

The early 1970s were a watershed period in the history of the Self-Defense Forces. Defense policy and the operations of the Self-Defense Forces changed dramatically both before and after these years.[1] Events unfolded rapidly both in Japan and abroad, and the links among them were complex. National strategy and policy toward the United States–Japan Security Treaty established new ground rules that would permanently affect the way the Self-Defense Forces operate.

Two events made it clear that the 1970s were not going to be as placid as the 1960s: the oil crisis of 1973 and Nixon's floating of the dollar. Together, these two events dramatically rewrote the diplomatic and political map that Japan had been operating from since the end of World War II.

What Japanese call the "Nixon shock" was actually a series of events. In July 1971, the United States government announced that President Nixon would visit China to revive diplomatic relations between the two countries. Then, in August, Nixon announced that the United States would halt the conversion of dollars for gold in order to defend the value of the dollar. Both of these decisions were crucial for Japan and left the Japanese government gasping in a vacuum. As time went on, their effects proved to be even greater. The American government's acknowledgment of the Beijing regime left Japan, which had followed America's lead by refusing to recognize China, out in the cold. Japan's stance with regard to the world's most populous country had been difficult diplomatically.

The severing of the dollar's link to gold had put a different kind of pressure on Japan. Japan's economic players had accepted a fixed rate of ¥360 to the dollar as an immutable fact; a floating rate threw all the familiar methods of planning out the window. A near panic ensued. The Tokyo Stock Exchange plummeted and dollars were sold frantically in the foreign exchange market. This rough shock therapy, though, put an end to the post-Occupation era of Japanese diplomacy and economics. Japan was no longer a protected nation.[2]

The oil crisis of 1973 had a lasting impact that structurally affected the Japanese economy and, with it, every aspect of Japanese living standards. When war broke out in the Middle East in October 1973, the Arab oil-producing countries put pressure on industrialized nations by boosting the price of crude oil and by restricting imports to countries friendly to Israel. The Japanese economy was thrown into an instant panic. Factories shortened their working hours, newspaper's decreased the number of their pages, and neon lights went dark. Housewives had to search for basic products such as detergents. Japan's high-growth sixties had been driven by cheap energy and the switch from coal to petroleum, but that had increased dependence on foreign sources of energy. By 1973 that dependence had become extreme, and the effects of the cutback in the availability of oil were correspondingly severe. The go-go sixties became a fading memory. Japan now faced energy conservation and slow growth. Japan's approach to security and defense had to change as well.[3]

Seven months after Nixon's 1972 visit to China, Japan and China announced in a joint communiqué that they would resume full diplomatic relations. The countries formally ended their state of war and Japan abrogated its treaties with Taiwan. China suddenly ceased to be Japan's primary hypothetical enemy, as assumed under the United States–Japan Security Treaty, and the buildup of the Self-Defense Forces lost its primary rationale. Positions that had been clearly defined throughout the Korean War, the Taiwan Strait crisis, the Laotian civil war, and the Indochinese wars, with China as the trouble-making puppet-master and America as Asia's guardian, became less sharply drawn. This blurring of previously sharp lines provided Japan with a more conducive environment for its diplomatic relations within Asia. The resumption of relations between China and the United States was widely considered a precondition for ending the fifteen years of war that had gripped Vietnam, Laos, and Cambodia and hopes for peace rose throughout Asia.

For Japan's defense policy and the United States–Japan Security Treaty system, however, the fading of the communist Chinese threat did not necessarily imply détente. While American military power on the Asian continent receded, American sea power grew, and the United States clearly planned to continue its forward defense strategy. Even as it pulled massive numbers of ground troops from Vietnam, Cambodia, and Thailand, it maintained its very large sea and air facilities in the Philippines. Before long, the United States had a network of island bases, from Diego Garcia island, in the center of the Indian Ocean, to the Philippines, Guam and Saipan, Okinawa, and the Japanese mainland. The threat that replaced China in military planning arrived in the form of the gradual buildup of Soviet naval forces in the Pacific. Détente on the Asian mainland was counteracted by a confrontation between the United States and the Soviet Union in the surrounding Pacific.

This shift in America's Asian strategy from the mainland to the high seas, from ground troops to sea and air power, strongly affected cooperation under the United States–Japan Security

Treaty. The equipment, strategic planning, and deployment of the Self-Defense Forces changed. The United States entrenched itself further in Japan by stationing large, well-equipped Marine units in Okinawa, which had by then reverted to Japanese sovereignty, and by making Yokosuka the overseas base of the carrier Midway. The Soviet naval buildup had produced a strong navy, and for the first time the United States government asked Japan to take up the task of defending sea lanes. The United States–Japan Security Treaty was gaining a breadth and depth that had been absent in the 1960s.

The rise in oil prices caused by the 1973 oil crisis meant that Japan could no longer sustain the heady growth of the 1960s. In 1974, the Japanese economy contracted for the first time since the end of World War II. A surge in consumer prices was also having a negative effect on Japanese living standards. The usual doubling of defense expenditures every five years looked at the very least unrealistic. The reestablishment of diplomatic relations with China in September 1972, and the signing of the Vietnam peace accord in February 1973, lessened Japan's sense of threat, and it became more difficult for the government to justify defense expenditures.

The 1973 oil crisis complicated policy-making on yet another level. It had made Japanese aware of another type of threat, variously termed petroleum security and resource strategy. Petroleum was the lifeblood of the Japanese economy and the sea lanes were the veins through which it flowed. It was natural for elements of the financial community to raise the security of sea lanes as a national security concern. After Britain's Labor cabinet had declared in 1968 an intention to retreat from east of Suez, Keidanren chairman Takeshi Sakurada and others proposed defense of the Malacca Strait as a national security goal. The oil crisis had exposed Japan's economic fragility and it was Japan's right, the Keidanren concluded, to defend itself through military means.* Had Soviet aircraft dropped into the Malacca

Strait a few barrels painted gray and black, to resemble mines, the price of oil delivered to Japan would have doubled overnight and the yen would have tumbled dramatically.

This rather pessimistic assessment, a threat to the sea lanes, turned out to contain little substance. In fact, the real story was quite different. American and Soviet nuclear deterrent strategies involved the deployment of nuclear-powered submarines and surface warships over the world's oceans, and Soviet vessels commonly plied Japan's oil routes. This, however, reflected Soviet nuclear strategy rather than a threat to Japan. The crisis lacked substance, because no country, especially the Soviet Union, was likely to attack Japan by itself. The appearance of menace existed, however, and this scary illusion was exploited. The economic community knew how vulnerable Japan was on the sea, not only for transport of resources, but for transport of its finished products as well. The crisis felt tangible enough to arouse considerable concern among ordinary Japanese. The first plan that was proposed for protecting the sea lanes was to place oil tankers in convoys escorted by warships. That was quickly subsumed into the American anti-Soviet naval strategy and was transformed from an object-oriented plan involving convoys to a territorial approach involving the protection of sea lanes. The territorial approach then developed into the idea of securing entire geographical areas, drawing Japan toward activity in areas outside Japan.

Therefore, despite the promises for a shrinking military and greater peace that were held out by the two worldwide shocks of the early 1970s, Japan found itself moving in the opposite direction. While support for the peace constitution and opposition to becoming a military power remained strong within

---

*Editor's Note: After the American withdrawal from Vietnam, Soviet naval and air units manned some of the abandoned bases.

Japan, there were no political forces allowing those tendencies to be actualized. Of course, authorities at the Defense Agency continued to search for a new defense policy that reflected the age of détente and slower economic growth. Out of these concerns came the idea of the standard defense force, which emphasized a base level of defense strength rather than one that escalated in lockstep with the defense efforts of Japan's neighbors.

In July 1972, Kakuei Tanaka had just been appointed to the post of prime minister after seven years of the Sato cabinet. Tanaka moved quickly to establish relations with China and then, on October 9, quickly pushed the long-delayed Fourth Defense Buildup Program, for 1972 to 1976, through the National Defense Council and cabinet conference. It was quite irregular to start a long-term plan halfway through its first fiscal year. This move was necessary because the rancorous debate over Yasuhiro Nakasone's defense plan and its subsequent failure meant that Nakasone's successors needed time to craft a new plan that was tailored to détente and clean of any suspicion of a revived Japanese militarism.

When Nakasone's plan was discarded, Japan's defense budget was decreased from ¥5.8 trillion to ¥4.63 trillion. The Fourth Defense Program emphasized that the defense of Japan was to hold fast to the system of the United States–Japan Security Treaty. The treaty therefore dominated defense thinking yet again. The Fourth Defense Program acknowledged the overall directions of détente and multipolarity, but also counseled against undue optimism:

> Although the interests of three major nations, the United States, the Soviet Union, and China, continue to overlap and intersect in Asia in complex ways, we have not yet reached a stable situation of détente. Many sources of tension still remain between other Asian nations. Although we feel that under these circumstances the likelihood of total war or the

> eruption of a large-scale armed conflict likely to develop
> into such a war is reduced, we cannot exclude the possibility
> that an armed conflict of limited location or duration may
> yet occur.

While the Defense Agency recognized that détente prevailed in the world as a whole, it concluded that these conditions were not yet mature in Asia and the Pacific. The Japanese found it necessary to continue the expansion of Japanese defense strength.

The Japanese public reacted fiercely. Although world tensions were relaxing, the defense budget continued to increase by large amounts every year. The Japanese people felt uneasy about this trend, especially about the doubling of the budget that occurred during each of the first four buildup programs. In the first Diet session after the Tanaka cabinet was formed, opposition parties ferociously battled the government's fourth program, asking the government to state clearly where the limits of defense strength lay. A beleaguered Prime Minister Tanaka asked the Defense Agency to study the question to define the limits of defense strength in peacetime, and he promised to present the Diet with numerical limits on Self-Defense Forces equipment and personnel.

The Defense Bureau, a part of the Defense Agency under Secretary Takuya Kubo, was responsible for drafting the government's response to the Diet. Kubo had worked in government policy since the Nakasone days and had come to believe that Japan needed to move away from the concept of a required defense force, which entailed the accumulation of weapons and equipment in order to respond to a threat. If defense strength continued to increase in response to threats, the escalation would never end. At this point Kubo concluded that Japan's levels of defensive strength should be detached from the idea of threat in favor of a new approach in which, when there is no threat of invasion, reserve troops would be prepared, through education and training, rather than readying an emergency rapid response force. Asked to produce numbers for the upper limit of defense strength, Kubo proposed this new approach to defense policy instead. Kubo's approach was first publicized as a personal opinion, then renamed a post-threat approach, and was finally elaborated into the standard defense force concept.

The opposition still wanted its numbers. As Tanaka tried to come up with numerical limits on defense strength, he met with strong opposition from the uniformed services. Defense strength has always been a relative concept and the military leaders believed that setting an absolute limit was impossible. They also warned that it was dangerous to equate détente with peace. Defensive power, they stated, is meant to be deployed in dire emergency, so it is not conducive to a simple upper limit. The generals also strongly opposed Kubo's idea of redirecting the Self-Defense Forces toward a concentration on troop education and training. If war capability cannot be used instantly in the event of emergency, they argued, its existence is meaningless. The military men tried to protect the prerogatives they enjoyed under the older concept of a required defense force, which made the capability to respond instantly in case of emergency the ultimate rationale. Finding a common ground between the required defense force concept and the standard defense force concept, which was based on the post-threat approach, was extremely difficult.

Still, the Defense Agency attempted to comply with Tanaka's directive. Well past its deadline, in February 1973, the Defense Agency responded with an opinion paper entitled "Concerning Peacetime Defense Strength." The Defense Agency's opinion described the goals for peacetime defense strength as: "to provide functions now lacking and to modernize equipment, although this will generally be accomplished by the completion of the fourth defense strength provision five-year plan." The paper gave specific numerical figures for quantitative defense strength, which were as follows:

- Ground Self-Defense Force: five district armies, thirteen divisions, and 180,000 men
- Maritime Self-Defense Force: five district fleets, four or five escort flotillas, and approximately 250,000 to 280,000 tons
- Air Self-Defense Force: three air district units, eight air wings, one hybrid air wing, and approximately eight hundred planes

In that paper the Defense Agency defined peacetime: "We assume that the international situation today is generally on a course of a relaxation of tensions, so a situation like that prevailing today is termed 'peace.' In peacetime, we should emphasize education and training, disaster assistance and other civil aid, improving the treatment of troops, and promoting research and development."

The opposition parties, the Japan Socialist Party, the Clean Government Party, the Democratic Socialist Party, and the Communist Party, had three types of objections to the Defense Agency's paper. First, the document was presented as the opinion of the Defense Agency, not of the government. Prime Minister Tanaka said that he had no intention of making the paper formal government policy. The opposition countered by declaring that there was no point in discussing a Defense Agency work estimate for which the government as a whole took no responsibility. The government wanted to present an opinion that would relate future policy to the fluid international situation, with the lightest possible restraint. The opposition parties accused Tanaka of breaking his word.

The specific figures given in the paper for the three branches of the service were called "goals," not "limits" or "upper ends." This semantic hedging was a response to opposition from the military. The chiefs of staff of the Ground, Maritime, and Air

Self-Defense Forces strongly opposed giving specific figures for a limit. If the Defense Agency had to produce figures, the chiefs of staff felt that it would be better to give the minimum below which the Self-Defense Forces would not go. They therefore tried to reverse the limits to indicate the base for a future military expansion. The result was a compromise, using the word "goals" instead of "limits." The opposition, of course, had been looking for a ceiling on military expansion, and were unsatisfied with this compromise. In his Diet testimony, Defense Bureau Secretary Kubo stated, "Although we do not consider these upper limits, so long as conditions of peace prevail they can be considered upper ends that will be adhered to." It was an initial step, but the opposition parties demanded more. They still focused on the fact that the government had broken its promise.

The figures presented by the Defense Agency contained the seeds for future expansion. The thirteen divisions and one hundred eighty thousand men described for the Ground SDF were, after all, already the target goals of the Fourth Defense Buildup Program. For air power, the figure of eight hundred strategic aircraft was virtually identical to the 770 planes envisioned in the fourth program. The naval figures called for an outright increase in tonnage of forty thousand to seventy thousand tons. When asked if it was not self-contradictory to preface a call for military expansion by saying, "The international situation today is generally on a course of a relaxation of tensions, so a situation like that prevailing today is termed *peace*," the government debaters collapsed into disorder; the session dissolved into chaos and the government suspended debate.

After a series of similar experiences in the Budget Committee of the lower house, the peacetime defense strength approach was abandoned. The opposition parties knew that giving their approval to this approach would effectively rubber-stamp an increase in the Self-Defense Forces. Abruptly, all of the opposition parties became eager to avoid further entanglements with the issue. The Japan Socialist Party, the Clean Government Party, and the Democratic Socialist Party jointly resolved to seek a retraction of their statement. Some within the government felt it would be ignominious to withdraw at the opposition parties' request the proposal that they had drafted at the opposition's initiative, but in the interest of legislative effectiveness the measure was withdrawn. Tanaka stated, "The government does not intend to formally adopt this proposal regarding limits of defense strength at this time. There are many issues that we must study from a variety of standpoints, so on this day of February 1, we withdraw the position paper entitled "Concerning Peacetime Defense Strength" and all supporting materials that the director general of the Defense Agency has presented to this committee."

The attempt to set forth a policy that would serve as a brake on the government's relentless expansion of defense strength had failed. The resistance of the military and the fickleness of the opposition parties were too much to overcome. But because the Tanaka government had never been actively in favor of setting limits on defense strength, political damage to the government was not severe. The public image of the opposition, however, suffered damage by the episode. The opposition had requested the plan themselves, and yet when presented with numbers that they had not expected, they simply rejected the plan. This reversal was similar to that which occurred during the debate over the basic national defense policy. When the Police Reserve was being transformed into the larger Security Force and then to the even larger Self-Defense Forces, Masashi Ishibashi of the Japan Socialist Party had similarly pressed the government to clarify the basic national defense policy as a means of slowing the military's continual expansion. When the Kishi cabinet presented its policy, the socialists cowered at the thought of confronting it and forfeited a chance to slow down the military expansion. By failing to use its most powerful weapon, civilian control, the Japan Socialist Party abdicated its responsibility as an opposition party.

After the oil crisis, financial impropriety brought down Kakuei Tanaka. The Liberal Democratic Party then turned to a new face; Takeo Miki was elected party president in December 1974 and was subsequently voted in as prime minister. He appointed Michita Sakata, a man known for his expertise in education and cultural issues, to be the new director general of the Defense Agency. "Clean Miki" and the new director general aroused expectations of a fresh and honest approach to defense policy. Takuya Kubo was soon elevated from Defense Bureau secretary to deputy director of the Defense Agency, where he was responsible for administration of policy. Under Miki, Sakata, and Kubo, the Defense Agency drafted a national defense program outline using Kubo's standard defense force concept and the principle of keeping defense expenditures under one percent of GNP. The one-percent figure was formally adopted to guide defense policy and budgets. Like the "left-wing troika" of the 1930s, Mitsumasa Yonai, Yoshio Yamamoto, and Shigeyoshi Inoue, these three men formed a kind of dovish troika in the 1970s that set about crafting a new defense policy and giving the military a human face.

When Michita Sakata took up the post of defense agency director general, he was concerned about the secrecy with which the Defense Agency had always set policy. No matter how technical the problems of defense might be, he believed they were of concern to the life and liberty of every Japanese, and he felt it was important that the entire Japanese people understand these problems. And yet despite Japan's material progress, there existed no way to gauge the population's desires and to reflect them in policy. Without some form of input, the Japanese people would continue to be uneasy and suspicious. Sakata decided to create a new method of making policy in defense administration. To advise him in drafting a policy to succeed the fourth Defense Buildup Program after it expired in 1976, he established the Forum on Defense Issues, a committee composed of eleven prominent civilian experts, with whom he met a total of six times.

The question of what would follow the fourth program was an important question not only for the Defense Agency but for the entire Miki cabinet. Hope for peace was growing throughout Asia. Détente took hold in international society, Japan and China continued to normalize relations, and North and South Korea talked under the auspices of the Red Cross. But the economic crisis that was caused by the oil crisis of 1973 still left uncertainty about the future. While still not completed, the fourth program's budget had already ballooned over the allotted ¥4.63 trillion to ¥5.6 trillion as inflation ravaged the economy. (In terms of 1972 prices, however, the budget was ¥500 billion under target.) Neither the international situation nor the government's finances were conducive to a long-term fixed expansion of the military budget.

Sakata believed that the standard defense force concept was the basic model needed to guide defense policy from 1977 and beyond. This belief, however, required the abandonment of the basic premise of defense against a threat, such as a second Korean War or the communist Chinese threat, which had underpinned every plan from the first to the fourth.

Although Chinese and North Korean threats were outmoded, Sakata anticipated difficulty in obtaining the cooperation of the military in drafting a new defense plan. Given the intensity of the resistance that military officials had demonstrated over an upper limit of defense strength, it was virtually certain that they would strongly oppose any defensive formulation that was not rooted in the concept of an emergency response to a hypothetical enemy.

Previous defense planning had estimated threat based on invasion in a local conflict using conventional weapons. Using a so-called threat ladder, defense authorities ranked conflict in six stages: (1) total nuclear war; (2) unlimited war with conventional weapons; (3) full-scale limited aggression; (4) small-scale limited aggression; (5) covert armed actions; and (6) indirect aggression. The third stage was the basis for Japanese defense planning. Under the fourth program, the military calculated weapons requirements based on an enemy threat of that scale. In his defense White Paper, Defense Agency director general Nakasone had stated that Japan's goal was the preparation of defense strength in conventional weapons sufficient to effectively respond to a limited war. This was an attempt to move up the threat ladder from (3) to (2); Sakata, on the other hand, tried to move a step down the ladder from (3) to (4). If the military raised its estimates of the threat, the government would still revise military strength downwards. The new assessment of needs ignored developments in opponent forces and instead organized the Self-Defense Forces at a standardized level.

Given the government's intention to standardize Japan's level of defense strength, Sakata's Forum on Defense Issues signified more than a desire to conduct the process of defense policy decision-making in the open; it also was an attempt to demonstrate to the military that the Japanese people supported the standard defense force concept. The forum was composed of the following eleven people:

Hideo Aragaki, writer

Isamu Arai, vice president, Small Business Finance Corporation

Kazushige Hirasawa, writer and NHK (Nippon Hoso Kyuokai) panelist

Hisao Kanamori, chairman, Japan Economic Research Center

Yoshikatsu Kono, chairman, Tokyo Metropolitan Administrative Research Institute

Masataka Kosaka, professor, Kyoto University

Kenya Murano, president, Ken Research Institute

Kenji Ogata, director in charge of general affairs, Nippon Telegraph and Telephone Public Corporation

Keiichi Saeki, president, Nomura Research Institute

Fusako Tsunoda, writer

Nobuhiko Ushiba, advisor to the Ministry of Foreign Affairs

The forum had members from many fields, but there were no former members of the imperial military or of the Self-Defense Forces. The military expressed its dissatisfaction with the composition of the forum, perhaps recognizing that this group would be different from the government-dominated councils of the past. The forum met six times over a period of three months, and a report of its proceedings and the findings of its individual members were compiled under the title "Considering Japanese Defense Policy." Seen as a whole, this report succeeded almost completely in doing what Sakata and Kubo wanted: articulating a consensus of Japanese opinion. For the most part, the forum was of the opinion that rather than seeking continued quantitative expansion through a fifth and sixth program, as the Self-Defense Forces desired, it was more appropriate to hold defense spending to within one percent of GNP and work for a force that was smaller but more effective. In its conclusion, the report stated: "We can understand that the members of the Self-Defense Forces seek an expanded defense capability in order to fulfill their responsibilities; however, the constant maintenance of a force that is able to respond to any and all conceivable concordances of events may become an endless task. It is not in the end appropriate for Japan to determine the extent of its defense strength based solely on military requirements." This conclusion summarizes the overall outcome of the forum's deliberations and was an expression of complete support for the standard defense force concept.

One member of the forum, Kyoto University professor Masataka Kosaka, appended his own individual findings, which supported the opinions of Sakata and Kubo:

> The central function of the Self-Defense Forces is "denial capability," and the SDF requires personnel and equipment in keeping with that objective. "Denial capability" refers to the ability to deny an external enemy an *easy* approach to national territory. Specifically, this means (1) preventing a fait accompli through surprise attack, and (2) being able to field a defensive effort that an enemy cannot overcome unless it mobilizes a very extensive military effort. This means that the ability to prevent any and every possible attack is not a requirement.

This statement embodies the central premise of the rationale behind a standard defense force; Sakata and Kubo wanted to make sure that its ideas would take root as a new guiding principle of defense thinking.

The effort to win the military establishment over to this new way of thinking began as soon as of the forum's report was complete. Sakata convened the council to consider the issue of defense strategy after the Fourth Defense Buildup Program. The chiefs of staff of the Ground, Maritime, and Air Self-Defense Forces were all in attendance, and the government was represented by Deputy Director Kubo.

Kubo was one of the former officials of the Ministry of the Interior who had led the Self-Defense Forces since the days of the Police Reserve. He had entered the ministry in 1943, became chief of the Kanagawa Prefecture Police Department, and then entered the Security Board in 1952. He was promoted back and forth between the Police Agency and the Defense Agency, and when he became secretary of the Defense Bureau under director general Nakasone in 1970, it was already his third term of service in the Defense Agency. Thereafter he was intimately involved in the discussion of defense policy and was widely considered to be the ablest theorist within the agency in matters of defense policy formulation. In February 1971, Kubo circulated opinion papers under the title "KB Personal Papers." The Defense Agency accepted Kubo's concept of a standard defense force, but the all-important military was not as receptive to his ideas.

In April 1975, Kubo directed the military to draw up a plan for defense expenditures after the end of the Fourth Defense Buildup Program. He presented the military with a basic outline of a plan, but did not make clear how situation assessments and defense models might dictate levels of standing defense strength. When the Forum on Defense Issues completed its report in September, Kubo issued a second directive. Addressing the director general and the three chiefs of staff, Kubo described the role of defense policy under the standard defense force concept and the idea of maintaining a standing defense strength. The conference met in the director general's office five times in September and October, but Kubo was ultimately unable to bring the military around to his new point of view.

The new standard defense force concept was built around certain assumptions about the international climate:

(1) The United States–Japan Security Treaty system would probably continue to have force in the future.
(2) The United States and the Soviet Union would continue to avoid nuclear war or any large-scale armed conflict that might develop into a nuclear war.
(3) There was little possibility of Sino-Soviet confrontation being resolved, although relations might be partially improved.
(4) The United States and China would probably continue their rapprochement.

(5) The situation on the Korean peninsula would generally remain as it was, with no major armed conflict.*

Kubo based his assessment of the international climate on the idea that the crises and threats to Japan would lessen or would at least be limited so long as the prevailing international climate did not deteriorate. Kubo advocated maintaining balanced Self-Defense Forces rather than responding to any particular threat, and proposed that the maintenance of a base defense strength would be enough to effectively respond to any situation up to a limited and small-scale aggression. This is why it was called the "peacetime defense strength" proposal.

Kubo's estimate of threat effectively downgraded the older standards by one notch on the threat ladder. Where the previous standards had called for Japan to be able to respond to a full-scale limited aggression and to match the defense strength of its possible enemies, in other words, to employ the required defense force concept, Kubo foresaw no urgent threat in the international climate and called for a balanced Self-Defense Forces that maintained a peacetime array of military capabilities that would enable them to deny an external enemy an easy approach to Japan's national territory. By keeping a close eye not only on the offensive strength, but also on the aggressive intent of potential enemies, Japan could make the full-scale limited aggression that was the starting assumption of older policies extremely unlikely to occur. And should it occur, overt signs that would precede such an aggression, such as the movement of troops and matériel, would make aggressive intentions apparent. Consequently, preparations for a limited and small-scale aggression would be sufficient to provide for security.

---

*Editor's Note: Kubo's thinking here departs from Western approaches because he considered international conduct to be a continuum, whereas Western theorists usually factor in the unthinkable, like North Korea's possession of nuclear weaponry.

Japan and the Japanese people could feel safe without an endlessly growing military.

The essence of Kubo's argument was that the Self-Defense Forces should focus on maintaining high quality, particularly a high quality of core personnel. According to Kubo, if strength levels were quantitatively insufficient, personnel could be regrouped at any time around core battalions to create a strong fighting force.

Kubo's theories of defense were innovative in two ways. The first, of course, was the severance of the link between defense strength and response to threat. The weakness of this theory was that it might be difficult to shift from the base level of defense to a new heightened level should Japan's situation change very rapidly. But the theory had an important advantage in that it allowed full use of defensive principles that were unique to Japan in combining a force specialized in home territory defense with the geographical advantages of an island nation. It was a theory for a new era of crisis management. An idea of such restraint could not have been developed by men who operate weapons, but could only have arisen from a system of civilian control.

The standard defense force model itself illustrates how revolutionary civilian control was for contemporary Japan. From 1868 to 1945, all military affairs had been entrusted to the military; military men gathered together in the emperor's war council made all decisions. Not even the prime minister could interfere in the relationship between the emperor and the military. Although the cabinet revised three times the imperial defense policy that was set forth as the supreme military strategy in 1907, it had no authority to change decisions concerning national defense policy, troop levels, and deployments that were made by the high command of the army and navy.

Assessment of the threat facing the Police Reserve was likewise out of the hands of the cabinet, since it was handed down from GHQ. The Mitsuya exercises and Bull Run strategy, again, were war plans drawn up by the military. Since it was created by a civilian, Kubo, the standard defense force model represented a new page in the military history of modern Japan. For the first time, the administrative institutions of the cabinet were estimating the quality and quantity of military threat, setting the levels of defense strength, and giving them as requirements to the Japanese military.

The military's pride was wounded by the new civilian role in military affairs. The conference convened to consider the report of the Forum on Defense Issues found it hard to reach a conclusion. A series of articles published by the *Mainichi Shimbun* serve to illustrate the atmosphere behind the scenes at the conference. It described a meeting in the director general's office on September 15, 1975, as follows:

> "Just, just let me say something here!" Ground SDF chief of staff Miyoshi cried out as though he couldn't hold back after listening to Kubo discuss the meaning of the standard defense force concept.
>
> The director general intervened. "Mr. Kubo, if you keep talking so long, no one else will have a chance to speak," Sakata said. "Mr. Miyoshi, speak as long as you want."
>
> "We are military leaders. We spend our whole lives training to be ready in event of war. There's no way you can get us to agree to your supposition that the purpose of the Self-Defense Forces is something other than to fight," Miyoshi said quite vehemently.

The remaining problem on the director general's agenda at that point was whether the standing defense force should have four or five active escort flotillas. It and other disagreements had stymied the conference.

> "It's not a matter of numbers," Air SDF chief of staff Tsunoda said. "We disagree over the fundamental way of looking at the international situation and the very purpose of having defense

strength. We must always consider the worst possible scenario. But you, Mr. Kubo, keep hitting the same note: 'Haven't
we kept the peace for thirty years with a smaller defense
establishment?'"

Kubo's response to the military officers was always the
same. "I'm not saying my approach is necessarily the best. If
you can show me some basis for your arguments that I can
accept, I will withdraw my proposal."[4]

The military failed to present an alternative plan that was
acceptable to Kubo. The conference met five times in the director general's office, but ended each time in deadlock. Each
adjournment saw an even clearer division in their respective
paradigms of diplomacy and defense, until finally Defense
Bureau secretary Kou Maruyama asked the participants to recognize that the discussion was not productive and to simply
bring it to an end.

The disagreement between Kubo and the military men had
become emotional. The military men were not used to theoretical debates, or to being compelled to sit and be lectured to.
When challenged to present a counterproposal to Kubo's plan,
they were unable to coordinate their positions. Each branch of
the service would come up with its own assessment of threat
and invasion scenarios that justified its own agenda. Simply
adding up the requests of the three branches led to a budget figure that was easily in excess of two percent of GNP. Each chief
of staff was so intent on the needs of his own branch of the SDF
that the chiefs together were unable to develop a unified plan.
And since they knew that Kubo was well aware of this, they
became that much angrier.

In the end, Sakata handed down a decision on his own. He
let the chiefs of staff say all they wanted to, and then, having
heard it, Sakata ordered them on October 29, 1975, to draft a
national defense program outline to follow the Fourth Program
to be based on Kubo's standard defense force concept. He had

devoted all of his efforts since taking office to this new attempt at determining policy. That fact, the international situation, and public opinion all made any other decision impossible. Sakata could not envision any threat to Japan within the next ten years or more. Given the period of slower economic growth, ballooning defense expenditures were undesirable and it was rational to seek some kind of equilibrium in defense capabilities for a peacetime situation. Such reasoning would be persuasive to the Japanese people. The figures that had been presented to the Diet in 1973 as the limits of peacetime defense strength were used as the basis for a standard defense force.

LOCKHEED AND THE P3C

A 1958 government decision to buy F-104C fighter planes from Lockheed was heavily influenced by Yoshio Kodama, a prominent member of the right wing. Kodama's influence was apparent yet again in the 1970s.

The Defense Agency had developed a domestic antisubmarine patrol plane (the PXL). PXL research funds were approved in the 1970 budget and a contract was signed with Kawasaki Heavy Industries to oversee development. The next year, research funding was increased and work began on prototypes of the equipment that the plane would carry. Suddenly, after an October 1972 meeting of members of the National Defense Council under the cabinet of Kakuei Tanaka, all work on a domestic PXL was halted and new plans were drawn up for the plane's development.

Takuya Kubo, who was secretary of the Defense Bureau at that time, stated, "We at the Defense Agency are completely in the dark about where the decision was made to restart the process," strongly suggesting that the factors behind the decision to reevaluate plans for the PXL had nothing to do with defense. Kubo later partially retracted this statement, saying that he "remembered incorrectly," and two days later, in a meeting with a foreign special envoy, Tanaka said that he was leaning toward an import for the PXL. Plans for the PXL had shifted from a domestic plane developed by Kawasaki Heavy Industries to the P3C, produced by Lockheed. In 1977, the government formally decided to purchase the P3C.

In July 1973, Lockheed had signed a contract with its longtime "market development consultant" Yoshio Kodama, agreeing to pay Kodama ¥2.5 billion in compensation for his assistance in negotiating a firm contract between Lockheed and the Japanese government for fifty new P3-model planes. The United States government decided at the same time to approve export to Japan of Lockheed's P3C, which carried the most advanced antisubmarine patrol equipment of the time.

Even after the doubts about the Lockheed deal surfaced, the Defense Agency did not begin an investigation. The subsequent death of Kodama meant that the details of the Lockheed negotiations would remain a mystery.

In July of that year, Prime Minister Miki presented the proposal for the national defense program outline to the National Defense Council. The prime minister was the chairman of the council, which considered the proposal on seven occasions. After studying the new defense model, and exactly one year after Sakata's directive, the council and cabinet adopted the national defense program outline along with an appendix that stipulated specific figures for unit composition and major equipment. Prime Minister Miki noted that, "The maintenance of a stable equilibrium is the chief aim of Japan's defense capabilities. To achieve sufficient vigilance during peacetime with such a level of defense, and to be able to effectively respond to events up to a limited and small-scale invasion is an appropriate goal."

This level of defense was considered to be virtually on the same level as that achieved at the completion of the fourth program. The scale of the hypothetical invasion was thereby dropped one level, from a full-scale limited invasion to a limited small-scale invasion. The basic principle of the standard defense force concept, including the specific numbers that the appendix had stipulated for troop strength and front-line equipment, was incorporated into the national defense program outline. The debate over the required defense force concept and the long-term fixed defense buildup was finished.*

Sakata announced the adoption of the new defense program in a press conference:

> In the debates over the outline in the National Defense Council, I feel we finally left behind the Cold War outlook in our discussions of Japan's future security. Peacetime vigilance was emphasized, targets set forth clearly for a standing level of defensive strength, and a change was made from increasing

---

*Editor's Note: No country near Japan had the amphibious lift needed to invade that country. Invasion almost certainly was a euphemism for Soviet border incursions from Sakhalin Island, then and now held by Russia and claimed by Japan.

the numerical strength of the Self-Defense Forces to maintaining and improving their quality, thus giving fiscal stability the importance it deserves. The outline is not only a compendium of the government's approach to security, it is also a question asked of the Japanese people by the government. I hope it is a step forward in creating a consensus among the Japanese people over defense.

The Kubo model had been adopted as the basis of the defense policy to succeed the fourth program. On November 5, one week later, the National Defense Council and cabinet endorsed the concept of keeping defense expenditures to within one percent of GNP. At that point, the new national defense policy was complete. It consisted of the standard defense force concept, an operations program plan, and figures for the standing troop levels, with funding limited to one percent of GNP.

THE MIG 25 INCIDENT

On September 6, 1976, a Mig 25, the most advanced Soviet fighter of its day, piloted by First Lieutenant Victor Belerenko, entered Japanese airspace and landed at Hakodate Port. The lieutenant expressed a desire to defect to the United States and requested asylum. Japan granted the request and three days later Belerenko flew to America.

The incident was a blow to the Japanese defense establishment because it exposed the weakness of the Japanese air defense system. The Mig 25 had gotten by the Self-Defense Forces' early warning system and reached a civilian airport without being challenged by

Japanese interceptors. Thirty-nine minutes before it landed, the Air SDF radar picked up the image of a plane of unknown nationality. Thirty minutes before landing, the SDF launched two F-4EJ fighters at Chitose Air Base to approach the unidentified plane, but their radar lost the Mig after thirty seconds. They picked the plane up again fifteen minutes before it landed, then lost it again and never thereafter detected it. When Hakodate air traffic controllers reported a jet fighter in the sky overhead, the F-4EJs changed course toward it, but the Soviet plane landed nevertheless.

While the search for a single defecting plane is quite different from the detection of an invading force launching a surprise attack, the Defense Agency considered the incident to be a failure of the early warning system against low-flying intruders and faulted the poor visibility from the interceptor aircraft.

A C-5A Galaxy transport plane was requested from the United States military to transport the captured Mig 25. The plane was taken to Hyakuri Air SDF Base, where Japanese and American experts examined the airplane in detail. According to procedures agreed to by the two sides, the Mig 25 was then returned to the Soviet Union by ship.

The incident showed the extreme difficulty of detecting low-flying intruder aircraft, and there were calls for the addition of a flying radar site to the early warning system. The government added an E-2C early warning aircraft to the national defense program outline, which was then being drafted, and implemented the addition promptly.

Japan had groped for a defense policy after the Nixon shock, the oil crisis, and the backlash against the Nakasone program. The government finally succeeded in producing the national defense program outline, with only a slight detour in the debate over the limits of defense strength. Finally, the outline was able to live up to the Japanese people's expectations for a peacetime approach to defense strength, but it was able to do so for only a very short time.

Changes occurred just when the Defense Agency was finally winning its program's adoption. Pressures from within and outside Japan quickly forced defense policies in exactly the opposite direction from what had been envisioned. No sooner had the standard defense force model been implemented than pressure for a military expansion began anew. The outline rapidly began to crumble under a combination of domestic political changes, international changes, and the policy's own internal weaknesses.

The first factor in this change was the Miki cabinet's political weakness. Takeo Miki was a member of a very small faction of the Liberal Democratic Party, Michita Sakata was not a faction member at all, and Takuya Kubo was consumed by a fascination for theoretical issues and ideas. They did not have the political clout within the LDP to be able to bring off effective political implementation. The shrinking of a military force is an uncertain enterprise unless it has a strong political base and national support. When it came to reducing the size of the Self-Defense Forces, these three men lacked the necessary political muscle, notwithstanding their careful theorizing. Though the Self-Defense Forces claimed that they were converting to a peacetime model, the changes were completely superficial. The weak political base of the reformers within their own party enabled the military to avoid compliance. Once the short-lived Miki cabinet had disbanded, the military knew it had outlasted its foe and welcomed the new and hawkish Fukuda cabinet.

The second factor affecting the defense plan was a new strategic environment. The nuclear competition between the United States and the Soviet Union was spreading to the northwest Pacific, and the United States government wanted Japan to expand the territorial range and duties of its military forces under the United States–Japan Security Treaty. Since one of the foremost goals of the outline was to provide the matériel required for the reliability and maintenance of the security treaty and its smooth operation, there was no way not to comply. The ceiling that the standard defense force concept had established, therefore crumbled. The shift of naval strategies by the United States and Soviet Union in the Pacific contained a threat to the United States, not to Japan. The growth of missile and submarine technology meant, however, that the oceans surrounding Japan were the site of this conflict, therefore the environment of this bloodless naval war seamlessly became subject to the provisions of the United States–Japan Security Treaty. Kubo had not foreseen this development, and the premise that the security treaty allowed for a smaller military was now turned on its head.

Additionally, although force limits had been set, there were no stipulations as to quality. Quite the contrary, there was a codicil that stated: "Due consideration shall be given to qualitative improvements to enable a response to more advanced technologies in other countries." This one sentence ate away from the inside at attempts to contain defense spending. It was no impediment to introducing top-of-the-line American aircraft such as the F-15 as the next generation of fighter after the Fourth Program, or the P3C as the next antisubmarine patrol plane (the PXL). All the most prominent equipment was steadily upgraded. It became difficult to see how the transition from the required defense force concept to the standard defense force concept resulted in any real changes at all.

In the end, the standard defense force concept was illusory.

Lowering the estimation of threat and shrinking the military for a peacetime role started as a grand experiment but was distorted midway through until the end result was indistinguishable from the older model. Although contemporary Japan's only civilian-crafted strategy remains on paper, it was gutted at the policy stage and exists in name only.

15

New Guidelines for the "Soviet Threat"

As Takuya Kubo formulated his concept of a standard defense force and the opposition sought to limit defense spending, changes were afoot in Asia and the Pacific. American strategists saw three major changes in Asia during the early 1970s. First, the Chinese threat was replaced by a Soviet threat. Second, the strategic battleground moved from the Asian mainland to the Pacific Ocean. And third, the domino theory of communism in Southeast Asia was replaced by nuclear deterrence as a strategic focus.

In 1969, President Richard Nixon presented his Guam Doctrine, according to which America would not intervene in ground conflicts in Asia. In 1973, the Paris Accords led to an American withdrawal from Vietnam, and in April 1975, Saigon fell and the South Vietnamese government collapsed. These events all illustrate the change in the American military strategy for Asia and the Pacific. American troops vanished from Southeast Asia. A huge new military base was constructed on the atoll of Diego Garcia in the Chagos archipelago, a British possession in the Indian Ocean, for American naval and air power. The Seventh Fleet added the Indian Ocean to its traditional Pacific base of operations. Two large bases in the Philippines,

Subic Bay Naval Base and Clark Air Force Base, supported large naval and air forces. Japan had approved the continued use of bases in Okinawa after the reversion of sovereignty, and Yokosuka was earmarked both as a home port for the carrier Midway and as a forward base of operations for the Seventh Fleet.

The United States assumed its next enemy in the Pacific would be the Soviet Union. The Chinese People's Liberation Army counterbalanced Soviet ground troops. The Soviet threat was its sea and air power and the site of confrontation in the Pacific was the sea lanes. The concept was bruited about in the Western media. As post-Vietnam America redeployed its armed forces to the northwest Pacific and to islands throughout the Pacific Ocean, the main American strategic principle became "presence and power projection," the ability to make its naval and air power felt over an expanded region from the Arabian Sea to the Pacific.

Another factor motivated change in the military situation in the northwest Pacific. Nuclear weapons had been shifted from land to sea, and had now reached the Indian Ocean as well as the northwest Pacific. America had relied for some time upon a strategic triad of delivery systems for its nuclear deterrent that consisted of strategic bombers, intercontinental ballistic missiles (ICBMs), and submarine-launched ballistic missiles (SLBMs). SLBMs were the last delivery system to be developed and had come to be considered the most important of the three because they were mobile and hard to detect, and they had high survivability.

Though deployment of seaborne nuclear weapons had begun under President Kennedy, it was Nixon who aggressively pushed the idea. *U.S. News and World Report* published the following account on April 13, 1970, when Nixon had been in office for barely a year:

A massive shift in United States nuclear strategy, a movement
from land to sea, is being weighed at the White House,
spurred by Soviet deployment of awesomely huge missiles.
The change in strategic thinking is the product of the
most thorough review of American defenses since the development of the A-bomb. It has been underway since shortly
after President Nixon assumed office. Under consideration is
this major proposal: Nuclear missiles and bombers would be
largely removed from the United States. Instead, some
nuclear weapons' bombers would be dispersed on carriers,
and the nuclear missiles in surface ships and submarines, all
sailing random patterns across the world's oceans.

During the 1970s, the majority of American strategic
nuclear warheads, roughly twelve thousand, were transferred to
strategic nuclear submarines. As the warheads were moved into
the sea, they were predominantly retargeted from military
installations to major Soviet cities. Even before the Seventh
Fleet added the Indian Ocean to its field of operations, strategic
nuclear submarines carrying Polaris missiles already possessed
the ability to launch an offensive against Moscow from the Arabian Sea. Many more tactical nuclear weapons were mounted
in surface ships and placed in aircraft carriers' magazines,
including bombs mounted on planes, anti-air and antiship missile warheads, torpedoes, depth charges and mines. The primary
duty of American surface ships became anti-Soviet deterrence,
and the freedom to use international waters took on a life or
death character.

Though not as dependent on the ocean, by the latter half of
the 1960s, the Soviet Union felt similarly compelled to gain
strategic nuclear equality at sea. It not only had to prevent underwater missiles from being fired at its cities through constant surveillance and, in the event of emergency, by attack; it also had to
place nuclear submarines of its own in the seas in order to be
able to level an equivalent threat against the United States.

The route from the Indian Ocean through the Malacca Strait

to the South China Sea and Japan Sea became an important logistical route for the Soviet navy. By the late 1970s, Delta-class Soviet nuclear submarines with the ability to target New York and Washington with nuclear-tipped ballistic missiles would move noiselessly under the surface of the sea of Okhotsk, not far from the Hokkaido coast. Conventional naval power was clearly not capable of protecting the logistical sea lanes that extended from Vladivostok to the Indian Ocean and of keeping the Soviet nuclear submarines that lay hidden beneath the Sea of Okhotsk under surveillance. The existing strategy of forward defense was no longer convincing. A new naval strategy was required. Japan became the natural focus of that strategy because of its geography, economic strength, the United States–Japan Security Treaty, and American respect for the capabilities of the Self-Defense Forces.

Some aspects of America's post-Vietnam transition touched Japan, but there is no evidence that any policy maker on the Japanese side made any serious attempt to include these changes in Japan's calculations, despite American efforts. In 1972, for example, American secretary of defense Melvin Laird stated, "[The increased level of Soviet naval presence in the Indian Ocean] is naturally something that America is concerned about, but it is also of concern to Japan. Tankers headed to Japan are constantly plying the Indian Ocean. Japan naturally must have the highest interest in maintaining this route." He also expressed dissatisfaction over lack of reciprocity in the way the United States–Japan Security Treaty was instituted. These changes in the strategic environment and the new importance of the United States–Japan Security Treaty did not, however, lend any particularly new charge to the debates in the Diet or the Forum on Defense Issues. Japan's course after the Fourth Program, and America's after Vietnam, seemed to be evolving in divergent directions.

In 1975, those two directions were forced to intersect. Post-Vietnam America was asking more of Japan. Soon after the fall of Saigon on April 30, 1975, Japan–United States summits were held between Prime Minister Miki and President Gerald Ford, the respective heads of government, and between Michita Sakata and James Schlesinger, the heads of their respective governments' defense establishments. They established a common view of the situation and of the United States–Japan Security Treaty that opened up the standard defense force concept and the national defense program outline. Kubo's ideas of discarding the evaluation of threat as a guide to levels of defense equipment and the importance of a "peacetime defense strength" were swept easily away by the new situation in the Pacific and the concomitant "Soviet threat."

Defense Secretary Donald Rumsfeld's national security report for 1976–77 and the "United States Military Posture Statement for Fiscal Year 1977," issued by General George Brown, chairman of the joint chiefs of staff, in advance of a Japan–United States summit, both placed greater defense responsibilities for Japan high on the agenda for countering Soviet naval power in the Pacific:

> Improving Japan's capability in anti-submarine warfare in the western Pacific is in Japan's interest. The United States wants to pick up the pace of Japan–United States cooperation in this area. We must emphasize that the United States is devoting increasing attentions to constant surveillance of the Soviet Pacific fleet and protecting routes to the Persian Gulf. (National security report)
>
> Peace and stability in Asia depend on Japan's stability, and this in turn is partially related to the maintenance of a close United States–Japan Security Treaty relationship. In specific terms, our policy is to prod Japan into maintaining a military force able to protect Japan from airborne attack and naval incursion and into developing its antisubmarine capabilities to supplement the defense of our important Pacific logistical lines. (Brown report)[5]

The expectations for a broadened application of the United States–Japan Security Treaty are clear. The duties of the Self-Defense Forces were given a new focus. This was a major change from the description of the relationship with Japan in the previous year's national security report, which only mentioned the importance of maintaining American bases in Japan and of modernizing of the Self-Defense Forces. At this time the 1973 Middle East war had accentuated economic nationalism among the Persian Gulf countries, but the Iranian revolution had yet to occur and the United States and Iraq were not yet in conflict over the resources of the Middle East. A fundamental object of the United States naval strategy at this time was the ability to deploy nuclear weapons in the Indian Ocean, and the United States government was indicating to Japan that the United States–Japan Security Treaty pertained to this conflict.

Although the August 1976 Miki-Ford and Sakata-Schlesinger meetings resulted in no specific commitments about sharing of duties and military cooperation (statements on the latter were especially vague), both parties confirmed that the United States–Japan Security Treaty relationship had become closer and both prepared the ground for ties to become even closer yet. Miki and Ford discussed conditions in Asia following the end of armed conflict in Indochina. They acknowledged that, "The United States–Japan Security Treaty is an indispensable element to the basic structure of international politics in Asia and its continued maintenance contributes to the long-term interests of both countries," and resolved that concerned authorities in the two countries would discuss within the United States–Japan Security Treaty committees the form that cooperation between the two countries would take.

In their meeting, Sakata and Schlesinger agreed to establish a permanent "emergency communication coordination institution" and to make defense summit meetings between the United States secretary of defense and the Japanese director general of the Defense Agency a yearly occurrence. Secretary Schlesinger discussed United States–Soviet détente, saying, "The American presence is useful for maintaining a balance of forces in the world, including Asia, and that is connected with détente. Détente, deterrent forces, and military power are three noncontradictory things." He emphasized that the current détente would not exist without a balance of power and requested Japanese understanding and support of that position.

This view of détente and the overall anti-Soviet stance was a world apart from the standard defense force concept. Détente, in the dominant Japanese view, was the conclusion of the SALT I treaty between the United States and the Soviet Union, the warming of relations between the United States and China, and the end of the Indochina War. For Japan, this felt like a distinct lessening of tension and made Japanese feel that it was possible to drop the standards of threat down one level on the threat ladder. The Americans clearly felt otherwise. Détente, they felt, was the reward for an expanded American presence and for maintaining a favorable balance of power vis-à-vis the Soviet Union, and they wanted greater Japanese cooperation in this effort.

This was in direct contradiction with the standard defense force concept. Kubo's approach presumed lower tensions, and that détente and the United States–Japan Security Treaty would endure unchanged. But the security treaty was changing, so when American and Japanese versions of détente collided, the American version was bound to prevail, since the continuation of the security treaty was the basic assumption of Japan's defense planning.

At the Sakata-Schlesinger meeting, Sakata explained Japan's stance toward defense. "We were not able to complete the Fourth Program because of the oil crisis. In subsequent planning, the views of the Forum on Defense Issues have been incorporated to create a model of defense that emphasizes front-line equipment, naturally, but also quality over quantity, modernization of equipment, endurance, and rear support. Prospects for the Air SDF look bright, but the introduction of new aircraft presents some problems; for the navy, antisubmarine capabilities are a priority for increase." Sakata proposed establishing the cooperative institution that the Miki-Ford talks had agreed upon. Sakata was speaking one way to the United States and a completely different way to the Japanese people. He omitted crucial elements of the new defense model. As a result he and Schlesinger decided to establish an institution for studying Japan–United States cooperation in emergencies without ever defining or identifying whether the emergency that cooperation envisioned was an aggression against Japanese territory or part of the United States–Soviet conflict over nuclear deterrence in the Indian Ocean or the Pacific.

The Japan–United States Defense Cooperation Subcommittee was established as a subsidiary body to the United States–Japan Security Treaty Conference Committee. It began formally with a first meeting in August 1976, a few months before the national defense program outline was adopted. The purpose of the newly established subcommittee was "to create guidelines regarding measures to be undertaken to ensure coordinated joint action of the Self-Defense Forces and the United States military in event of emergency." In other words, it was to create joint Japan–United States operations planning. The American and Japanese military establishment had conducted secret operations coordination for the Flying Dragon and Bull Run plans of the 1960s, but never before had such coordination been a legitimate part of the security treaty organization. On the Japanese side, its members were to be the Foreign Ministry's North American Bureau secretary, the Defense Agency's Defense Bureau secretary, and the director of the joint staff council. On the American side, its members were to be American ambassador to Japan and the planning chief of American forces in Japan.

The third subcommittee meeting, held in December 1976, adopted the following agenda for research and consultation:

(1) Questions regarding a direct attack against Japan or situations of imminent risk of same.
   a. Basic concept.
   b. Questions concerning coordination of functions (strategic functions, information functions, rear support function, etc.).
(2) Questions regarding situations in the Far East other than those of item (1) that have a major impact on Japan's security.
(3) Other topics (joint exercises, training, etc.).

Once these topics were settled, they had to be studied in greater detail, so the subcommittee formed three specialized subsections; one each for operations, intelligence, and support, to grapple with specific issues. All heads of these subsections were drawn from the American and Japanese militaries. Their members and purviews were as follows:

- Operations Section: command and coordination, preparation for operations, ground operations, sea operations, air operations, telecommunications
- Intelligence Section: information exchange, intelligence activities and other cooperation systems, security
- Support Section: all matters pertaining to support activities, support activities functions

These three sections, all staffed by military men, did the actual work that the subcommittee had been set up to do. They also constituted an officially sanctioned operations coordination office, the seed of a joint command. When they had learned in the 1960s that the Mitsuya exercises provided for the establishment of an operations coordination office "in the event of a threat to Japan's security or international peace and security in the Far East," upon consultation between the chairman of the joint staff's council and the commander of American forces in Japan, the opposition had mercilessly hounded the Sato cabinet. Now, however, an operations office with virtually the same framework and functions was operating openly as a regular institution under the United States–Japan Security Treaty. Other military men participated in the section meetings and drew up an operations plan for emergencies and responses. They presented the results, entitled "Guidelines for Japan–United States Defense Cooperation," to both the United States and Japanese governments in November 1978. The report came to be known as "the Guidelines" and set the direction and content of security treaty cooperation thereafter.

The essential character of the Guidelines was to give real military meaning to the joint defense clause of Article 5 of the United States–Japan Security Treaty, which concerned actions opposing armed attack against either Japan or the United States in territories under the jurisdiction of Japan. Strangely, eighteen years had passed since the signing of the security treaty and, despite the strong emphasis in the treaty on American emergency assistance, no official forum for actual planning had been established, nor had any operations studies ever been conducted. Compared to the close, detailed plans drawn up by the North Atlantic Treaty Organization (NATO) for emergency assistance between the United States and the allied nations of Western Europe, the carelessness of the effort in Asia is striking. The reason for this approach was that, at least militarily, there was no comparable tension along Japan's periphery that would necessitate joint operations plans like those of NATO, so symbolic support was considered sufficient. The sudden decision that a joint United States–Japan defense was needed resulted from the intensified confrontation between the Soviet Union and the United States over the deployment of nuclear weapons in the northwest Pacific Ocean rather than because of any increased threat to Japanese territory. The Guidelines thus were developed not because Japan felt a pressing threat that required a joint defensive effort, but because of the larger situation in the Pacific.

The Guidelines consisted of three sections:

(1) Posture to prevent aggression.
(2) Measures to be taken in the event of armed attack against Japan.
(3) Cooperation between Japan and the United States should an event in the Far East outside of Japan have a major impact on Japan.

Section 1 stipulated how aggression would be deterred. America would "maintain a nuclear deterrent as well as a rapid response force for forward deployment," while Japan would ensure the efficient operation of the Self-Defense Forces. Together, they would maintain the utility of American military bases in Japan. The idea was that by making Japan's close cooperation with the United States clear, any aggressive intent could be warded off. The presence of the Soviet Union in an official document as a hypothetical enemy was never so clear; the document did everything but name the Soviet Union.

Section 2 described measures that Japan and the United States would undertake jointly should deterrence fail. "The Self-Defense Forces will undertake defensive operations primarily in Japanese territory and adjoining waters and airspace," while "the United States shall operate so as to supplement functions that the Self-Defense Forces do not have." It was explained in terms of offense and defense. The main mission of the Maritime Self-Defense Force, for example, was "antisubmarine warfare and protection of shipping in the seas surrounding Japan," while the United States Navy's mission was "to force the invading military force to retreat by means that include the use of mobile striking power." Regarding command in battle, the Guidelines stated that "forces shall move as ordered by their respective command systems," but also recommended that a coordinating organ be established "for the effective joint implementation of operations" as a standard measure when actual war broke out. Despite the familiar talk of burden sharing and command coordination, the Guidelines represented a step not even imaginable in the days when the Mitsuya and Bull Run exercises became major controversies.

The guideline of section 3, which dealt with the cooperation between Japan and the United States should an event in the Far East outside of Japan have a major impact on Japan, dealt with the issue of territory under the jurisdiction of Japan. This was a thorny problem, because it explicitly went beyond the scope of Article 5 of the United States–Japan Security Treaty. At first glance section 3 appears to be similar to Japan's provision of bases to support the wars in Korea and Vietnam, but the document also mentions the possibility of research into how Self-Defense Forces bases could be jointly used by the United States military and how other accommodations could be provided. Providing domestic bases could easily expand to providing support services such as transport, supply, and protection. If the United States and Japan intended to oppose the Soviet threat jointly, the line of conflict would be extremely long, from the Indian Ocean to the northwest Pacific. Since deterrence is an ongoing confrontation of forces during either war or peace, and if deterrence is considered to be armed conflict, then the "provision of other accommodations" sought from Japan would become unavoidably wide-ranging. Here, the Guidelines were mapping out yet another new direction.

Only a small portion of the Guidelines was made public. There was absolutely no disclosure to the Japanese people of the details of the plan, or of specific measures regarding joint operations, but the plan's outline was clear. The Guidelines were such a major turning point in Japan–United States defense cooperation that they amounted to a revision of the United States–Japan Security Treaty, first in the sense that the United States and Japan would have a single strategy for emergencies that presupposed the Soviet Union as the enemy in the sea and air space around Japan, and second in the sense that the security treaty was being transformed from a bilateral treaty solely for the defense of Japan to a collective security agreement aimed at the Soviet Union. The research and liaison institutions established between the two militaries made joint operations planning and joint exercises a regular occurrence and implemented the security treaty as though it were a two-nation version of NATO.

This push for Japan's military expansion could never be reconciled with the standard defense force concept. But so long as the security treaty was the cornerstone of the national defense program outline, Japan could never be free of the American world view and anti-Soviet strategy. No one could have guessed how quickly the United States–Soviet Union confrontation would escalate in the northwest Pacific. Kubo was certainly not alone in missing it. But the result was that the interaction of the national defense program outline and the new involvement in America's anti-Soviet strategies in the Pacific led not to the peacetime defense levels that Kubo had sought, but to a policy of military expansion.

THE DEFENSE WHITE PAPERS

The first defense White Paper was produced under director general Yasuhiro Nakasone in 1970. The entire document is only ninety-four pages, but it was the first report on current military strength that has been presented by the Japanese government to the Japanese people during modern times. After a period of five years, Director General Michita Sakata issued the second such White Paper, and the format of an annual report was adopted thereafter. By the nineteenth report in 1993, the complete document, including related materials, had reached 377 pages. The increasing size of the annual defense White Papers mirrors the growing importance of defense in Japan over the last twenty years.

A White Paper is a typical government document and is not written in a very interesting style. It does not read as though it is intended to sell taxpayers on the government budget, like the national security report produced by the United States government. Rather, it is a bureaucratic attempt to justify the government's defense policy in light of the international situation. After 1980, the desire to play up the Soviet threat led to exaggerations and distortions in estimates of Soviet military strength that have caused the reliability of these reports to be called into question.

Reading all of the White Papers one after the other, though, does provide a picture of changes in defense policy over the course of twenty years. The reports are certainly indispensable sources for any study of the history of the

Self-Defense Forces. After Nakasone's White Paper, there are four major shifts in tone in the defense White Papers:

1976–1977: The peacetime defense strength White Papers promote a base level of defense strength.

1978–1984: The Soviet threat White Papers present a campaign emphasizing a danger to Hokkaido.

1985–1989: The Ron-Yasu alliance White Papers return to a concept of defense strength based on perception of threat.

1990–1993: The post–cold war White Papers emphasize instability in Asia and international contributions.

The 1976 and 1977 White Papers were a product of the first age of détente. They were drafted under the Sakata-Kubo line and are almost completely devoted to explaining the concept of the standard defense force. Only during this period do phrases such as "emphasize nonmilitary elements" and "reservations about the current state of the Self-Defense Forces" appear. These phrases indicate a desire to break with the past practice of basing defensive strength on threat perceptions of enemy strength, which prevailed through the first four defense buildup plans.

After the Miki cabinet was replaced and the defense establishment was placed firmly behind the Japan–United States Guidelines, the Fukuda and Ohira cabinets successively turned cold shoulders to efforts to increase domestic defense production that were not in keeping with America's new Pacific strategy. Instead, the White Papers concentrated on the Soviet threat. The 1978 description of the northeast Asian military situation focused on Soviet Far Eastern military strength for the first time. This forthright approach met with praise from military leaders such as General Hiroomi Kurisu. The characterizations of the Soviet military threat became gaudier and more outlandish each year, and references to the standard defense force concept became harder and harder to find as weight was placed on evaluation of "capabilities." By the 1981 defense White Paper, the concept of a base level is mentioned only once, as "the so-called standard defense force concept."

Once Nakasone became prime minister and articulated a common fate for Japan and the United States, an effort was undertaken to build up the Self-Defense Forces. The 1985 defense White Paper contains a section on the characteristics of the area surrounding Japan, in which the periphery of Japan is described as the Soviet Union's "primary route to the Pacific Ocean," which meant that "the strategic location of Japan is very important in the trans-Pacific military rivalry between the Soviet Union and the United States." Based on this geopolitical assessment, the paper proclaimed Japan to be allied to the United States and opposed to the Soviets. In its description of Japan's position and geography as an "innate block" to Soviet military access to the Pacific, not even the slightest trace of the standard defense force concept can be detected.

16

A General Speaks

Many defense taboos fell by the wayside in the 1970s, particularly in the second half of the decade. The Mitsuya exercises had thrown the Diet into a state of confusion, but the Japan–United States Defense Cooperation Subcommittee, which formulated the same kind of Far Eastern emergency plans that were found in the Mitsuya exercises, operated publicly from the start without arousing any opposition. The hypothetical enemy envisioned by this enterprise was very clearly the Soviet Union's Far East military force. This implication collided with the government's public interpretation of the constitution, that Japan envisioned no specific enemy, and yet no one challenged the government to explain the contradiction. As taboos fell, the government even overlooked declarations by military staff members that the current incarnation of the Self-Defense Forces would continue the traditions of the imperial military.

The sense grew within the ruling party that debates in the Diet on defense and security issues had to be based on reality and facts, not on ideology and rhetoric. The twenty-five years since the end of World War II had produced a deep sense of powerlessness and weariness in the Japanese people over the relentless expansion of the Self-Defense Forces and the extensive cooperation under the United States–Japan Security Treaty, and the Liberal Democratic Party (LDP) knew it. Some taboos began to seem irrelevant.

In November 1978, the government adopted the guidelines produced by the Japan–United States Defense Cooperation Sub-committee. It was the third year of the Fukuda cabinet. Discussion was open. The ruling LDP, the opposition parties, and even the military men each brought their own viewpoints to bear on the Self-Defense Forces and on defense issues in general. Surprising rightist declarations were followed by calls to acknowledge the legality of the SDF and for it to operate outside the law in times of emergencies. Military men criticized defense policies openly, calling the fundamental governing principle of civilian control of the SDF into question.

Takeo Fukuda, who replaced Prime Minister Miki, enjoyed a long-standing reputation as a hawk. He had forcefully promoted the Blue Storm Society, an anti-Soviet political grouping of LDP hawks formed in the 1970s. He made no attempt to conceal his distaste for the smaller military that Miki, Sakata, and Kubo had worked to create. In his yearly policy address, he became the first prime minister to place national defense at the forefront of concerns, and he expressed a passionate desire to build up defenses. He aggressively welcomed dialogue with the uniformed services, and told the top officers of the SDF that the Self-Defense Forces had "great duties and responsibilities" because nationalism was causing "continuing international instability." He also called military officers to regular talks at the prime minister's residence, a practice that had not been followed for fourteen years. There was a new closeness between government and military, and Fukuda's hawkishness redirected policy back toward the required defense force concept.

At the Clean Government Party's yearly conference in January, party chairman Yoshikatsu Takeiri looked forward to the realistic possibility of coalition governments in the 1980s by saying, "Refusing to accept the Self-Defense Forces means disarming the country, and the Japanese people will not accept that. The right to self-defense is not effective without a minimum level of ability to maintain territorial integrity." About the Self-Defense Forces themselves, he said, "The ability to maintain territorial integrity has achieved the latent consent of the people," and indicated that he favored an open acceptance of the SDF. This did not mean that he approved of the government's Self-Defense Forces policies, but it was the first time that the Clean Government Party had separated itself from the Japan Socialist Party's (JSP) position that the SDF was ipso facto unconstitutional.

The LDP met this change in policy with jubilation. Fukuda, who was in Kyoto, immediately phoned Takeiri. "I just saw your address on television. I must indicate my great respect," he said, welcoming the Clean Government Party's turn to a more pragmatic position. LDP secretary general Ohira also freely expressed his joy, calling the Clean Government Party a "friendly party" for the first time, and praising it by saying that the prospects for the progress of democracy in Japan had become brighter. Only one of the opposition parties, the Democratic Socialist Party, had ever accepted the SDF, calling for "defense under the constitution" and "a United States–Japan Security Treaty without American troops in Japan." The Japan Socialist Party, the largest opposition party, responded to the Clean Government Party's move toward recognizing the SDF quite differently, declaring that the forces represented a return to prewar conditions and were likely to draw Japan into war. There were now a variety of viewpoints, a kind of multipolarity on the security treaty and on defense policy, among the opposition parties.

Bold words began to flow from within the government. After observing the touchdown ceremony of the First Air Squadron of the Ground SDF on January 8, Defense Agency director general Shin Kanemaru said in his address, "Some say the Self-Defense

Forces must not present any threat to foreign nations, but what kind of defense is it if it does not threaten enemies?" This statement aroused considerable criticism. Under Kanemaru, the 1978 defense budget had increased 12.4% over the previous year to ¥1.901 trillion, and the F-15 fighter and the P3C antisubmarine patrol plane had both been approved as the latest upgrades. His mood was ebullient, leading perhaps to this slip of the tongue. But he then continued by saying, "I believe Japan, South Korea, and Taiwan share a common fortune," which was more than a simple overstatement. The opposition parties immediately called for his dismissal. Kanemaru symbolized the new Fukuda cabinet's lean to the right.

In the suit brought by residents of the area surrounding the American base at Atsugi, seeking stronger restrictions on aircraft noise levels, the government was the defendant. Its January 18 brief on the suit against Atsugi airplane noise stated, "Residents of surrounding areas must endure a little excess noise in the interests of national defense," indicating that it was a natural state of affairs that local residents should endure a certain degree of pollution from the base. The brief emphasized that the benefit received by the nation and the Japanese people from the use of the base by the United States Navy and the Self-Defense Forces should not be compared with the benefit of a quieter life for a portion of the Japanese people if freed from noise. This national interest argument advanced the public utility of the Self-Defense Forces and was made only a few days before Fukuda delivered his pro-defense administrative policy speech, representing the beginning of a period in which national rights overrode civil rights.

When Ground SDF general Hiroomi Kurisu, chairman of the joint staff council, then began talking of extralegal powers for the SDF, huge ripples were caused not only by what he said but also by the fact that his views so perfectly mirrored the country's turn to the right. From the very start, Kurisu spoke directly to the media through numerous interviews with reporters. He startled the defense establishment by seeking to be treated in the same way as cabinet ministers and Supreme Court judges. When the informal decision was made in October 1977 to elevate him from Ground SDF chief of staff to chairman of the joint staff council, he said, "As the highest officer of the Self-Defense Forces, the chairman of the joint staff council should be a prime minister's appointment through the emperor's attestation. When I receive my appointment, I will go to the emperor." His outspokenness began immediately.

> A theory has been advanced that there are two different types of militaries, offensive and defensive, and that the former threatens peace while the latter makes peace possible. In reality, it is difficult to make such a clear distinction. The history of war shows that only offense can win. We cannot effectively respond to offensive actions that pose a threat from areas outside Japan's sphere through defensive measures alone. Weapons that do not make potential adversaries feel that their bases and strategic supplies might be at risk are clearly ineffective as a deterrent to future offensive intentions. The concept that a military effort devoted exclusively to defense is compatible with maintaining a deterrent effect is highly problematic.

This was a criticism of the Self-Defense Forces' rule dedicating itself solely to defense; it touched on the heart of defense policy doctrine. It was difficult to dismiss as being simply a spontaneous remark, coming as it did from a Defense Agency director general. Kurisu's comment appeared in the press about the same time that Kanemaru was asking, "What good is a defense that doesn't threaten the enemy?" which agreed with the sentiment of Kurisu's statement. Defense Agency bureaucrats had little effective means of countering these statements. General Kurisu had effectively used Fukuda's and Kanemaru's hawkishness to gain a voice. Shin Kanemaru later complained, "Chairman Kurisu kept getting his statements into weekly magazines without even clearing them through channels."[6] Kurisu's next public statement concerned the SDF's authority to exercise power outside the legal system in times of emergency. In the July issue of *Shukan Post*, he was asked whether, under the existing legal system, the Self-Defense Forces required the command of the prime minister to mount any war operations, regardless of the emergency. Kurisu responded by describing a scenario in which the SDF did not receive an order to mobilize after a surprise attack.

> That is the case. We can do nothing. However, should such a situation occur, it is hardly conceivable that the Defense Agency, the National Defense Council, and the cabinet would merely be standing idle. [If we received no order, the implications would be ominous.] The military staff would probably act on its own authority, extralegally, as it were. That is a form of justifiable defense. In such a case, I would certainly expect that the Japanese people would be of a mind to permit such extralegal action on the part of the Self-Defense Forces. I believe it is possible that a situation could occur in future that would place the SDF in a position that it would be unable to reconcile itself to not taking action simply because the legal system had ceased to exist.[7]

Giving examples such as emergency scrambles to confront aircraft violating Japanese airspace and ongoing captures of Japanese fishing vessels, he stated that the current Self-Defense Forces Law had many inadequacies and was unable to gain the Japanese people's confidence. In an emergency, the first line of commanding officers would be forced to respond extralegally. He further stated that local units had the necessary resolve to take action. This was a clear message from the highest-ranking military officer to units on the front line that in emergencies they need not obey the law. At this point, even Kanemaru felt that Kurisu had gone too far and had to be replaced. Kanemaru describes the process leading up to Kurisu's dismissal:

> I called Deputy Director Maruyama of my office and told him that I had decided that I must have his (Kurisu's) resignation. Maruyama replied that he would discuss the matter thoroughly with the defense officials and the top brass and asked me to wait for two days. Two days later, I waited until Maruyama reported that he had obtained Kurisu's complete agreement. I then called Kurisu himself to my office and told him that if he didn't resign I would fire him. He promptly pulled a letter of resignation from his jacket.[8]

On July 25, Kurisu was no longer the chairman of the joint staff council. His remarks on operating outside the law had proved too great a challenge to the principle of civilian control for him to stay on. Yet the matter was far from over. Criticism by military officers continued thereafter and no one else was punished like Kurisu, so Kurisu effectively achieved his goal. Although he himself had lost his position, the ideas he had voiced had a life of their own and they continued to have a major effect on defense policy.

Kurisu had argued a general hypothesis from an extreme case. It was a way of using the extremely unlikely possibility that the Soviet Union might invade Japan to point out certain inadequacies in the current system. "Extremely unlikely" is clearly not synonymous with impossible, but to enact a legal system on that basis during peacetime would effectively turn the nation into a defense-oriented state, if not a garrison state, a most odious prospect to the lower-middle class. Although Kurisu's tone was calm and reasoned, his ideology resembled that of the pre-war imperial military.

The standard defense force concept was still operative at that point, and it measured threat realistically as a combination of capability and intent. It held that if an enemy's aggressive intent became pronounced, movement toward launching a surprise attack would be physically observable. On this basis, the government had decided to adopt "a posture of sufficient vigilance for peacetime" and field the capability to repel a limited and small-scale aggression. This all presupposed that the situation envisioned by Kurisu, a surprise attack calling for SDF operations outside of the law, was highly unlikely. The only way to effectively respond to the unlikely scenario presented by Kurisu was to turn the nation into a major military power. The prevailing defense wisdom thus considered it wiser to field a military sufficiently vigilant to prevent a surprise attack. The idea of matching an opponent's defense strength and putting enough troops on the front lines to repulse a surprise attack had been fundamentally discarded. Although this new attitude had prevailed only over the heated opposition of the military, the chairman of the joint staff council and the chiefs of the three branch staffs had ultimately agreed to this premise and the Diet had formally adopted it. Kurisu's sentiments were a backlash arising from earlier resentments, another reflection of the unhappiness that the military still felt about the entire standard defense force concept.

The sole reason Kanemaru gave for Kurisu's dismissal, however, was that Kurisu had opposed the principle of civilian control. His basic commitment to the military was not called into question, nor his loyalty to the chain of command or to the defense model. If the reason for his dismissal were that he disagreed with the standard defense force concept, rather than that he had gone outside the institution, then it would have been an example of civilian control in action, but the incident ended without a debate of Kurisu's ideas. After his resignation, he became a hero to hawks who wished to see an expanded role for the military. His book, *The Soviet Union as a Hypothetical Enemy: How We Would Respond*, is a prime example of this current of thought. In a real sense, Kurisu was more of a danger once he was freed from the restraints of his position.

The repercussions of the Kurisu affair began to make themselves felt almost immediately. The Defense Agency had begun a study of how the three branches of the Self-Defense Forces would respond to an emergency that would involve United States–Japan operations. This effort received an extra impetus from the Kurisu affair, and expanded from a study of emergency operations in event of war to an investigation of the emergency legal system itself. On September 29, 1978, two months after Kurisu resigned, Prime Minister Takeo Fukuda addressed the lower house. In response to a question on the connection between the emergency studies and response to a surprise attack, Fukuda stated, "In my opinion, the Self-Defense Forces exist to handle emergencies and it is the government's duty to study emergencies. [However,] we must also consider the unlikely possibility that a surprise attack could occur prior to the study's completion." He thus linked the legal and operations studies and promised that both would be the object of the research.

The government wanted to pursue a study of the emergency legal system that presupposed an unlikely but nevertheless possible surprise attack. The study's effects would necessarily cast a shadow on civilian lives and rights under the constitution. The destruction of the balance between military requirements and basic human rights was a very real possibility. The Defense Agency's emergency research quickly grew from an agency project focusing on operations to a project of national significance focusing on the enactment emergency legislation. Although the government stated that enacting emergency legislation had no connection to Kurisu's statements, Fukuda himself said, "We cannot completely rule out the possibility of a surprise attack. For that reason we need to fully study what we would do in that event."

It is difficult to argue that the two positions were unrelated. Government officials affirmed the necessity of an espionage law and the Self-Defense Forces' right of belligerency. Rationales that placed military requirements above basic human rights followed one after the other from government sources. Kurisu's statement was like putting out a fire with gasoline, and led to the successive breaking of many defense taboos. Fukuda's attitude toward the firing of Kurisu evinced a certain gratitude. He invited Kurisu to the prime minister's residence for parting words, at which time he told him, "Thank you for your long service. After you take off your uniform, I hope you will be able to consider defense issues from a new perspective." Fukuda also directed Deputy Director Maruyama to set up a venue for him to converse at length with uniformed officers of the Self-Defense Forces.

It became clear after Kurisu resigned that the government and the military were drawing closer together, and that the governing party and military officers were using each other. Retired military staffers and Liberal Democratic Party factions jointly established a think tank. It became the chief strategic planning group of military expansionists and a pressure group for increasing the defense budget. It also became a source of silent military pressure on the bureaucrats of the Defense Agency, developing into a kind of deterrent. The balance of power between the two moved steadily to the military.

In 1980, two years after Kurisu's dismissal, an organization called the Japan Strategy Research Center was inaugurated with Kanemaru as its president. Both Kanemaru and the center's director, Noboru Minowa, belonged to the LDP's Tanaka faction. Minowa had been a deputy director of the Defense Agency and was involved with Fukuda's Blue Storm Society. More visible, however, was the gaudy presence on the board of former military officers, who included the previous and other past chairmen of the joint staff council, the previous Ground SDF chief of staff, a former Maritime SDF chief of staff, and other former Self-Defense fleet commanders and air squadron commanders. Ryuzo Sejima, a counselor from the prominent financial company Ito Chu, was an advisor to the group. Kurisu himself was not a member. The stated purpose of the center's founding was "to make proposals illuminating strategic situations and security policy by surveying and studying specific issues relating to Japanese national security."

Kanemaru had been a hawk his entire political life, as evidenced by his controversial statements. In the extraordinary executive staff meeting of the Defense Agency after Kurisu's dismissal, Kanemaru stated that, "I understand that former chairman Kurisu spoke as he did after serious consideration of the responsibilities of his office and the relation of the fundamental duties of the Self-Defense Forces in time of emergency to laws that serve as the basis for its actions. I deeply regret being forced to ask for his resignation." Since nationalist Diet members within the Liberal Democratic Party also voiced dissatisfaction with Kurisu's dismissal and the military expressed unanimous support for Kurisu's statement, Kanemaru probably became involved in the establishment of the Japan Strategy Research Center as a way to reaffirm his position as a hawk and to seek a peace with members of the military. This act not only repaired his own standing with the military, but was the start of a new government-military relationship as well. The military had secured a beachhead in the most powerful of the LDP factions, so it was able to direct civilian control through the Defense Agency, while the government for its part was able to employ the knowledge and information of military experts to share in a beneficial relationship with the defense industries. It was an relationship of mutual benefit.

In private life, the main character of the Kurisu drama, Kurisu himself, promoted his own views in a larger arena. As a result of the situation he had created, those who followed him in the military were able to increase the size of the military through the new relationship with the government. Military requirements were now evaluated according to the old formula, the required defense force concept.

In March 1979, Ground SDF chief of staff Shigito Nagano delivered remarks before a group of financiers indicating that the increased strength of the Soviet Union in the Far East required a revision of the national defense program outline. Though Nagano was criticizing established policy in public with outsiders, exactly as Kurisu had, he received no punishment. When he retired in 1980, he joined Kanemaru's Japan Strategy Research Center as a managing director. The second chairman of the joint staff council after Kurisu, Air Force general Goro Takeda, gave an interview with the magazine *Hoseki* while sitting as chairman, in which he likewise criticized a solely defensive military. He received a warning from the director general, but then had his statements printed up for distribution within the section. He raised questions about the three non-nuclear principles, saying that Japan was completely defenseless against the Soviet Union's nuclear weapons. He also criticized government policy, and said that the national defense program outline was fundamentally flawed. The authorities remained silent. After his retirement, Takeda, too, joined the Japan Strategy Research Center as a director.

The Kurisu statements clearly led to a change in the relationship between the Defense Agency bureaucrats and the military, and the application of civilian control. This was a key juncture in the history of the Self-Defense Forces. The military gained broader freedom to state its opinions and the Defense Agency dropped its restraints. The Liberal Democratic Party no longer appointed persons with expertise in defense strategy, like Takuya Kubo, to the posts of Defense Agency director general and deputy director. All discussions of the principles of defense and strategy were turned over to the military. Not surprisingly, 1978 was the year in which Japan adopted the Guidelines for Japan–United States Defense Cooperation for its emergency operations planning. The domestic changes were, if anything, of greater importance, since Kurisu's declaration effectively ended in turning defense leadership over to the military. Just as the Guidelines had essentially amounted to a second revision of the United States–Japan Security Treaty, so too did the changes inspired by Kurisu cause repercussions that fundamentally altered defense administration. These two developments of 1978 presaged the 1980s, a decade when defense reigned supreme.

THE VOICES OF GENERALS

If the Self-Defense Forces were buffeted in the 1970s by Yukio Mishima from the right and Makoto Konishi from the left, in the 1980s the major drama affecting the Self-Defense Forces was the rebellion of the generals. Since the 1960s, each decade had been colored by a single event. In the 1960s, it was the first revision of the United States–Japan Security Treaty. In the 1970s, it was the reversion of Okinawa. In the 1980s, it was the invasion of Afghanistan. The 1960s saw the left ascendant. In the 1970s, the left and right contended equally, but in the 1980s, the right reigned supreme. The sense of crisis over the Soviet threat was whipped up by the generals' rebellion and was used to scold the Japanese people for being "blinded by peace." Regional wars, including Afghanistan in 1979, the Falklands War between Britain and Argentina in 1982, and the Israeli invasion of Lebanon in 1982, pushed the generals into a frenzy and gave renewed power to pro-defense forces and those harking back to the traditions of the imperial military.

The first person in uniform to publicly take issue with the government's defense policy was Ground SDF general Hiroomi Kurisu, but the same type of criticism came in wave after wave from many sources, as though Kurisu had broken a dam of discontent. The military was particularly critical of the national defense program outline. When Shigeto Nagano became chief of staff for the Ground SDF in March 1979, after General Kurisu's dismissal, he gave a speech to financiers pointing to the major buildup of Soviet forces in the Far East that was radically altering the military situation in Asia for the worse. In noting that the Far East situation was in a state of flux, he publicly called for a gradual revision of national defense program outline. The government had stated previously that the situation had not changed sufficiently to warrant revising the outline, so these remarks were a departure for the military. After retiring from the SDF the following year, Nagano amplified these statements, urging that the SDF's solely defensive posture be abandoned. "The Self-Defense Forces must quickly develop an offensive capability able to launch tactical counteroffensives against the bases from which attacks and bombardments are launched." He proclaimed the need for "forward defense" and advocated raising defense expenditures to two percent of GNP as he marked out for himself a new political career. Later he became a member of the upper house for the Liberal Democratic Party.

The rawness of language reached its height when Takehiko Takashina became chairman of the joint staff council after Nagano. Immediately after he ended his short tenure in November 1979, he stated before a gathering of an assembly of former unit members, "You would have to be sick or blinded by peace not to realize that the Soviet Union poses a threat to Japan. If you look at the Soviet threat realistically, our current defenses are plainly inadequate. Japan is perfectly sited to block Soviet access to the Pacific, so we are the first prize they will want in event of war. Only a real dupe wouldn't be able to guess what the intentions of the Soviet Union are." The point was to criticize the assumption underlying the national defense program outline, that any change in enemy intentions would be detectable beforehand, enabling Japan to respond.

After Kurisu and Takashina, Air SDF general Goro Takeda assumed the post of chairman of the joint staff council. He distributed his personal views within the Defense Agency while still in his position, aiming once again at the national defense program outline. "There is a fundamental flaw in planning to repulse a limited and small-scale aggression through our own power." Citing the figure that the Soviet Union had deployed one-third of its strategic nuclear forces in the Far East, he said that Japan was completely defenseless against nuclear weapons, raising a strong objection to Japan's three non-nuclear principles. Takeda also criticized in magazine interviews, the solely defensive posture of Japan's military. Unlike Kurisu, he was merely issued an intradepartmental warning.

There are countless other examples of military officers speaking out against government defense policy during this period. It is hard to say exactly how much influence these statements had on actual defense policy. The Guidelines for Japan–United States Security Cooperation are a clearer example of pressure on policy makers; however, the criticism of military leaders was indispensable in creating the prevailing atmosphere. When Nakasone became prime minister, these voices faded away. The generals' voices proved to be the vanguard's trumpet heralding military ascendancy in the 1980s.

17

Defense of the Sea Lanes

The easiest way to see how far the United States–Japan Security Treaty system expanded cooperation between the Japanese and American militaries outward from Japanese territory is to look at how the defense of sea lanes became a political issue. Sea lane defense opened the door to military expansion. A sea lane is almost any shipping route on the open sea, so, for the purposes of defense, their extent, both in theory and in practice, goes on almost without limit. Naming sea lanes as an appropriate object for self-defense makes the scope for military action extremely elastic. All that defense authorities have to do then is to later provide a geographical definition of the sea lanes and describe the military operations that are to occur within or along them. The concept of sea lanes thus leant itself nicely to Japan's defense buildup of the 1980s.

In military jargon, "sea lane" is akin to "communications lines" and "logistical lines." The United States Navy uses the expression "sea lines of communications" (SLOC). The SLOCs that connect the American west coast to Hawaii, Hawaii to Guam, and the Philippines to Yokosuka are the veins and arteries of the United States military in the Pacific. If these lines were cut, fuel, ammunition and food could not get to operating ships. Under United States Navy doctrine, the capability to resupply at sea is vital to maintaining a fleet as a fighting force. The SLOC for the Soviet Union from its Indian Ocean units to Vladivostok, was likewise of vital importance to the Soviets.

The debate over sea lanes in Japan, however, had little to do with maritime routes of resupply for the military. Instead, sea lanes were important to Japan for protecting movement of maritime imports of resources, principally oil, in times of emergency. Since Japan is so dependent on imports for everything from foodstuffs to energy, the call to defend transport routes resonated as an issue after the oil crisis made Japan's vulnerability tangible for the first time since the war. The main questions were how to carry industrial resources and the necessities of life to Japanese ports, how to protect the routes, and how to compose the convoys. That was the importance of sea lanes in the Japanese debate. Defense of sea lanes seemed appropriately commercial for an economic giant.

Why did the definition of sea lanes change in this manner? First, the rebuilt Japanese military was dedicated solely to defense; there was no need for defense of sea lines of communication, whose existence was predicated on foreign campaigns. Second, the memory of American submarine attacks on commercial shipping and the complete cut-off of materials during World War II left a lasting and visceral memory in the Japanese people. Convoy protection was, therefore, supported by defense policymakers. The Maritime Self-Defense Force considered the protection of tankers to be the easiest way to justify expansion from a coastal navy to a blue water navy.

The idea of Japan defending sea lanes went back before the 1973 Middle East war, because Japan's near-total dependence on foreign energy had become obvious. The maritime route that protection policies advocated during the late 1960s and early 1970s had more in common with the British navy's protection of Atlantic convoys during World War II. Sea lane defense was advocated by financiers and by survivors of the imperial military who remembered Japan's days as a naval power. It was also reminiscent of Nakasone's proposal, in which he talked about control of the oceans around Japan as a reason to expand Japan's military.*

In initial discussions, sea lane defense strategies were synonymous with convoy escorts. Convoys of dozens of large tankers were to be escorted by several warships that would provide protection all the way to Japanese ports. The range for this activity was set at one thousand nautical miles from Japan. Takuya Kubo said when he worked as Defense Bureau secretary under director general Nakasone, "The southeast route extends in a corridor about one hundred miles wide from Tokyo Bay in the direction of Saipan for one thousand miles. The southwest route goes through Osaka and Kyushu to the end of the Ryukyu island chain in a corridor also about one hundred miles wide whose exact length slips my mind at the moment, but is also nearly one thousand miles."[9]

This was probably the first recorded government position on the geographical extent of sea lanes. Nakasone's proposal called for an antisubmarine mopping-up force centered on two helicopter carriers that would defend convoys. This proposal faltered with the rest of Nakasone's agenda, as described earlier, and the system of escorted convoys and defense of sea lanes appears thereafter only in theoretical discussions of policy.

Sea lane defense next raised its head in the late 1970s. The concept of escorted convoys was dropped in favor of "defense of routes." This discussion was raised after the oil crisis, when the

---

*Editor's Note: American naval officers at a 1958 conference in the Philippines were surprised to learn from their Japanese counterparts that the teachings of Alfred Thayer Mahan had been offered in Japanese naval schools since 1897. Mahan claimed that a dominating naval force was necessary for national greatness.

financial community was not the only group concerned with protecting resource flows. Vice secretary of the Liberal Democratic Party Etsusaburo Shiina also expressed the concerns of the political world: "Most of Japan's resources, in the case of oil, ninety-nine percent, pass from the Persian Gulf through the Indian Ocean through the Malacca and then Taiwan Strait on their way to Japan. Any minor disruption, even an isolated terrorist incident, would have a major impact on Japan's energy picture. Defense is not limited to territorial integrity alone. We must also consider how to defend Japan's interests as they exist in tankers at sea."[10]

The heightened interest in Japan's energy security at this time overlapped with American desires to make Japan adopt a larger share of ocean defense within the framework of the United States–Japan Security Treaty. The Japan–United States summit led to the establishment of the Defense Cooperation Subcommittee and the adoption of certain guidelines. The main topic of this discussion was how Japan and the United States would handle the sea lines of communication of the Soviet navy that extended from the Persian Gulf to the Indian Ocean through the Malacca Strait and then the Taiwan Strait on its way to Vladivostok. The strategic planners pointedly noted the exact overlap of this line with Japan's petroleum sea lanes. They were well aware that the Soviet sea lines of communication were a product of the rivalry with the United States in naval strategic nuclear weapons and were not a measure of the Soviet Union's capability to disrupt Japan's trade and transport. They did look at the two as part of a combined threat from the joint enemy of Japan and the United States.

Convoy defense was discarded as a model in favor of defending belts of sea lane. With this extension of the object of defense from convoys to sea routes, the policy became more aggressive. Indirect defense of ships shifted to direct defense of maritime space. Defense limited to direct protection of convoys could be defined as exclusively defensive, a simple extension of Japan's home territory to include its convoy ships. In the case of limited defense, war could only be precipitated by enemy action, the approach of submarines, or torpedo attacks against Japanese ships. Once defense was extended to ensuring the safety of the sea routes themselves, however, warships would be moving independently of convoys, searching, pursing, and attacking enemy submarines approaching the thousand-mile-long, hundred-mile-wide sea lanes. The success of such an effort would then guarantee the safety of Japanese ships. This change required a great deal more offensive capability, including larger and more advanced warships and aircraft. For the Maritime Self-Defense Force, defense of sea lanes would be the thin end of the wedge for a major building program.

From the American perspective, there were no more effective means of pressuring Japan than this. Japan had become more dependent on ocean trade for its industrial resources and necessities of life than ever in the past. The Japanese people were also well aware of this state of affairs. The increase in Soviet activity from the Indian Ocean to the Japan Sea was also a very visible reality. From the perspective of the nuclear rivalry at sea, the undersea competition in submarines and the need to defend sea lines of communication were an American crisis. If that fact could be downplayed, however, while the overlap of the Soviet Union's sea lines of communication and Japan's sea lanes was played up, the nature of Japan's dependence on sea lanes and the expanded scope of operations by the Soviet navy could be combined to create the appearance of a Japanese crisis as well. America used this sleight of hand to nudge the initial goals of Japan–United States cooperation under the Guidelines in a favorable direction. The Sea Lanes Crisis came to be a major buzzword.

The gradual expansion of the Soviet navy has coincided with an ebb in the American ability to expand its efforts on the front lines of the western Pacific to an all-time low. In event of emergency, there is probably only a fifty-fifty chance that the United States would be able to supply and communicate with American troops in Asia and the Pacific in the initial stages of war.[11]

An extremely large number of warships would be required to protect convoys operating over the long maritime transport routes. The United States Navy has instead adopted an offensive approach to push the enemy into a defensive position. The United States Navy and the Maritime Self-Defense Force coordinate so that they do not duplicate each other's efforts. This enables American warships to operate independently. The Maritime SDF's antisubmarine P3Cs are deployed so as to fulfill this duty.[12]

Defense Agency sources have made it clear that the Americans requested that "Japan increase its maritime defense strength and work to ensure that it can defend the sea lanes in Japan's vicinity through its own efforts" during the Japan–United States security conference that met in Hawaii from late July through early August. The Defense Agency took these American requests as a call for increasing the anti-submarine and air defense capabilities of the Maritime Self-Defense Force. Americans had been calling for increased Japanese efforts to defend the security of sea lanes for some time, particularly in the United States Congress, but the exchange of opinions in Hawaii represents the first request between governments in a formal venue such as the administration-level conference.[13]

The assumptions common to all these statements were a crisis in the northwest Pacific and the need to divide the burden between Japan and the United States. Throughout the 1960s, the United States Navy had looked at the Maritime SDF as something akin to the anti-submarine unit of the Seventh Fleet. With the move of the United States–Soviet rivalry over deployment of nuclear weapons at sea to the northwest Pacific, the United States now saw the Maritime SDF as an independent regional naval presence that could be responsible for entire areas under the Guidelines. Having begun its current incarnation with cast-off coastal patrol vessels from the United States Navy, the Maritime SDF greeted its new role with excitement, though it also felt the heavy weight of this new responsibility.

In May 1981, Prime Minister Zenko Suzuki visited Washington, D.C. Questioned at a press conference at the National Press Club about whether Japan would defend sea lanes to ensure its petroleum supply, Suzuki stated for the first time that it was Japan's responsibility to defend sea lanes up to one thousand nautical miles.

> Because we are so poor in resources, ensuring the security of transport for resources from abroad is a life-and-death matter for Japan. Since the United States Seventh Fleet is in charge of security in the Indian Ocean and the Persian Gulf, it cannot be in the environs of Japan. It is natural, then, that Japan defend this region, since it is on our front doorstep. Our policy of defending the region surrounding Japan out to a distance of several hundred nautical miles and sea lanes to a distance of one thousand nautical miles is something we intend to strengthen in future in keeping with the provisions of the constitution and within the scope of self-defense.[14]

This pronouncement came to be known as Suzuki's Sea Lane Defense Doctrine and would come to be considered as a public commitment to America. Suzuki later explained that it was merely a description of what the government had always thought, not a new commitment to share responsibilities, but the Americans had already latched onto it as gospel.

SENDING TROOPS OVERSEAS

The Japanese government has defined the dispatch of troops overseas as "dispatching armed units for the purpose of armed actions to the land, territorial waters, or air space of another nation." Adhering to this definition would appear to prevent the recurrence of any aggression such as that launched against Asia earlier in the century. Since the government does not consider the following cases to constitute the deployment of troops overseas, however, it is not possible to affirm that the Self-Defense Forces will never be sent abroad in some new form.

(1) Dispatch to other countries of troops whose purpose is something other than armed action. The dispatch of Self-Defense Forces to another country to rescue Japanese citizens held as hostages would fall into this category.

(2) Air attack of a foreign base when self-defense could not be performed without fighting an enemy base. "When there is no other alternative, attacks on enemy bases should be permitted and considered as an issue separate from the question of the dispatch of troops abroad."[15]

(3) Actions of the Self-Defense Forces in international waters, such as the defense of sea lanes and minesweeping in the Persian Gulf are not a dispatch of troops abroad. "Actions taken to remove mines judged to have been cast adrift in international waters, where they might pose a

threat to Japanese shipping, to ensure the safety of said shipping route is not an armed action and is thus possible under the Self-Defense Forces Act."[16]

Of the scenarios described above, the second is highly improbable, but it is rather easier to imagine the Self-Defense Forces being dispatched for missions like those described in items *1* and *3*. The Japanese government has in fact been asked by the American government to engage in action of the type described in *3*. With any expansion of the range of Japan's international activity and the increased likelihood of conflict in the form of terrorism or guerrilla actions, the chance of events falling into gray zones that are just outside of the government's definitions is steadily increasing. The possibility of sending nonmilitary units of Self-Defense Forces troops (medical, communications, transport, and engineering corps) to take part in United Nations peacekeeping operations is also under study at this time, which adds an entirely new aspect to the debate.

Looking at Suzuki's explanation, it is possible that he was referring to the one-hundred-nautical-mile-wide, one-thousand-nautical-mile-long corridor for the defense of convoys that Kubo described in his Diet testimony in the early 1970s. The same conditions would apply, that is, the right to individual self-defense and to protection of maritime transport routes through convoys. The Americans, however, did not understand Suzuki's comment in this way. They regarded it as part of a joint effort at deterrence of the threat posed by the Soviet navy based on principles of burden sharing and division of territorial responsibilities. They took Suzuki's words as a public affirmation that Japan was adopting an unlimited collective security concept of Self-Defense and abandoning a solely defensive posture. If his explanation was genuine, Suzuki's statements were astonishingly ill considered. It was no time to bring up outdated concepts of convoy defense to provide security within sea lanes when nuclear submarines had changed the nature of the threat. And it was decidedly unrealistic to expect Suzuki's words to be taken at face value.

The Americans latched onto this new "commitment" from the prime minister to place sea lane defense at the top of their list of priorities vis-à-vis Japan at the next United States–Japan Security Treaty the following June. They pressed Japan for a major naval and air force buildup. The Americans presented the figures shown below as desired force levels for the SDF. The figures in parentheses are the corresponding numbers from the national defense program outline.

- missile destroyers: 75 (60 antisubmarine destroyers)
- offensive (hunter-killer) submarines: 25 (16)
- P3C patrol planes: 125 (100)
- interceptor squadrons: 14 (10)
- support fighter squadrons: 6 (3)
- early warning plane squadrons: 2 (1)

THE MIYANAGA SPY INCIDENT

The Miyanaga spy incident involved former Ground Self-Defense Force General Yukihisa Miyanaga and a Soviet military attaché, Colonel Kozurof, and it has come to be known by either of their names. Miyanaga and two SDF staff members had passed information to Kozurof, a reputed member of the GRU, Soviet Military Intelligence. The information included the *Monthly Bulletin of Military Affairs* and copies of official telegrams relating to the Ministry of Foreign Affairs. The Japanese men were charged with violating the Self-Defense Forces Act and with suspicion of theft. After the affair's discovery, Kozurof returned to the Soviet Union. The incident occurred on January 18, 1980, shortly after the Soviet Union invaded Afghanistan, when perception of a Soviet threat was at its strongest and received a great deal of coverage. Since this was the first time an incident of spying for a foreign power was discovered among currently-serving Self-Defense Forces officers or high-ranking retired officers, it led to calls for better protection of classified information. After the incident, the Defense Agency established a committee to study the information classification system and installed electronic locks on sites where top-secret documents were stored.

Miyanaga had specialized in the Russian language since the days of the imperial army and had been kept for a period in Siberia after the end of the war. After entering the Security Forces in 1952, his duties were to assess the military strength of the Soviet Union as a hypothetical enemy, gather informational materials, translate documents, and analyze data. He was considered to be the SDF's ablest Soviet expert. Since he was already knowledgeable about Japan's anti-Soviet defense preparations in the north, he was allowed free access to the Ground Self-Defense Force's Central Counterintelligence Command even after he retired. He had involved his former subordinates in passing sensitive documents to the Soviets in a scheme that seemed straight out of a John Le Carré spy thriller. Public security authorities disclosed information definitely indicating a much larger scandal immediately after the affair was discovered. Ultimately there were no further developments within the Ground SDF. Since very limited materials were made public in the trial, the scope of the overall affair is not completely known, even today. Miyanaga was found guilty of all charges and sentenced to a year in prison, while the other defendants were sentenced to eight months each. Although Miyanaga's motivations were never made clear, he did not receive a great deal of money.

BOX

All militaries are protective of their secrets, and intelligence units doubly so. The three branches of the Self-Defense Forces and the joint staff council each has its own intelligence-gathering department in addition to the Defense Agency's intelligence division. The most active of these are the Ground SDF's Central Counterintelligence Command, Intelligence Department, Coastal Monitoring Command, and Electronic Surveillance Command, which have offices throughout Japan and are involved in the gathering and analysis of written, personnel, and electronic information.

There is another secretive intelligence group called the JCIA, the Second Office of the Ground SDF staff's Intelligence Department. Although it is technically part of the Ground SDF,

J2, as it is usually called, is actually operated as an internal bureau of the Defense Agency (and used to be called the Cabinet Intelligence Office). Its headquarters are at the Ichigaya Army Garrison, and it employs eleven hundred people. It also has a branch office in Hokkaido and conducts electronic surveillance of the Soviet Union. It delivers its information through the Defense Agency to the prime minister's office. When the Soviet Union shot down Korean Airlines flight 007 over Sakhalin in September 1983, J2's electronic eavesdropping and decoding confirmed the entire process down to the ground command communicating with the fighters and directing them to fire on the airliner. This information was the basis of United States Secretary of State George Shultz's announcement of the incident.

The activities of J2 were briefly visible again when South Korean Central Intelligence Agency (KCIA) operatives kidnapped South Korean opposition politician Kim Daejung from his room in the Tokyo Grand Palace Hotel and took him back to Korea in August 1972. Before his capture, Kim Daejung was being watched by the head of a Japanese private detective agency, a former first lieutenant recently retired from the Ground SDF staff's Intelligence Department. He had opened the detective agency after his retirement and two weeks later received a request from the first secretary of the South Korean embassy, thought to be the mastermind of the kidnapping, to keep an eye on Kim Daejung's whereabouts. Since the Japanese government also wrapped this affair up quickly through a political resolution with South Korea, all of the facts of the incident and the extent of the SDF's involvement are unknown.   _| Box

America also asked Japan to introduce Patriot surface-to-air anti-aircraft missiles and to increase Japanese stocks of ammunition to a sixty- to ninety-day supply, including missiles, torpedoes, and mines. Ammunition stocks are crucial to fighting a protracted war, and the stocks at that time (about eighty-five thousand tons), were judged to be sufficient only for one or two weeks. The request was also unprecedented.

After Suzuki's public commitment to the United States, Japan–United States defense cooperation began to expand around the goal of defending sea lanes. Although the Japanese government superficially protested *sotto voce* against the excessive expectations of the Americans, it did not object to the defense of sea lanes being placed in the framework of the Guidelines for joint study. The next year, in 1982, joint operations research began between the Japanese and United States militaries. Once the concept of a joint defense had been accepted, the rest fell into place. Japan had already dropped any consideration of convoys to protect tankers. Now the two-dimensional concept of defense of Japan's southeast and southwest transport routes as linear zones had to be shifted into the further complexity of defending not a line, but an entire plane.

The meaning of the expression "sea lane defense" had gradually altered from denoting the defense of a ship, to defense of a route, to defense of an entire region, all without changing a word. Instead of defending cargo ships carrying crude oil or flour, Japan was now defending the aircraft carriers of the Seventh Fleet and high-speed transport ships carrying missile warheads and aircraft fuel north of the Philippines and west of Guam. The goal of sea lane defense became a larger area and a more powerful opponent. The idea of a territorial defense or of a solely defensive military now seemed almost quaint.

After the research for a joint effort at sea lane defense with the Japanese military began in 1982, the national security report under Secretary of Defense Caspar Weinberger stated a hope that Japan would contribute to the security of the Pacific region by defending sea lanes up to a distance of one thousand nautical miles. The Reagan anti-Soviet buildup was just hitting its stride with an across-the-board modernization of nuclear and conventional weapons and the construction of a six-hundred-ship navy. American naval demands on Japan for the northwest Pacific under the United States–Japan Security Treaty were correspondingly lofty. The regular Japan–United States conferences would soon become the scene of unrelenting pressure in this direction.

As it moved toward sea lane defense operations, the Japanese maritime fighting force quietly became a Pacific blue water navy. By the 1980s, its participation in Pacific naval exercises such as the Rim of the Pacific Joint Exercise (RIMPAC), and the Pacific Exercise (PACEX), would come to seem quite ordinary.

18

The Late-Blooming Military Power

The Self-Defense Forces could not have asked for two better sources of foreign pressure for expansion than what they got in the 1980s—Afghanistan and Ronald Reagan. It was a decade of fair weather. When the Soviet Union invaded Afghanistan in December 1979, there was mention of a "northern threat" that Japan had not heard since the fears of a Soviet invasion of Hokkaido. When Ronald Reagan took up residence in the White House, his talk of the Soviet Union as an evil empire created a new age of confrontation in the world. Détente was dead; the Japanese people and the architects of the standard defense force concept were derided as fools. The Self-Defense Forces were invited into new territories in the budget process, in the scope of military operations, and in the scale of joint Japan–United States exercises. Supported by its enormous economic power, Japan was suddenly well on its way to becoming a military power.

In the midst of all this, Yasuhiro Nakasone became prime minister of Japan. The Soviet threat, Japan's strategic position, and a Japan–United States alliance were Nakasone's old themes, and the age gave this military expansionist a chance to enter the national arena once more. He saw that Japan's steady progress as a major economic power was now resulting in Japan being called upon to shoulder international responsibilities in line with its abilities. For Nakasone, who was proud of his ability to improvise a performance to the tenor of the times, it provided him a most suitable stage, and the Self-Defense Forces were his partner in the dance.

Eleven years had passed since Nakasone's resignation as the Defense Agency director general. During this time he had become a formidable Diet member and the leader of a Liberal Democratic Party (LDP) faction. He kept himself in the public eye. He continued over the years to accumulate a colorful record of public pronouncements. In 1973, when he was the minister of international trade and industry, he created a stir by saying that "Japan is a kingdom in the east of Asia," and when he participated in a 1978 debate at Tokyo University's May Festival as the secretary general of the LDP he said about the thirty-year-old constitution, "A generation has passed. So isn't it now time for the Japanese people to say how well they think it has performed? We need to reevaluate it. That is the democratic process."[17] As ever, he was passionate about the need to revise the constitution.

He naturally also had plenty to say about Kurisu's various remarks and about emergency legislation. While recognizing that Kurisu had to be dismissed as chairman of the joint staff council in order to protect civilian control, he also said, "Since the prime minister is the commander in chief, Prime Minister Fukuda himself should have been the one to ask for [Kurisu's] resignation by summoning him and allowing him to speak his mind." About the issue that Kurisu had raised of whether the Self-Defense Forces could act outside the law, Nakasone was sympathetic: "The two defense laws do not stipulate what to do in time of emergency. The resolution of this question properly belongs in the political arena, but this is an age of breaking taboos." When the debate over enacting emergency legislation was at its height, Nakasone was an ally of the hawkish elements in the party.

> Obviously we cannot protect the country if in the event of an enemy invasion of Hokkaido tanks still have to drive on the left, stop at red lights, and ask permission before crossing private property. The newspapers are all in a lather that enactment of emergency legislation will infringe terribly on civil rights, but should an enemy land and we move jointly to protect the country, the suppression of some civil rights is quite obviously necessary for the public good.
>
> Japan should not become a militarist state, but we need to be fully competent to defend ourselves and be able to mount an honest defense effort. It is also important that we enable the Japanese and American militaries to work together for mutual defense in time of emergency.

Nakasone could feel in the air that Japan's political center of gravity was moving from left to right. When he ran against Masao Ohira for the leadership of the LDP in November 1978, he proclaimed himself a neonationalist who wanted to depart from the economics-first philosophy of the past and bring "the inclusive national unity and development that is the primary function of politics" to the fore. It was a position based on his reading of the times. By declaring that there had been a turn to the right, he announced that the even match between left and right of the 1970s was a thing of the past and he challenged the conservative factions led by Ohira, which had been the mainstream since the days of Shigeru Yoshida. Nakasone's appointment as prime minister in 1980, thus augured the biggest turn to the right in defense policy that postwar Japan had seen.

Nakasone fought two general elections during his five years as prime minister, once losing the LDP's majority and the other time achieving a historic victory. He chose South Korea as the destination of his first trip abroad, and shortly after his inauguration he also met with General Secretary Mikhail Gorbachev.

He then hosted the Tokyo Summit, further heightening his image as an international political leader. In domestic politics, he continued to challenge tradition and called for a "general accounting of postwar politics." He publicly worshipped at controversial Yasukuni Shrine, pushed for an espionage law, and proclaimed himself in favor of constitutional revision. Although implicated in both the Lockheed and recruit scandals, he astutely shrugged them off and preserved his political life. As prime minister he showed the most passion in breaking down taboos in the areas of the United States–Japan Security Treaty and national defense.

Although he now looks like something of a Don Quixote tilting at windmills, he mounted his attack on the Soviet threat with a vengeance. His defense policy was very popular with the "Western free world," but by the time his efforts began to bear fruit, the Cold War was over and the world was on the cusp of embracing a new period of détente. Nakasone sent the Self-Defense Forces abroad, gave a new dimension to the United States–Japan Security Treaty, and freed the Self-Defense Forces from their shackles and chains, if only for a while.

The defense industries, though, welcomed the advent of a Nakasone administration with open arms. On November 24, 1982, when Nakasone won a crushing victory in the Liberal Democratic Party election for party president, and it became clear that a Nakasone cabinet would shortly take office, the Tokyo Stock Exchange immediately responded to the news with a rush on defense-related stocks. Mitsubishi Heavy Industries was particularly popular. It had been gaining for days beforehand in anticipation of a possible Nakasone victory. It gained a further ten percent in only two days. Mitsubishi buyers were probably happy that someone who had been a Defense Agency director general was finally prime minister, but they also clearly were anticipating that a more hawkish cabinet would lead to a larger defense establishment.

Nakasone did not let them down. When he was Defense Agency director general, Nakasone had won the confidence of the defense industries with his three policies: (1) a basic policy of purchasing, production and development; (2) a policy of promoting the defense industry; and (3) a research and development promotion policy. A mere ten days after becoming prime minister, Nakasone decided to create a special exception to the limitations on weapons exports that would enable the defense industries to sell military technology to the United States. The defense industries rejoiced. "Because of the United States–Japan Security Treaty and our mutual defense support agreements, the United States and Japan have a special relationship that makes the exchange of military technology between us natural." The alteration of this one-way channel into a two-way street not only rendered the three principles of weapons exports meaningless, it also created a danger of shifting the focus of Japan's advanced technology from civilian industries to military industries. The government emphasized that it would not lift weapons export restrictions toward any country other than the United States. The lowered barriers helped pave the way for joint development of the FSX, the new generation of fighter aircraft, and Japanese participation in the Strategic Defense Initiative (SDI). Mitsubishi Heavy Industries was the prime Japanese beneficiary of both of these government-backed projects, so the wild expectations of the stock market that led to a rush on Mitsubishi after Nakasone formed his cabinet were proven to be realistic.

Bearing this offering of weapons technology, Nakasone visited Washington, D.C., in early 1983, where he had his first face-to-face meeting with President Reagan. There he made remarks that left an indelible impression affecting both the Japan–United States defense cooperation and the Self-Defense Forces. With one particular astonishing phrase, he also shocked the Japanese public—he called Japan "an unsinkable aircraft carrier."

This statement was made in an interview with *Washington Post* editor Katherine Graham and others and was reported in the January 19 issue of the *Washington Post*. Graham asked Nakasone, "How do your views on the Constitution and the defense of sea lanes differ from those of your predecessor, Zenko Suzuki?" Nakasone's answer was of unprecedented directness for Japanese prime minister.

> **A:** I have served as Defense Agency director general, so I have my own views as to Japan's defenses. In my opinion, the Japanese archipelago should stand as a powerful bulwark against infiltration by Soviet Backfire bombers, like an unsinkable aircraft carrier. Preventing infiltration by Backfire bombers should be our number one defensive priority. Our second priority should be to maintain total control over the four straits that surround Japan to deny Soviet submarines and other warships passage. Our third priority should be to ensure the security of the sea lanes. We should expand our oceanic defenses by several hundred nautical miles. This attempt to ensure the security of the sea lanes should focus on the region between Tokyo and Guam and between Osaka and the Taiwan Strait.
>
> **Q:** You have just mentioned defense against Backfire bombers and containment of Soviet submarines. Do you believe these to be the defensive responsibilities of Japan?
>
> **A:** Japanese governments have historically been vague on these issues. My government, by contrast, is extremely clear on them. I do, however, feel there is no need to declare them.[18]

Nakasone and President Reagan discussed the Soviet naval and airborne threat in the Pacific and the strengthening of United States–Japan defense cooperation more extensively than ever before. When the president then said, "Call me Ron," he was clearly excited by the understanding Nakasone had demonstrated. The efforts at defense cooperation during this period came to be known as the Ron-Yasu alliance.

Nakasone's "unsinkable aircraft carrier" comment constituted a major departure and turning point not only for Japan's defense but also for Nakasone's personal political beliefs. It is hard to detect any glimpse of these during his previous incarnations as Defense Agency director general or while a party president candidate. The opposite sentiment seems more evident in his ideas on Japan's position in the United States–Soviet Union nuclear rivalry. Was this really the same man who had once said, "I am such an extreme nationalist that the Americans regard me as a dangerous person"?[19] The political chameleon seemed to have added another protective color.

Since Nakasone's comment was a public expression of views regarding Japan's defense, it forced Self-Defense Forces operations and strategy and Japan–United States defense cooperation to abandon the past practice of equipping the SDF against a specific aggression in favor of joint anti-Soviet deterrence. Although the outlines of this effort had been hammered out as guidelines under the Fukuda government and the sea lane defense had been adopted under the Suzuki government, Nakasone's statement put Japan squarely within the larger American anti-Soviet deterrence strategy. Japan was now a complete subscriber to the theory of "deterrence and balance of power."

Nakasone's strong words appear to have taken Katherine Graham, of the *Washington Post*, by surprise, since her follow-up question was basically seeking a confirmation of what Nakasone had just said. Any American reporter familiar with the issues would have known that the Soviet moves in the late 1970s to increase its naval and air forces in the northwest Pacific and the neighboring Sea of Okhotsk were a response to the United States–Soviet contest over strategic nuclear deterrence, so the question should not be taken at face value. It was common knowledge that the Soviet Union had based the aircraft carrier Minsk in the Far East to protect its strategic nuclear weapons. These missiles were aimed solely at the United States mainland; logical targets for the Backfire bombers were the surface ships of the forward-deployed Seventh Fleet. This under-standing of the underlying situation in the northwest Pacific was common to American policymakers and journalists alike.

Nakasone's description of the Japanese archipelago as a bul-wark against Backfire bombers and bottlenecks to pen up Soviet submarines was heartily welcomed by the United States. Although Japan's two previous prime ministers, Masao Ohira and Zenko Suzuki, had demonstrated a superficial agreement with the American position on the Soviet military stance, they had always conditioned their statements on defense coopera-tion with the concepts of regional defense and the principle of individual self-defense. They had never described the Soviet military in the Far East as the common enemy of Japan and the United States. The strong pledge that the nationalist Nakasone had made was considered a happy miscalculation in two senses. The backlash was intense. Nakasone denied his words, saying that he hadn't used the expression "unsinkable aircraft carrier" and that his idea of closing ocean straits did not go beyond defending the archipelago or Japan's right to individual self-defense. But like Suzuki's comment on defending sea lanes, once the words were out of his mouth he could not take them back.

It is fair to say that Nakasone's grand gesture after his return to the top guaranteed that defense would be the biggest topic of his administration throughout the 1980s. Nakasone's political rebirth and the start of the Ron-Yasu alliance signaled the final death of the standard defense force concept. Under Kubo's détente-era plan in the 1970s, Japan did not fundamentally direct its defensive efforts at any particular hypothetical enemy. Under Nakasone's formulation, the "Soviet Union's inte-grated military buildup" necessitated that "Japan maintain an appropriate defensive force to ensure its own security."[20]

The Soviet Union was now at the forefront of Japan's defense activity. Kubo incorporated Kyoto University professor Masataka Kosaka's concept of "denial capability," the ability to deny an external enemy easy approach to national territory, into his thinking about Self-Defense Forces fighting potential; Nakasone preferred to talk about deterrence. The difference between the two concepts could not be clearer. Deterrence and the balance of power were his guiding precepts in seeking the level of defense to be maintained during peacetime. Deterrence indicated a level of military power sufficient to make an enemy think that it could not succeed in an attack on Japanese soil, and the balance of power was to be maintained at that level.

It was only to be expected that the Nakasone cabinet would remove the brakes on defense policy. Nakasone brought the notion of "response to threat" back to the center of defense policy. Units could no longer simply "maintain sufficient vigilance" but again had to be able to "respond immediately to emergencies." The government discarded the budgetary restraint on defense spending of one percent of GNP and tried to shift defense budget planning from yearly to five-year plans. All of these measures were the products of the Miki cabinet, so it is understandable that they were discarded en masse. Nakasone was setting the clock back to the days of the required defense force concept. And he was perhaps trying to borrow a little of Reagan's authority to enact the Defense Buildup Program that he had been unable to get through in his Defense Agency director general days.

Five years became the basic planning period for defense budgeting in 1986. A decade had passed since both this system and the required defense force concept were abandoned after the Fourth Buildup Program. Nakasone tried to abolish the yearly planning system and the limit of one percent of GNP for defense spending together, but the opposition parties opposed him and elements within the Liberal Democratic Party opted for a more cautious approach, with the result that removal of the one-percent limit had to wait until the following year. The adoption of an interim defense buildup plan by the cabinet was given priority and a five-year plan totaling ¥18.4 trillion was adopted. It seemed inevitable that at some point during the five years of the plan this figure would exceed the one-percent limit, so the two issues were essentially settled at once.

The defense establishment had long awaited the restart of the five-year defense planning system. After the end of the fourth program, defense budgeting had become a yearly affair and the Defense Agency was no longer able to make decisions on purchases of front-line equipment like fighters, warships, tanks, and missiles in five-year chunks. The eight-year design-and-build cycle for a major weapons system made single-year budgeting extremely inappropriate. Although defense authorities revised five-year plans internally once every three years under the title "53 (1978) interim work estimate" and "56 (1981) interim work estimate," the estimates had no official standing and were regarded solely as in-house equipment wish lists. It was a stroke of good fortune for Nakasone that his cabinet was formed just as one of these plans was being debated, the 59 (1984) interim work estimate, which covered the period 1986–90. It was an excellent opportunity for the hawks to revive the five-year system.

The Reagan administration held out the same hopes for the 59 interim work estimate. America had engaged the so-called evil empire in a major arms race, but budgetary difficulties made it difficult to sustain an arms buildup commensurate with the size of the world and its immense oceans. Japan was an obvious place to look for help, given Japan's great economic strength, its pivotal location in anti-Soviet strategy, and its reliance on oceans. Japan's mammoth trade surplus with the United States was also used as a source of pressure in the United States Congress to get Japan to do more on defense.

The United States Department of Defense and congressional leaders wanted an increase in Japan's sea and air forces to enable it to defend sea lanes up to one thousand nautical miles away. They wanted Japan to abolish or revise the impediments to that increase, namely, the national defense program outline and the one-percent-of-GNP limit. It was apparent that the reasons for doing so had more to do with anti-Soviet strategy than with Japan's defense. Defense secretary Weinberger called the levels of fighting strength under the outline "outmoded" in his 1983 "Report on Allied Contributions." The 1984 update of this report referred to the 59 interim work estimate being prepared by the Defense Agency, stating that if the plan were sufficiently refined, the target of defending sea lanes to one thousand nautical miles would probably be reached by 1990. A defense buildup beyond the outline was suggested. Assistant Secretary of Defense Richard Armitage said, "Japan is no longer simply the cornerstone of American policy in Asia; it is a global partner." He also expressed a lack of faith in the targets of the outline: "Japan's prime ministers have historically made it clear that the object of their defense policies is Japanese land, territorial waters, airspace, and sea lanes up to one thousand nautical miles. In view of the close proximity of the threat to the Japanese archipelago, however, the fighting potential of the Self-Defense Forces is deficient, both in number of warships and aircraft, and in lack of ability to keep fighting for any length of time."[21]

Nakasone could not resist American pressure since he had visited Washington and reached an official concordance of views with the Reagan administration on opposing the Soviets. The 1959 interim work estimate became less of an in-house reference document for the Defense Agency and more of a commitment to the United States and proof of a pledge. It was elevated to the status of an interim Defense Buildup Program, a government defense buildup plan that was binding on fiscal planning authorities. In September 1985, the cabinet adopted a five-year plan for ¥18.4 trillion in spending.

As the interim work estimate became an interim defense program, spending got further and further away from the one-percent limitation. Although the cabinet did not adopt this policy change at the same time as the interim program, it was only a question of time. Defense spending for fiscal 1987 increased 5.2% over the previous year (¥3.5174 trillion), pushing defense spending to 1.004% of GNP, thus exceeding the limit by ¥13.4 billion. After eleven years, Miki's fiscal restraint had collapsed. The cabinet resolution applied a new standard to defense spending: "Defense-related costs for a given fiscal year within the period [of the interim defense program] shall be determined within the framework of the requirements plan set forth in said plan." Thereafter a total amount was specified. Not becoming a military power and building a moderate defense strength were the only limitations on the stipulation of that all-important total. Effectively, all rules were off.

Nakasone said, "I struggled long and hard with the question of whether to hold fast to the one-percent limit or whether to reach the goals of the five-year plan. In the end I decided that defense was more important. We have to at least meet this minimum standard." While he showed a remarkable ability to bend to public opinion, at the same time he also said that "the change from [defense spending of] 0.997% [of GNP] to 1.004% [of GNP] is not going to transform Japan instantly into a militarized state. In fact, the two figures are virtually the same."[22]

Nakasone had always opposed setting a percentage or ratio limit on defense spending. In his first defense White Paper issued in 1970 when he was Defense Agency director general, he had stated that "it is not always appropriate to keep the defense budget proportional to the increase in economic strength or as a fixed percentage of the gross national product or the national budget," and declared himself opposed to GNP-based restrictions. In that sense, when he succeeded in going beyond the one-percent limit, he had again achieved a goal outlined seventeen years before. Discarding the limit meant switching from a quantitative restraint that could be easily gauged by anyone to a qualitative restraint that depended on more subjective criteria. When he heard about Japan's new defense budget, United States defense secretary Weinberger stated that "Nakasone can be credited with breaking through the one-percent limit and getting the 5.2% increase in the budget [over the previous year]. We welcome it on all counts."

THE NADASHIO ACCIDENT

At 3:38 P.M. on July 23, 1988, in the center of Uraga Channel in Tokyo Bay, the submarine Nadashio of the Second Submarine Flotilla of the Maritime Self-Defense Force, under Commander Keisuke Yamashita, collided almost head-on with the Daiichi Fuji Maru, a large pleasure-fishing boat captained by Manji Kondo. The Daiichi Fuji Maru rode up over the spherical bow of the Nadashio and sank stern first. Thirty passengers and crew drowned. The Daiichi Fuji Maru had forty-eight passengers on board for a Sunday fishing expedition and was en route from east Kanagawa to the waters off Oshima Island. The Nadashio had just finished a fleet exercise off the Izu Peninsula and was sailing on the surface en route to its home port of Yokosuka when it cut across the path of the fishing boat heading south on the Uraga Channel.

The Yokohama Regional Sea Disaster Trial Court found in its first judgment, on July 25, 1989, that "the accident was caused by insufficient vigilance in the Nadashio's lookout as it headed west to Yokosuka Port, which prevented it from taking action soon enough to avoid hitting the

Daiichi Fuji Maru." The trial court also found that the Second Submarine Flotilla of the Maritime Self-Defense Force, to which the Nadashio belonged, "had not provided sufficient instruction on keeping watch to submarine crew members, which is one of the primary tasks of safe navigation, or on course selection and early evasion," and it sought a remedy of this situation through a formal recommendation. Although it found Commander Yamashita personally responsible, it did not issue a judgment against him. As a result the prosecutor objected and sought a new trial. A second trial was held in the High-Level Sea Disaster Trial Court, with similar results.

The Nadashio accident occurred in broad daylight on a calm day in Tokyo Bay, and after the accident the Self-Defense Forces took more than twenty-one minutes before notifying the Maritime Safety Board that an accident occurred. The revelation that the submarine was unable to mount an effective rescue operation exposed the slackness of the Maritime Self-Defense Force and prompted savage criticism.

It was also suspected that Commander Yamashita had tampered with the ship's log to correct the time of the impact in order to evade responsibility. Observers expected that a suit would be brought in a criminal court after the sea disaster trial. The incident remains a running sore within the electorate.

RECRUITMENT PROBLEMS

No fighting force can function without personnel. The quality and training of those personnel are vital. Hand-to-hand combat has mostly vanished; modern warfare increasingly uses electronics and artificial intelligence, even in individual weapons. Therefore the standard for evaluating soldiers is no longer whether they are healthy and can carry heavy loads. Knowledge of and ability to use precision weapons are more important in today's soldier.

Japan's Self-Defense Forces are completely volunteer, with no conscription, and ordinary soldiers, as opposed to the officer candidates graduating from the Defense Academy, are engaged "by appointment," with short-term contracts that must be renewed once every two years for the Ground SDF, and once every three years for the Air SDF and Maritime SDF. There is therefore no long-term employment stability within the forces. There are tracks available for long-term appointment, but it requires a great deal of commitment to rise from the ranks of private, airman, or seaman apprentice to officer status. In bad economic times military pay can seem fairly decent, but in a good economic climate, it is difficult to find young people to whom being a soldier in the Self-Defense Forces looks attractive.

The strength of the Ground SDF is set at 180,000, but as of November 1989, the organization has been able to recruit only 85.2% of this number (153,061 men). For ordinary soldiers, the complement is only 72% of the target. This means that every four-man tank crew is missing one person. Since the officer corps is 96% staffed and the ordinary soldiers are 72% staffed, the SDF is a top-heavy organization. The large-scale employment of women as soldiers is now being studied.

Nevertheless, the military continues to seek major weapons that demand highly trained personnel for operation and maintenance. The SDF's military expansion is beginning to seem like a nouveau riche mansion, gaudily decorated, but without a staff to keep it up. A shortage of recruits could ultimately slow down military expansion.

 DEFENSE ACADEMY ATTRITION

Until the fifteenth class was graduated from the Defense Academy in 1971, cadets almost always accepted a Self-Defense Forces commission. There were usually no decliners, or perhaps only one. Prior to the fifteenth class, the highest number to decline was four, in the fourteenth class. The year 1974 marked a turning point, when suddenly twenty graduates of the twentieth class declined appointments. By the late 1980s, the numbers had grown even greater. The total and average numbers of decliners per decade grew as follows:

Defense Academy Class	Total number of declines	Average Percentage of class
1st–10th	4	0.4
11th–20th	82	8.2
21st–30th	259	25.9
31st–34th	194	48.5

Clearly, Defense Academy students were leaving the Self-Defense Forces in increasing numbers. One reason was that Defense Agency authorities were spending more time lobbying for front-line items and devoted correspondingly less energy to training cadets. In the 1980s, as the wild growth of defense spending took center stage, the lack of interest in personnel and education was even more pronounced, contributing to a constant understaffing of educational facilities and a higher rate of commission refusals among Defense Academy graduates.

The economic boom is not in itself sufficient to explain this phenomenon. There are many reasons graduates refuse appointments. In the thirty-fourth class, which was graduated in the spring of 1990, sixteen graduates refused appointments in order to take over family businesses or otherwise respond to family emergencies, seven elected to pursue private sector employment, and three went on to graduate schools. Among the twenty-nine graduates who listed some other reason, ten said that the Self-Defense Forces were not attractive, eight found themselves personally unsuited to the life, and four felt a lack of confidence in their ability to perform as officers.

Students of the Defense Academy are paid a monthly stipend of ¥74,800 as a student allowance above and beyond state-supplied room, board, and clothing. This totals ¥1.7 million over four years. This large expenditure has led some to call for recovering expenses from those who refuse commissions or requiring a specified period of service after graduation. Defense Agency director general Yozo Ishikawa stated in a March 1990 upper house Budget Committee meeting that the agency would be studying specific measures to lower the rate of appointment refusals in future.

The deepening of the Ron-Yasu alliance and the recognition of the Soviet Union as a common enemy in the Pacific caused the scale and subject of the joint exercises between the two nations to show a remarkable change and expansion. The exercises became joint exercises in a true sense for the first time.

American and Japanese forces have held joint exercises as far back as the inauguration of the Self-Defense Forces. The exercises provide an illuminating record. A special minesweeping exercise was the first such exercise and was held for four days starting on April 25, 1955, south of Kuroshima outside Sasebo Harbor. Japan and the United States had also held joint training sessions when the ships were lent to Japan, but the Kuroshima exercise was the first joint operations exercise held with the United States Navy.

The success of the minesweeping exercises emboldened the Self-Defense Forces, and special antisubmarine exercises were also held starting in 1957 as the first joint exercise in warfare techniques. The Japanese learned antisubmarine strategy from the Americans with the expectation of its use against nuclear submarines in the future. The first special antisubmarine exercise began on September 16, 1957, and lasted four days. It was called Exercise Baseball (EBB) and was held off the southern coast of Shikoku. The idea was that Japan and the United States were playing catch with warfare tactics and opinions. A baseball was even thrown from an American oiler to a Japanese destroyer to start off the exercise.

Joint Japanese-American exercises started at sea. Until the mid-1970s, the exercises were only occasional occurrences designed largely to provide the Self-Defense Forces with the opportunity to practice with an indulgent instructor. There was a wide gap in the fighting and organizational capabilities of the two militaries. The United States was then putting its main efforts into fighting, first in Korea, then in Vietnam. It did not have many resources left for the joint exercises with the Japanese.

In the 1980s, the situation changed. America's Pacific strategy no longer centered on its role as Asia's policeman, but on the rivalry with the Soviet Union over control of the seas. The contest centered on the northwest. The confrontation consisted mainly of keeping a deterrent force constantly visible in the field and deploying a force capable of rapid response to emergencies. Japan's military presence and geographical location made Japanese cooperation vital. The framework of the joint Japan–United States exercises within this new strategic environment expanded, beginning conceptually in the days of the Guidelines, in the late 1970s, and reaching full-fledged reality with the joint exercises of the 1980s. Nakasone's statements were a true signal of that change.

The Maritime Self-Defense Force felt the greatest effect of this change. It had been at the forefront of the expansion under the shift to sea lane defense. In the days when the Seventh Fleet ruled the Pacific Ocean uncontested, the Maritime SDF was only effective as an antisubmarine force for the several carrier groups of the Seventh Fleet, and even that was a stretch. By taking responsibility for the defense of sea lanes north from the Philippines and west of Guam, the Maritime SDF had gradually transformed itself into a blue water navy and a competent partner of the Seventh Fleet. Having started its first tottering steps with a loan of ships from the United States, the Maritime SDF now was equipped with a force that, but for the lack of aircraft carriers, was not so inferior in surface warships, submarines, and antisubmarine patrol planes to the United States Navy in the western Pacific.

Japan's participation in the Rim of the Pacific Joint Exercise (RIMPAC), showed how far Japan had come in making a transition to a blue water navy, which now operated away from Japan's shores as a matter of course. RIMPAC had begun in 1971 as an exercise for the defense of the southern Pacific among the nations of the ANZUS treaty, namely, Australia, New Zealand,

and the United States. With the shift in United States strategy after the Vietnam War, RIMPAC took on the color of a collective security exercise in the western Pacific, including Japan. Canada and Japan joined the ANZUS exercises to create a grouping of industrialized countries of the West. The exercises ranged across a wide swath of ocean from the California coast to the Hawaiian archipelago, and lasted for over one month. Although they could not be linked in any sense with an individual Japanese self-defense, a solely defensive posture, or a water's edge defense, the SDF nevertheless participated fully.

The size of the participating force increased rapidly after RIMPAC 84, held in 1984 shortly after the Nakasone administration began. The RIMPAC 84 contingent was half again as large as at the previous RIMPAC. The Japanese contingent at RIMPAC 86 was a powerful hunter-killer antisubmarine group consisting of eight destroyers, one submarine and eight P3C antisubmarine patrol craft, large enough to be considered an escort flotilla, the basic tactical unit of a fleet. The destroyer group was called the New 8.8 Fleet because it was the newest fleet, and had eight helicopters and eight ships, one destroyer with antisubmarine helicopters, two destroyers with fleet anti-aircraft missiles, and five ordinary destroyers. The Japanese contingent was organized as a protective force for the American carrier group. Since its exercise role was to repel any kind of attack by aircraft, surface ships, and submarines against the carrier Ranger, as well as to attack the enemy coast, it is difficult to see how it can be explained in terms of a solely defensive posture or individual self-defense. Even given how excited the military was about training in fighting skills for use in actual warfare it is hard to see the change of the exercise to an open sea, multinational, joint Japan–United States exercise as anything other than a move toward collective self-defense.

The government's official explanation was magnificent–participation in a collective self-defense was, of course, previously considered to be prohibited by the constitution, but operationally the government now defined collective self-defense in a narrow, exceptional way at the same time that it was flexible and broad with the definition of individual self-defense. A multilateral joint exercise now fell within the range of individual self-defense. In the case of the RIMPAC exercises, the government cited Article 5, paragraph 21, of the Defense Agency Establishment Act as legal grounds: "The performance of education and training required to fulfill its duties." Regarding the multinational character of the exercise, the government said, "For Japan, we consider it an exercise with the United States, the organizer of these maneuvers," meaning that the Self-Defense Forces had no relationship with the forces of any other nation, even should they find themselves in the same area of ocean.[23] Since they were far away from Japan and isolated at sea, the Japanese could not know exactly what they were doing, so the possibilities for verbal evasion were endless. In the end, the distance between the record in the Diet and the actual exercises grew and grew and the exercises disappeared from view. It is axiomatic that the Japanese language is not designed for clarity of expression. In the history of security and defense issues, the use of techniques for accentuating vagueness reached new heights with the debate over RIMPAC participation.

RIMPAC was not the only step up in exercise activity, nor were the exercises limited to the Maritime SDF. The Maritime SDF held sea operations every year, starting in 1984, with American carrier fleets. Small-scale joint exercises, such as special antisubmarine exercises, had continued since 1957's Exercise Baseball, but Japanese and American fleets had never been combined before. The sea operations were also scheduled to overlap with the North Atlantic Treaty Organization (NATO) naval exercises in the Atlantic in 1986. During the Seoul Olympics, the Maritime SDF held sea operations in the Japan Sea to aid United States Navy efforts to keep pressure on North

Korea. Collective self-defense was becoming ever more of a reality and exercises were taking on more of the flavor of actual warfare.

The Air SDF also drew closer to the United States during their joint exercises. The backbone of the Air Self-Defense Force had always been American aircraft, from the first generation F-86F to the F-104J, followed by the F-4EJ and finally the F-15J. Japan and the United States had a long-standing student-teacher relationship. After the cabinet adopted the Guidelines in 1978, the North Cape exercise started a new era for joint air training exercises. In 1979, the SDF took on fighters from the United States Air Force stationed in the Philippines to gain experience in fighting other types of aircraft. In 1982, a sophisticated joint exercise in electronic warfare was held with B-52 strategic bombers based in Guam carrying hydrogen bombs. These were more practically oriented than previous exercises; they shifted from war technology to war tactics. Like the Maritime SDF, the Air SDF also held joint exercises called Total Operations, which involved the entire force. On one occasion F-16 fighter-bombers were based at the Misawa Base. Even joint exercises with Air SDF F-15s and F-1 support fighters that included American F-16s based in South Korea came to be considered as falling within the scope of a solely defensive military. F-16s are equipped with precision sighting devices for nuclear bombs and in the event of an emergency would be used as nuclear bombers against the Soviet Union. Having these aircraft partici-pate in the joint exercises should have been considered a major violation, but the government considered them to fall within the bounds of Japan's right of individual self-defense and a solely defensive posture since they strengthened anti-Soviet deterrence.

The Ground SDF followed the same pattern in its joint exer-cises. It held close combat exercises and heavy-snow, cold-weather exercises on a regular basis with army infantry units from Hawaii and Alaska and with marines from Okinawa. Since Ground Self-Defense Forces do not leave Japan, they had not previously had any role in joint exercises under the Japan–United States security cooperation. Once the United States–Soviet Union nuclear confrontation heated up in the Sea of Okhotsk, however, the Ground SDF gained a role, since it concentrated its forces in Hokkaido. There were always generals who did not have a great deal of faith in the United States–Japan Security Treaty, but even they began to develop a closer relationship with the United States military after joint exercises started under the name Yama Sakura. During these exercises, OV-10 and A-10 offensive aircraft were flown in from American forces in South Korea without causing any particular concern.

After eighteen hundred days of the Nakasone administration, the Self-Defense Forces had become a different creature. No longer were they a force in the shadows. Now they were on the road to becoming a new Japanese military with an international role fitting for the expression that Nakasone was fond of using to describe Japan—The International Nation Japan. In the joint exercises, the terms "Japanese army" and "Japanese navy" were used without a second thought. Few people bothered to call the Ground SDF by its official name, the Japan Ground Self-Defense Force.

The 1987–88 survey of the International Institute for Strategic Studies, published in London, summarized the five years of the Nakasone administration:

> Nakasone's period of office had been a remarkable one. On the international stage, he moved confidently among Western leaders and relished the role of making Japan more visible. At home he exercised leadership to an unusual degree and courted personal publicity. He achieved a great deal. In November 1983 he speedily managed to get permission from Parliament to transfer technology to the United States, something that had been resisted for years. He set in train much closer cooperation between the Self-Defense Forces and United

States forces. He maintained consistent growth in defense spending and overseas aid, despite financial austerity in all else, and succeeded in lifting the ceiling on defense expenditure of one percent of GNP that had been in force since 1976. And in July 1987 he concluded an agreement with the United States for Japanese participation in Strategic Defense Initiative research. By such actions, backed by his constantly articulated view that Japan should play a proper part in Western security, he changed the terms of the domestic defense debate. Public awareness of the need for defense grew, helped, it must be said, by increasing Soviet military activity around Japan.

There was no small irony in the praise Nakasone received from Western sources considering his roots as a nationalist, so opposed to the Occupation constitution that he absented himself from the vote to adopt the United States–Japan Security Treaty. In the final analysis, the defense policy directed by Nakasone was that of a delayed transition to becoming a military power. The ultimate conclusion on the military expansion under Nakasone may be that the 1980s were a time when Japan began to move toward taking an international role by marching the Self-Defense Forces in a direction counter to the prevailing world current. The question for the future is how Asia, the Pacific, and the rest of the world will respond to that change.

THE SELF-DEFENSE FORCES
AND NUCLEAR WEAPONS

According to the government's interpretation, Japan can possess nuclear weapons without violating the constitution. If the words "nuclear weapon" are substituted for the phrase "war potential" in Article 9 of the constitution, the Japanese government's position would be as follows:

> The nuclear weapons prohibited in Article 9, paragraph 2, of the constitution are only those nuclear weapons covered in the literal definition of the words that exceed the minimum required for self-defense. For some years now the government has taken the interpretation that the maintenance of any nuclear weapons below that level is not prohibited by Article 9, paragraph 2.

According to Prime Minister Nobusuke Kishi's comments in April 1958 before the upper house Cabinet Committee, "We do not interpret the constitution as prohibiting nuclear weapons. The Self-Defense Forces are able to use weapons that allow them to maintain the minimum force required for self-defense. It is thinkable that nuclear weapons fall in this range, since there are an extremely wide variety of nuclear weapons."

In the early 1970s, the Tanaka administration also stated that it felt that the use of nuclear warheads on defensive weapons, anti-aircraft missiles, mines, and atomic artillery was constitutional. In March 1978, Prime Minister Fukuda stated before the upper house Budget Committee, "There are circumstances under which we could possess nuclear weapons. I believe the Supreme Court would support this view. I am the president of the Liberal Democratic Party as well as the prime minister and I cannot imagine that this approach could change as long as the LDP administration continues."

It is thus first necessary to understand that Japan's "three non-nuclear principles" did not develop from constitutional interpretations. It is more accurate to say that the government considers the decision not to possess nuclear weapons to be a policy choice. The government has linked the two as follows. "As a matter of policy, Japan does not possess any nuclear weapons under the three non-nuclear principles, but this issue is unrelated to interpretations of Article 9 of the constitution."[24]

In that sense, it is not so unreasonable for other countries to worry that Japan might develop an independent nuclear arsenal. The report entitled "Japan–United States Relations in the 1990s," written by the Congressional Survey Department in April 1989, contains the following paragraph: "An extremely important question is whether Japan will decide to possess an independent nuclear deterrent. For Japan to make such a decision, radical changes would have to occur in the current overwhelming opposition to nuclear weapons among the Japanese people. It nevertheless remains a possibility that should the Soviet Union continue to be viewed as hostile, Japan's opposition to nuclear weapons may eventually change."

This view is common in Asia. Certainly one of the reasons for this concern is the government's statement that possessing nuclear warheads is constitutional. Given Japan's latent potential, it is difficult to assuage fears that the country will develop its own nuclear weapons. As seen by other countries, the possibility of Japan's develop-ing nuclear weapons is more logically persuasive.

(1) The domestically produced H-2 rocket, which launched a two-ton satellite in 1993, can be converted to an intercontinental ballistic missile (ICBM).
(2) Japan can get as much plutonium 239 (the fuel for atomic bombs) as it wants from its thirty-seven domestic nuclear power plants.
(3) Creating atomic bombs is easily within Japan's tech-nological, scientific, and financial means.
(4) Most of the Self-Defense Forces' front-line weapons can be used as either nuclear or non-nuclear weapons, so the means of delivery are already in place:

F-4 fighters: B-47, B-61, B-3 atomic bombs
F-15 fighters: W-25 air-to-air rockets
P3C patrol planes: B-57 nuclear depth charges
SH-60 helicopters: B-57 atomic bombs
Asroc antisubmarine rockets: W-44 nuclear depth charges

No matter how often Japanese state that the three non-nuclear principles prevent nuclear development, for-eign countries refused to be convinced.

$E{\tiny\text{vents}} \atop {\scriptstyle\&} I{\tiny\text{ssues}}$ THE MILITARY USES OF OUTER SPACE

Space exploration has been linked to military applications from its very first days. From Sputnik to Strategic Defense Initiative, American and Soviet space programs have been linked to the nuclear arms race. Japan was the third country after the United States and the Soviet Union to launch a satellite into space, but of the three, only Japan has had a clean space effort, one that is non-nuclear and nonmilitary. This distinction has eroded somewhat since the mid-1980s as the Self-Defense Forces have come to rely on satellites. The impetus to make Japan's space exploration program nonmilitary came from two directions. The first was the inclusion of a statement at the beginning of the 1969 Space Development Corporation Act declaring the corporation's purpose to be limited to nonmilitary applications. The second was a resolution for the peaceful use of space that was adopted in the lower house debate over the space act. The military has been excluded from the effort.

This stricture began to fray in 1983 when the Sakura 2a communications satellite was launched and a plan was developed to use the Self-Defense Forces' Iwo Jima Base for communications. The government avoided stating whether the Self-Defense Forces' use of the base was for military applications and approved its use as a subscriber application under the Public Telecommunications Act. In the following year, the warships of the Maritime Self-Defense Force were permitted to use the United States Navy's Freatsat military communications satellite "as a communications route" and the government declared that if the satellite had general applications, "it was not against provisions for peaceful use."

This removed the ban on Self-Defense Forces commu-nications using satellites and resulted in the inclusion of satellite communications in the Defense Agency's Inte-grated Defense Digital Network. In 1989, approval was granted for a transportable earth station that used field relay of long-distance video via the Superbird communica-tions satellite. This enabled the Defense Agency to instan-taneously project images in real time from around the country to its central command site. The Self-Defense Forces continue to show a desire to possess and use not just communications satellites but spy satellites as well.

19

Looking Toward the Future

The new Japanese military is likely to be quite different from what has come before. The age changes and so do people. The postwar generation has taken the helm of the forty-year-old Self-Defense Forces as they have reached their maturity. The Nakasone administration oversaw not only a buildup, but a completion of a changing of the guard in the military command. There is no longer a single person in the Self-Defense Forces organization with any military record in the old Imperial Army and Imperial Navy.

In July 1984, the last imperial military second lieutenant, chairman of the joint staff council Sumio Murai, retired. In December 1985, the last Naval Academy graduate, Sasebo Regional District Headquarters commander Masao Shigeno, retired. In March 1986, the last Military Academy graduate, Ground SDF chief of staff Morio Nakamura, retired. In December 1987, the last ex–imperial soldier, chairman of the joint staff council Shigehiro Mori, retired.

The retirement of these men paralleled the rise of a new generation. Ground SDF chief of staff General Atsushi Shima was born in 1934, Maritime SDF chief of staff Makoto Sakuma was born in 1935, and Air SDF chief of staff Akio Suzuki in 1933. The

1990s is their time. All grew up when the military reigned supreme in Japan's affections and Japanese militarism took the country into invasions of Asia. They endured the total reversal of values that occurred after the war. When they chose their paths in life in the first class of the Defense Academy, the Cold War was at its height. They now stand at the command of the Self-Defense Forces. The eleven thousand graduates of the Defense Academy now account for twenty-seven percent of the forty-thousand-member staff and eighty percent of the general officers.

How this new generation responds to the post–Cold War world will determine the coming shape of the Self-Defense Forces. A new relationship is emerging between the Self-Defense Forces and the Japanese people. As we today witness the ongoing collapse of the Cold War system that triggered Japan's rearmament, the choices and decisions whether to continue as it has been or to try something new requires the involvement of all of the Japanese people.

20

After the Cold War

Over forty-five years ago, the Cold War broke out in Europe
and pulled war-battered Japan into a kind of rearmament. The
communist Chinese and North Korean invasion of South Korea,
effected with the Soviet Union's acquiescence, brought the Cold
War to Asia. Despite its best efforts, Japan could not isolate itself
from the conflict between East and West; the United States and
the Soviet Union had carried their rivalry to the distant corners
of the globe. The instant the Cold War reached Asia, Japan
became an integral part of America's strategy for containment of
the Soviet Union and of communist China. The promise of permanent peace remained, but the reality of a demilitarized country under the peace constitution had lasted a scant five years.

In Europe, the confrontation between the North Atlantic
Treaty Organization (NATO) and the Warsaw Pact stopped short
of combat, but in Asia the Cold War turned hot; instead of hostile armed camps staring at each other across Europe's borders,
Asia had full-fledged wars. Violent conflicts erupted between
the land powers: Korea, Vietnam, China, the Soviet Union, and
a sea power, the United States, on two peninsulas jutting into
the sea from Asia. A string of hot spots of nonconventional warfare erupted along this line of tension: the Taiwan-China spat,

the anti-British communist insurgency in Malaysia, and assaults on the neutrality of Laos and Cambodia.

The geopolitical fallout of the Cold War kept Japanese security policy in a push-pull relationship between hopes for peace and support for American anticommunism under the United States–Japan Security Treaty. Legality and pragmatism had become disassociated from ideals and sentiment. This was the political soil from which the Self-Defense Forces grew. During the 1980s, eighty percent of the Japanese public accepted of the necessity of the Self-Defense Forces, but for all that, comparable numbers consistently opposed revising the constitution to make the role of the military less legally ambiguous. The Self-Defense Forces were more popular for their role in rapidly responding to disasters such as typhoons and floods than for their role in national defense. And while government support for the three non-nuclear principles, not to possess, build, or harbor nuclear weapons, resonated strongly with the experiences of Hiroshima and Nagasaki, the same government gave its silent approval to calls at Japanese ports by ships of the United States Seventh Fleet suspected of carrying nuclear weapons. Japanese public opinion ran in two different directions.

Two contradictory forces worked at the heart of the Self-Defense Forces, the brake of the peace constitution against the engine of American pressure. Modern Japanese fears of Russian intentions also played against Cold War America's international anticommunism. Clearly, Japan's government had created the Self-Defense Forces not out of a national consensus, but in response to the Cold War in Asia, even if it meant violating the principles of the constitution. The American-Soviet conflict and a divided Korea created the United States–Japan Security Treaty system, which nourished Japanese rearmament. The government had begun rearmament not by following due process but by acting on its own, one small step at a time, presenting the Japanese electorate with a fait accompli, and then waiting for the de facto result to gain acceptance. The process was decisively different from the experience of German rearmament, even though Germany was also a defeated nation. When Soviet military forces lost the capability for major offensive action in the 1990s, Japan faced a major reevaluation for the Self-Defense Forces as its entire raison d'être collapsed.[25] The onset of peace brought a moment of crisis that called into question the very existence of the Self-Defense Forces.

The end of the East-West conflict signaled that Japanese policy makers would no longer tailor defense buildup targets to Soviet threats and to American demands. Rapid changes in the world situation, the new but still prenuclear defense environment surrounding Asia, and America's post–Cold War strategy complicated life for Japanese policy makers but gave the entire Japanese nation a chance to rethink security policy.

Too much water had passed under the bridge for the Japanese to return to the pacifism of the early postwar period. Besides, as bureaucrats the world over have learned, massive defense structures are too large to tear down. The small seed that General Douglas MacArthur had planted as the Police Reserve had grown into a military organization with the third largest defense budget in the world, if not the third strongest. The Self-Defense Forces had almost as many tanks as the British army and had the world's best coastal navy; the Air SDF had a number of F-15s that was second only to that of the United States Air Force, and more Patriot missiles than Israel. Japan was the only country outside of America, to have equipped four combat ships with the AEGIS Maritime Fighting System, a highly advanced system developed for fleet and offshore defense. Japan's warships averaged less than ten years of age, were scrupulously maintained, and defended sea lanes out to one thousand nautical miles. Best of all, Japan's military production system used domestic designs and production methods. Japan's admirals were eager to get an aircraft carrier into service.

When the Cold War ended unexpectedly, Japan's military expansion continued in high gear. Model 90 tanks designed to counter the Soviet T-80 tank had only just begun rolling off the production line in 1990. The government had poured over $30 billion into the development of the FSX, the next generation of fighter being developed by General Dynamics and Mitsubishi Heavy Industries. Money for a "large transport ship," the prototype for an aircraft carrier, had found its way into the budget. The second term of the interim Defense Buildup Program, the five-year weapons supply plan revived by the Nakasone administration during the late 1980s, found new life in 1991. Total defense spending was slated at ¥22.75 trillion. Defense officials optimistically believed that, unlike those of other Western nations, the Japanese economy could maintain mammoth spending. The Cold War did not cooperate.

Defense Agency authorities at first denied that the Cold War had ended. And when they grudgingly began to take note of what to others was quite obvious, they were unwilling to let go of the idea of two camps, East and West. The Japanese defense White Papers revealed, among other oddities, that defense authorities still considered Japan to be a potential battle ground between two still hostile camps.

The views contained in the White Papers were brazenly different from those of the rest of the world. For example, the 1989–1990 Strategic Survey of the International Institute for Strategic Studies described the world situation as follows: "During the past twelve months, the basis of the world's geopolitical structure has been radically transformed. These momentous events overturned the political and security arrangements that have existed since the end of World War II and brought into prospect a real moderation, if not yet an end to, the East-West confrontation."[26]

By contrast, the Japanese defense White Paper of the same year observed no such change in the Cold War: "The East-West conflict remains fundamentally one of opposition." It saw the basic character of the international situation as one of continuity rather than of change, a relationship of conflict rather than dialogue. Defense analyst Yuken Hironaka commented that "The application of New Thinking to Soviet diplomacy shows no sign of eliminating the worldwide military confrontation between the United States and the Soviet Union or the European confrontation between NATO and the Warsaw Pact. The basic military confrontation between massive military forces of the camps of East and West centered on these two nations has shown no real change."[27]

Japanese defense officials remained unaware, at least in the public's perception, that a momentous transition in world history was occurring. Referring to the depleted and demoralized Soviet military deployed near Japan, the Defense Agency said, "There not only still exists a latent threat to Japan, it constitutes a factor that is making the military situation in this area increasingly tense." The Defense Agency essentially saw Gorbachev's unilateral military dismantling as unimportant. In one small corner of the world, the Cold War lived on.

The following year, the Defense Agency finally got around to realizing that "the international situation, especially in Europe, is undergoing historic changes," yet an end to the Cold War, especially in Asia, was not seen as probable. "The situation [in Asia] is more complicated than that of Europe. It remains unstable and fluid in Korea, in Cambodia, and between Japan and the Soviet Union regarding Japan's Northern Territories. The immense Soviet military in the Far East is another reason for heightened military concern in this area."

This analysis was clearly self-serving. The budget process for the interim Defense Buildup Program was in full swing during the 1991 fiscal year, and the Defense Agency was not about to proclaim that the Cold War was over. It needed the Cold War until the cabinet signed off on the Interim Program. Rather than shaping defense policy to the situation, the Agency was trying to recast the situation to fulfill its own policy needs. Once the cabinet had approved the interim defense program, the Defense Agency officially declared in its 1992 defense White Paper that the Cold War was over:

> The dissolution of the Soviet Union means that the confrontation between East and West, which has shaped worldwide military affairs since the end of World War II, has truly ended. The postwar order of two superpowers, the United States and the Soviet Union, facing off with massive nuclear-armed militaries has collapsed; the high military spending caused by the tense confrontation between NATO and the Warsaw Pact is also fading, as the nations of the world make major progress in freezing or rolling back the size of their armies. The possibility of a war on a worldwide scale has receded into the distance. International society is now groping for a new order for world peace.[28]

Even with the Cold War's demise, however, the defense budget continued to grow under the Liberal Democratic Party administration. A Cold War–model five-year plan not only was adopted, it was adopted without question. The government sought no reductions in units or troops and no weapons systems under development were halted. While the defense White Paper had stated that there was "major progress in rolling back the scale of national militaries," the agency apparently did not intend to apply this statement to Japan itself. Two years later, in 1994, Japan remained the only Western nation without a plan for reducing the size of its military.

Though they have resisted acknowledging it, the Defense Agency authorities have been unable to hide their bewilderment at the Soviet breakup. The Soviet threat was the single most important rationale for the existence of the Self-Defense Forces. The Defense Agency's shock was akin to that felt when the socialist Soviet state replaced the Russian Empire. There would be no returning to the age when Japanese politicians debated a buildup of an autonomous defense force within the immovable framework of the Soviet threat and a United States–Japan Security Treaty.

Even stubborn officers whose thinking and careers had been molded by the Soviet threat received the message that they could not get by simply by clinging to the former threat of their old menace. The Soviet collapse and the Gulf War made them aware that, like it or not, the world had now begun to operate according to new rules. There was no Soviet threat to fuel a military buildup. The United States and Russia had become quasi-allies. American troops were drawing up plans to leave bases in the Philippines, where they had maintained a presence for almost one hundred years. The beginnings of dialogue between the United States and both North Korea and Vietnam were palpable.

The Defense Agency struggled to define a new role for itself, and a new image for the Self-Defense Forces. Having acknowledged in their White Papers that the Cold War was over, defense authorities concluded that failure to define a new role for themselves would jeopardize their very existence. Too, the long-established political order of Liberal Democratic Party rule and Japan Socialist Party opposition showed signs of needed change; and this in turn forced the pace of the defense policy transition. The defense establishment had to seize the initiative from anyone who might want to create a peace dividend by shrinking the military.

Two options presented themselves as possible directions for the Self-Defense Forces. One was greater participation in United Nations peacekeeping activities; the SDF had to venture into the unknown territory of "international contributions." The other was to stir Japanese concern that North Korea might have nuclear weapons, a throwback to much older defense modes. Once into the 1990s, the Defense Agency became visibly active in both these areas.

The Gulf War proved to be the opportunity for change. In August 1990 American authorities publicly requested Self-Defense Forces participation in the war. President George Bush telephoned Prime Minister Toshiki Kaifu frequently. President Bush asked Kaifu for a visible international effort from Japan, including the dispatch of the Self-Defense Forces. He communicated American expectations of Japan at a meeting with Prime Minister Kaifu, stating that the world would welcome Japanese efforts in transport, rear support, and medical support and that no SDF armed action would be required.

State department and military authorities followed up with more specific lists. They requested frigates to join in the picket line of the naval blockade, P3C antisubmarine planes for intelligence gathering, transport cooperation from the Air SDF, and the dispatch of minesweepers. The commander of the United States naval forces stationed at Yokosuka telephoned the director of the Maritime SDF staff at Roppongi in Tokyo.

> He asked, "Can we get you to send SDF minesweepers and resupply vessels to the Middle East?"
>
> The director was surprised. "You should know better than anyone that we can't, and that we haven't the ability. I can't say yes."
>
> "This is what Ambassador Michael Armacost, the commander of the Seventh Fleet, and the commander of United States naval forces in Japan are asking for. We want you to study the possibility."[29]

During the same period, American officials also requested that the Maritime SDF provide an escort for the carrier Midway when it left Yokosuka for the Middle East. The Americans insisted that the situation required a visible Japanese contribution, even if it that meant a reinterpretation of the constitution.

At that time, troops and matériel destined for the Middle East were shipped out from American bases in Japan at Okinawa, Yokosuka, and Sasebo. The United States–Japan Security

Treaty did not permit the use of American bases in Japan for regions outside the Far East, and the Persian Gulf was certainly not the Far East, but the tenor of the times did not allow them to even raise the issue. Japanese government authorities could do nothing but hang their heads in response to the furious rebukes from abroad.

In Tokyo, Ambassador Armacost was very active. In a meeting with commentators from the mass media, he was forthright in voicing American dissatisfaction with the Japanese government, noting that "Japan is a beneficiary of Middle East oil, but it is not bearing any risk." He pressed Keiichi Miyazawa, one of the most pro-American faction Liberal Democratic Party leaders: "Japanese will pay money, perhaps break a sweat, but never spill a drop of blood. Why is that?" He made a special point to try to persuade LDP secretary general Ichiro Ozawa, who had more power within the LDP than Kaifu, to dispatch Self-Defense Forces units. "We're not asking you to send troops to the front lines. All we ask is for rear support. This is an issue for Japan to decide, but we want you to share some of the risk with us and maintain a presence."

Ozawa agreed with the ambassador. The dispatch of Self-Defense Forces overseas when the constitution limited the SDF to the defense of Japanese territory was impossible, and everyone knew it. The Self-Defense Forces did not own a map of the Middle East, and none of its pilots had ever landed in Saudi Arabia. The SDF had no intelligence data, training experience, or equipment relevant to desert wars. Officers were not confident that they would even know how to handle prisoners. Like the warriors of the Edo Period (1600–1868), the Self-Defense Forces existed only to defend against foreign enemies invading Japanese soil.

Prime Minister Kaifu and LDP secretary general Ozawa pointed to the United Nations Peace Cooperation Bill as a response to President Bush's requests. The bill was designed to create a legal basis under which the Self-Defense Forces could provide transport and rear support for the multinational force. The effort failed completely. Reference to the United Nations was made in order to get around the prohibition in Article 9 of the constitution against "armed actions" and "collective self-defense." Although the article was worded to permit participation in United Nations actions, it was clear that what the government's efforts really sought were participation in the multinational force and support for the Gulf War. The Japanese people saw through this transparent effort to subvert the constitution, and the government withdrew its efforts.[30]

In the end, Japan did not send the SDF to participate in Desert Storm, nor did it send any matériel. Instead, it paid out $13 billion to help cover war expenses of the multinational force. About $1 billion of that was shifted out of the defense budget, so the Self-Defense Forces could be said to have participated in the Gulf War, in a financial sense. The experience also proved anew that Japanese bases were useful for a war in Asia. The Ground and Air SDF transported the forces, weapons, and matériel of the United States forces in Japan, a form of support never before provided. But the dominant impression left in the minds of those who wanted a contribution of blood was a bitter one. The SDF's first attempt at dispatch abroad thus ended with a major controversy and with the SDF still stationed in Japan.

The experience taught the Japanese government a lesson. The Bush administration expressed little gratitude. And though it had increased taxes to raise its $13 billion contribution, Japan gained little respect from the international community. The result was an opportunity to change the standards for overseas dispatch of the Self-Defense Forces.

At first, the Clean Government Party had advocated unarmed and nonmilitary cooperation as Japan's contribution to peacekeeping operations. This position was in direct opposition to the Kaifu administration's proposal. Immediately after the Kaifu bill was withdrawn, negotiations began to develop a three-party consensus. Initially, there was no change in the Clean Government Party's stance. Chairman Kiishi Ishida boldly stated, "As long as there is a Clean Government Party, we will ensure that any new global contribution is completely peaceful. If there is a movement to include the SDF from within the Liberal Democratic Party, we will meet it with resolve to destroy it." The November 1990 party conference passed four resolutions: (1) any new organization shall be permanently established and staffed with non-SDF personnel; (2) personnel shall be widely drawn from different fields and receive education and training suitable to their duties; (3) efforts shall be unarmed and nonmilitary and there shall be no participation in armed actions; and (4) these personnel shall be dispatched to United Nations peacekeeping duties based on United Nations resolutions.

As the three-way conference continued, however, the Clean Government Party began to show signs of moving toward inclusion of the SDF. In June 1992, Secretary Yozo Ishikawa announced that "there have been many calls for accepting the joint appointment of serving SDF personnel with current rank to the peace cooperation unit." This was a clear indication of a change in policy. Secretary Ishikawa explained the change in the Clean Government Party's attitude as follows:

> The Clean Government Party at first was studying this issue with the idea of not using the SDF in peacekeeping missions. We then sent a mission with the Diet's anti-SDF factions and an individual mission of our own to investigate how other countries handle peacekeeping work. After thoroughly considering the opinions of United Nations personnel and specialists in this field, we realized that we must employ the capabilities of the SDF in United Nations peacekeeping activities. We also went through full discussion within the party before arriving at a resolution to use the SDF within constitutional limitations.[30]

Only a year and a half after chairman Ishida had declared that the Clean Government Party would destroy any Liberal

Democratic Party move to include the Self-Defense Forces, the Clean Government Party had reversed itself completely. The original principles that the three parties had initiated their discussion around, separate organization, no SDF, and humanitarian aid, had been overturned in favor of using the SDF.

The Miyazawa administration was no longer alone. In the Diet, an overwhelming majority had now coalesced around the bill. The government went before the Japanese people and presented its case that it wanted to expand the role of the United Nations. The goal here was to ensure international peace and security in the post–Cold War world through human participation, including the dispatch of the Self-Defense Forces to United Nations programs to restore peace and serve humanitarian purposes. In the background, the administration felt confidence for having gained the Clean Government Party's support and sensed an opportunity to change the Japanese people's outlook on defense and security issues by changing its insistence on limiting defense only to peace in Japan. It also believed that other Asian countries would no longer look on the dispatch of SDF troops abroad as being synonymous with a threat of aggression.

The Japan Socialist Party, the largest opposition party, joined with the Japan Communist Party to state that the overseas dispatch of the Self-Defense Forces remained unconstitutional and that any international contribution had to be nonmilitary, civilian, and directed at public welfare. It was not able, however, to generate strong enough public sentiment to overcome the image of pragmatism that the government and LDP were able to project over a new international role and use of the SDF. Public opinion had vociferously opposed any participation or contribution to the multinational force against Iraq in the Gulf War, but favored human participation in United Nations peacekeeping activities in some form. Although still uncomfortable with sending the SDF, the electorate felt that some form of human participation was necessary.

Although public opinion had changed, the Japan Socialist Party had not. It was unable to come up with a specific counter-proposal for effective participation, despite its heated opposition to the overseas dispatch of the SDF. The party concentrated on portraying peacekeeping troops as being ultimately military in nature and argued that the United Nations was the tool of the United States. Although the Japanese public was uneasy and did have concerns about sending the SDF abroad, simpleminded Cold War–style propaganda could no longer persuade them. A consensus had arisen that it was natural for Japan to devise some kind of more meaningful participation in international society. Although there was also a consensus that the SDF should not be sent abroad, forces favoring the protection of the constitution resorted to overheated readings of Article 9 and they were unable to build a viable policy. The change of heart of the Clean Government Party and the Japan Socialist Party's inept response tipped the balance toward passage of the PKO Cooperation Act and set the stage for sending the SDF abroad.

The PKO Cooperation Act provided for a contingent of SDF troops with a maximum of two thousand personnel to be made an international peace cooperation unit, or a peacekeeping unit. The purpose stated in Article 1 was "to contribute positively to efforts for international peace centered on the United Nations in order to appropriately and rapidly cooperate with international peacekeeping activities and humanitarian international rescue activities." The unit's mission comprised three types of duties; peacekeeping activities, humanitarian international rescue activities, and material cooperation. Although generally known as the PKO Cooperation Act, the government called it the International Peace Cooperation Law, especially in statements made in English. The difference was that the government saw the act as not limited to peacekeeping activities, so the PKO Cooperation Act was not an accurate name. Should another event like the Gulf War occur, the Japanese government wanted the option of participating in a multinational force in the form of humanitarian international rescue activities and material cooperation. The rest may only have been a cover.

Although police officers and other members of administrative organizations were slated to serve in the international peace cooperation unit alongside SDF members, the law stipulated that a SDF officer would command the unit and that six job categories of the peacekeeping unit were set aside for the SDF. These military-only jobs were called the Peacekeeping Force, an internal unit of the peacekeeping organization. Use of weapons and armed actions were possible in all of these duties. Article 3, paragraph 1 of the PKO Cooperation Act described them:

(1) Monitoring cease-fires in armed conflicts and monitoring military withdrawals and implementations of disarmament.
(2) Occupation and monitoring of demilitarized zones.
(3) Checking the ingress and egress of weapons.
(4) Collecting, storing, and disposing of weapons.
(5) Assisting in marking boundaries such as cease-fire lines.
(6) Assisting in the exchange of prisoners between combatants.

As the text of the law indicates, and as has become clear from past practice in peacekeeping activities, these duties may require armed action and are always performed by troops. The task of ascertaining when armed action was necessary was to be determined by the special local representative of the secretary of the United Nations. This was based on the traditions of international peacekeeping organizations. It was a lesson gained from experience in regional conflicts around the world, from the Congo to Cyprus to Palestine.

While stipulating the mission of the Peacekeeping Force, Article 2 also stated that "the implementation of international peace cooperation duties shall not involve threats of armed force or armed actions." The law kept responsibility for command with Japan, stating that the prime minister would direct the force as representative of the cabinet. Naturally, this provision was added out of concern for Article 9 of the constitution. The government maintained that this meant the SDF could be assigned to peacekeeping duties without conflict with the constitution. In order to finesse the constitutional issue, a five-point basic policy was devised. So long as five conditions were satisfied, there would be no possibility of the dispatched SDF encountering situations requiring armed actions:

(1) A cease-fire agreement must have been reached between combatants.
(2) The combatants, which shall include the country which contains the region in which the peacekeeping unit will operate, must have agreed to Japanese participation.
(3) The peacekeeping unit must not be biased toward a given combatant, maintaining a neutral position.
(4) When one of the above principles is no longer satisfied, Japan may withdraw its presence.
(5) The use of weapons must be limited to the smallest extent needed to protect the lives of the unit members.

The government held that the SDF's participation under this law did not violate Article 9's prohibitions against armed actions or the dispatch of armed troops to other nations for the purpose of armed action because these five principles ensured the international character of the peacekeeping operations.

The bill found rough going in the Diet. There were many thorny issues that had to be resolved. Who would command, the United Nations or Japan? How could the bill be considered consistent with the constitution's explicit provision against armed actions? How could the organization retain control if the use of weapons was left to individual discretion? Who would decide how to apply the five principles, particularly the provision for withdrawal?

Many other questions arose, like rules of engagement and relationships with other militaries. The task of finding holes in the forty-year taboo against sending troops abroad solely through scholastic argument without resorting to constitutional amendment required lengthy and convoluted rhetoric. The Diet decided that "participation" of the Self-Defense Forces in peace-keeping operations was not acceptable, but "cooperation" was. "Armed actions" were unconstitutional, but the "use of weapons" was not. As to command, the United Nations could not *shiki* the Self-Defense Forces, but it was acceptable for the Self-Defense Forces to receive *shizu*. When pressed, the government authorities had to concede that both *shiki* and *shizu* translate into English as "command." The Diet had indeed become a venue for the finest sort of hairsplitting.

The government saw the difference between *shiki* and *shizu* with regard to the dispatched units as follows. The local United Nations commander had the authority to determine when, where, and at what duties the units from various countries are employed and where they are stationed. This authority was called United Nations command. The PKO Bill called this authority *shizu*. *Shizu* and *command* had the same meaning. The chief of headquarters of the international peace cooperation unit, i.e., the prime minister, would create and change an agenda for complying with the United Nations command, and the head of the Defense Agency would follow that agenda by directing (*shiki*) and monitoring the troops dispatched by Japan to make them perform international peace cooperation duties. In that sense, the troops sent by Japan would be under United Nations command.

The United Nations would command (*shizu*) while the prime minster and SDF commander would direct (*shiki*). This circuitous interpretation remained purposefully vague. At the least, it seemed likely to elude the understanding of the local commanders.

The government presented the following interpretation of the relationship between the use of weapons and armed actions:

(1) In general, the "armed actions" of Article 9, paragraph 1 of the constitution of Japan refer to combat actions that are part of an international armed conflict by Japanese physical or human organizations, while "use of arms" in Article 24 of the [PKO] bill refers to the use for which they were designed— machines, instruments, and devices whose direct purpose is to kill human beings or to destroy objects as a means of armed combat, such as firearms, explosives, and swords.

(2) The "armed actions" of Article 9, paragraph 1 of the constitution of Japan is a concept of the use of power that includes the "use of weapons;" however, "use of weapons" is not synonymous with the "armed actions" that this paragraph prohibits. For example, the defense of one's life or person or that of Japanese personnel at the same location, so-called self-preservation, is a natural right. The "use of weapons" for that purpose to the minimum extent necessary does not constitute the "armed actions" prohibited by Article 9, paragraph 12, of the constitution of Japan.

These arguments successfully persuaded enough politicians that the use of weapons by troops active abroad was justified. The key was that individual members would make decisions based on their personal circumstances on whether or not to use weapons, so the use of weapons was not subject to the decisions and orders of commanders. Justifiable self-defense was the criterion for use of weapons. The right to use weapons based on inherent rights would later be expanded in Cambodia to include actions in defense of foreigners.

In parallel to the debate over the bill, United Nations peace-keeping efforts in Cambodia, which had seen a cessation in twenty years of civil war, started in earnest in 1992. The four principal combatants agreed to a cease-fire in Paris and instituted a temporary eighteen-month United Nations administration. The United Nations Temporary Administration for Cambodia

(UNTAC) was formed and Yasushi Akashi was appointed special representative by United Nations Secretary General Boutros Boutros-Ghali and sent to Phnom Penh. UNTAC was a complex peacekeeping operation with a wide range of duties and authority, including military (receiving arms), police powers (restoring public order), electoral support, administrative reconstruction, monitoring human rights, returning refugees, and postwar recovery. It involved the participation of twenty-two thousand persons, making it the largest program the United Nations had ever undertaken, a grand experiment. The Japanese government speeded enactment of the bill, keeping in mind the imminent dispatch of Japanese, including SDF troops, to Cambodia. Because a Japanese, Yasushi Akashi, had been appointed the United Nations special representative, the government did not want this opportunity to slip away. It was the first time a Japanese had ever been assigned to lead a United Nations peacekeeping force, and the government wanted to use that excitement to get the bill passed. Because Cambodia is a Southeast Asian nation, the interest of Japanese was high.

The excitement did not eliminate the existing problems. The relationship among the peacekeeping force, armed action, and constitutionality remained a Gordian knot. The government had a long history of arguing that it could not participate in peacekeeping activities because they involved the use of force, which was not permitted by constitutional law. Now it called the same actions constitutionally permissible—even though a given peacekeeping force might be involved in armed action, participation in it was not unconstitutional if Japanese actions were not part of that armed action. This was not a very persuasive argument. It made the Japanese electorate uneasy and aroused the concern of other Asian countries. No solution seemed likely to be found.

This time the Clean Government Party took the initiative to break through the stalemate. In the Diet in February 1992,

Secretary Ishikawa proposed to Foreign Minister Watanabe that the legal system be left intact but the parts that stipulated the duties of the peacekeeping force be left out until a separate new law could be discussed. Troops would be sent, but not to peacekeeping contingents likely to be involved in armed actions. For the time being, the SDF would only assist in support areas such as medical duties, transport, and construction, or in humanitarian international rescue efforts. The Liberal Democratic Party, the Clean Government Party, and Democratic Socialists agreed on this proposal . Those duties of the peacekeeping unit for which it was stipulated in Article 12 that "no persons other than SDF members may request assignment," that is, the peacekeeping force would not be carried out until the law was revised. Nevertheless, the SDF would, in the end, be involved with all functions, great and small, of the Cambodian peacekeeping operation.

In October 1992, an engineering battalion of Self-Defense Forces troops, the Japan Engineering Battalion, was dispatched to Cambodia in two groups of six hundred to be employed in a one-year peacekeeping assignment under UNTAC. At that time, two groups of eight SDF officers each were sent to monitor the cease-fire. These 1,216 men were the first armed soldiers to go overseas from Japan since its defeat in 1945. The commanding officer of the first group was Lieutenant Colonel Ryuji Watanabe, an engineering officer of the twenty-first, or 1977, class of the Defense Academy, who was drafted from the post of vice minister of state for defense. The second in command was Lieutenant Colonel Yoshio Ishinoshita, an engineering officer, from the Defense Academy, class of 1976. The core of the first group was drawn from the Fourth Engineers Corps of the Ground SDF's Central Region Division; the second group was drawn from units of the Northern Region Division. Rather than asking for volunteers, the government ordered designated platoons into action.

The Japan Engineering Battalion set up camp in Takeo Province, to the south of Phnom Penh. Through sheer coincidence, this site had a historical connection to Japan. In July 1941, when Cambodia was still under French colonial administration, the Japanese army took advantage of the fact that Hitler had seized France to occupy southern Cambodia and to build an air base for offensive use in the coming fight with the United States and Britain. American president Franklin D. Roosevelt responded to imperial Japan's "occupation of French Indochina" by declaring an oil embargo against Japan. When the Pacific phase of World War II began in December 1941, the main force for the attack against Singapore was launched from the Cambodian base through Thailand and the Malay Peninsula. This base was thus one of the sparks of World War II. The Japanese troops, all from the Defense Academy era, were too young to remember this history.

UNTAC assigned the Japanese engineering battalion the task of repairing National Roads 2 and 3 and rebuilding bridges. The rain and heat were intense, but having brought more than three hundred vehicles, the Japanese did not experience any particular difficulty in their work. The region was peaceful and the cease-fire rarely broken; there were no Khmer Rouge attacks against the Self-Defense Forces. In March 1993, the first group returned safely to Japan; in September 1993, the second group joined them. Once the SDF became a part of UNTAC, its actions began to stray beyond legal limits and government promises. Conditions imposed during Diet debates proved meaningless. The facts on the ground created a fait accompli in steps. These changes occurred principally in three areas: in adding new duties and expanding old ones, in ambiguities regarding commanding officers, and in the evisceration of the five principles against armed actions.

The differences between the peacekeeping operation as written and as carried out were profound. The engineering troops became soldiers, and road repair duties became armed patrols. Although the government claimed that the force was adhering to the five principles, the SDF could neither suspend its operations nor withdraw. This situation peaked in May 1993, after the completion of elections for the Cambodian constitutional convention. The SDF was not only outside of Japan, it was outside of the law.

Japanese political forces in favor of protecting the constitution felt powerless, and lost their drive after the bill was enacted into law. Concern about SDF behavior in Cambodia was minimal, so the SDF was free to establish new precedents quite publicly. Only journalists paid significant attention, sending large quantities of information back to Japan. Most interest was in individual events and personal stories of soldiers' exploits and hardships, however, and little attention was paid to substantive problems. Opposition members in the Diet rarely raised the problems occurring in the peacekeeping operations.

Duties were expanding little by little to include the transport, medical support and resupply of non-Japanese troops, but at first the changes could still be dismissed as being done in the name of efficiency or convenience. When the SDF became involved in electoral support, however, it was clear to anyone who cared to notice that a substantive change had occurred. UNTAC pulled the six-hundred-man Japan Engineering Battalion from the road repair assignment and transferred it to peacekeeping duties, such as armed patrol, protecting election monitors, and protecting ballot boxes. The unit was transformed from an engineering corps into infantry troops. As the elections approached, the SDF troops abandoned road repair work and put on helmets and bulletproof vests and began carrying small arms. In the name of road surveillance and information gathering, they began daily armed patrols.

These added duties went through no process of legal approval or popular consensus. Treating the UNTAC flag as the imperial standard, the Japanese unit began to engage in duties that were in violation of Japanese law without any qualms whatsoever. It made one wonder why tens of thousands of words had been exchanged in Diet debates and what meaning the revisions and peacekeeping force freeze really had, if any. The overriding impression is that the Cambodian contingent had accomplished concretely in one year what had taken the SDF forty years of legislative conniving to achieve.

The changes and additions to the duties, some felt, were unavoidable due to the situation on the ground. Others felt that these developments lay within the discretion of the commanders and local responsible parties. Or that small infractions were permissible if they allowed Cambodia to hold general elections, especially since there were no SDF casualties. The end justifying the means is a popular approach. From the Cambodian and UNTAC viewpoints, these rationales were probably convincing. But if results measure the justifiability of these duties, then neither the five principles nor the implementation plan based on them were necessary. If the law constituted the Japanese people's consent to placing the six-hundred-man engineering battalion under UNTAC command, there were essentially no limits on changing the battalion's duties as the situation developed.

Japan's participation in UNTAC, nevertheless, was different. The SDF detachment was sent to Cambodia on the understanding that even though it was a military unit, it would be assigned nonmilitary duties within the framework set out by the five principles and that participation in the peacekeeping operations would not involve "armed actions." It was for that reason that the law was revised and the issue of the peacekeeping force postponed. Although certainly a degree of flexibility would be appropriate based on the circumstances in Cambodia and UNTAC requests, the discarding of the five principles and the venture into the military domain that had been specifically removed from the unit's mandate from the Diet was clearly over the line. Were contradictions to arise between the five principles, on the one hand, and the Cambodian situation and UNTAC requests, on the other, it was the explicit policy of Japan that the duties be suspended and the unit withdrawn.

This was more than an agreement arising from a simple legal discussion; it was an option that had just barely managed to emerge from constitutional restrictions and years of cabinet interpretations of the constitution. The Miyazawa administration clearly stated this to the Japanese public many times and said that it would keep these promises. But perhaps this is just another example of the process of piecemeal gains that the SDF has followed since its inception, expanding its prerogatives through a fait accompli.

Although participation in United Nations peacekeeping marked a new page in Japanese defense policy and in the history of the Self-Defense Forces, Japan's future international role does not seem likely to end with these missions. The responsibilities of the Japanese contingent in Cambodia were limited to a small, finite area with strictly defined duties. As United Nations peacekeeping has expanded to many new areas and to involvements in local conflicts, the scale and nature of United Nations commitments are changing dramatically. The responses to the civil wars in Bosnia and Somalia clearly demonstrate this. The trend leads from peacekeeping to peace enforcement.

After its one year of experience in Cambodia, the Defense Agency began to firm up a policy of taking on expanded duties in its "international contribution." The issue of changing the Self-Defense Forces from a solely defensive organization that does not operate outside domestic boundaries to one that can help establish peace through a contribution to the post–Cold War international order has begun to receive serious attention. To accomplish this, the Self-Defense Forces Act will probably have to be restructured, and another unit in addition to the Ground, Maritime, and Air Self-Defense Forces will have to be formed specifically to take part in international contributions.

Before this, however, when the next PKO participation is being studied, the PKO Cooperation Law will have to be revised to remove the freeze, so that ground troops can be sent. If Japan is selected as a permanent member of the United Nations Security Council, a constitutional revision to allow for its participation in United Nations forces will certainly be debated. This is the lesson that Defense Agency authorities took home from the dispatch of a contingent to Cambodia.

These new duties on the international front were very welcome to a Self-Defense Forces in transition. They allowed the SDF to avoid scrutiny from Japanese eager for a peace dividend, and provided the foundation for a "new front" under the auspices of the United Nations. Additionally, the sight in the Japanese media of Japanese soldiers rolling up their sleeves for peace in remote Asian locations helped rehabilitate the Self-Defense Forces' long-standing image in Japan as a shadowy player and has greatly helped its recruitment campaigns. One staff member said that the best thing to come of the new international involvement is that there are no longer any Japanese who don't know what the Self-Defense Forces are doing. Certainly nothing could be more helpful in getting rid of the ambivalent and negative impressions held by many regarding the Self-Defense Forces.

In the summer of 1993, a new phase in Japan's defense policy history began when the first non–Liberal Democratic Party government since 1955 took power amid great fanfare under Hosokawa. In an early speech Hosokawa told Japan that the world is the ocean, the age is the wind, the state is the ship, and the people its rudder. The new administration was a breath of fresh air, and it rose to unprecedented levels of popular support that ran above seventy percent. Expectations were high. The new coalition excluded the LDP after thirty-eight continuous years of rule and marked the end of the traditional Cold War bickering between revolutionary and conservative, left and right, Liberal Democrats and Socialists. "Post–Cold War" and "reform" were the new regime's catchwords, and it was widely expected that Hosokawa would oversee the creation of a new national consensus on Japanese security and draft a new defense policy.

The SDF accepted the new administration without qualms. Although this would seem natural for a military under civilian control, the new coalition included the Japan Socialist Party, which maintained that the SDF was unconstitutional. Resistance among the military must have existed. But after a long series of dramatic events in world affairs, including the tearing down of the Berlin Wall, and the collapse of the Soviet Union, SDF officers were quite aware that the march of history was unstoppable. They could hardly expect that this trend of drastic change would bypass Japan and the SDF alone. But no officers resigned, and there was not the slightest rumor of coup d'état, not even from the fringes. Since the new administration had promised defense policy continuity and full adherence to the United States–Japan Security Treaty, and the new Defense Agency director, Keisuke Nakanishi, was a former LDP man, the SDF was not particularly worried. But the winds of change were not all blowing in the SDF's preferred direction.

On October 31, 1993, Hosokawa attended an inspection of the troops at the celebration of the thirty-ninth anniversary of the founding of the three-branch SDF. Unlike past prime ministers, who had dressed in formal morning suits and read from hackneyed scripts prepared by government officials, Hosokawa wore ordinary dress and spoke without a written speech, holding the microphone in one hand. The prime minister, commander in chief of the SDF, looked directly at the troops and addressed both them and the nation. The content of the address was a far cry from what the LDP prime ministers had traditionally delivered. Hosokawa advocated a reduction in the military, and the audience knew that this was something quite new:

"The Cold War order that has shaped this last half century is gone. The international situation has altered dramatically. I believe that it is only natural that the demands of the age on Japan's defenses have also changed greatly. So now what should Japan's defenses be?"

Hosokawa answered his question with a clear call for revising the national defense program outline: "Almost twenty years ago, under the Cold War order, the national defense program outline was drafted as our basic defense program. Considering how far technology has come in the intervening years, it is doubtful that the program can respond appropriately to the demands we face today. We must rethink the outline."

Hosokawa also called for a reduction in the size of the military: "International society has changed astonishingly. Within that international society we are called to show leadership in taking the road to peace. And it is my belief that we must also show initiative in leading the way toward a world with smaller militaries."

This was Hosokawa's basic approach toward defense. His address at the inspection of the troops unveiled a desire to lead the way to a new consensus on defense, one with a smaller military. On the Asaka Training Ground in Saitama prefecture, where he gave this speech, it was a warm, gentle, sunny day. It was the first time that the SDF leaders heard that a military tightening was about to descend on them.

It was soon to become apparent, though, that the new administration in fact had no new defense policy at all beyond Hosokawa's few explicit words. There were no specific policies or programs waiting to be implemented. The parties had yet to work out a consensus over the direction of security policy for Japan in the post–Cold War world; thus the prime minister's speech never ventured beyond a declaration of principles and intent.

The new administration had taken power with only two issues; the formation of a non-Liberal Democratic Party government and political reform. It had not come to power with a single platform on international affairs and did not agree on the need to reduce the military. Part of the government consisted of former LDP politicians who advocated making Japan like other nations by taking the PKO Cooperation Law a step further. This faction included Ichiro Ozawa. It was an impossible task to reconcile this group on defense issues with their coalition partners, the socialists. The latter had been so opposed to the PKO Cooperation Law that they had used an "ox walk," an archaic stalling technique whereby Diet members cast their ballots with extreme slowness. One reason the SDF did not greet the new administration with alarm is that they knew that it lacked the cohesion on defense issues to institute any changes.

In the seven parties' joint statement of July 29, 1993, which formed the basis of their government, they placed more emphasis than the LDP ever had on Japan's role in the post–Cold War world and on the people's rapidly changing needs. But when it came to the most important policies, they were vague: "To honor the ideals and spirit of the constitution, to maintain continuity with existing basic national policies of foreign relations and defense, to bear the role and responsibility of world peace and reducing military size, and to build a nation that is trusted by international society."

This statement lent itself to interpretations of both continuity and reform, but the primary emphasis was on continuity. When Nakanishi took up the post of Defense Agency director, he described his aspirations for the agency: "The new administration will continue past defense policies. You of the SDF stand in the forefront of defending our nation's peace and independence, ensuring Japan's security, and fulfilling Japan's duties in international society. We of the SDF must devote ourselves to this cause." This statement was not much different from what incoming Defense Agency directors usually said.

The first task of the new director was to negotiate with the

Ministry of Finance to get the full amount budgeted for the coming fiscal year in the interim Defense Buildup Program drafted by the outgoing LDP. And while the six socialist members of the new cabinet stated that the current SDF exceeded the allowable bounds of self-defensive power and was unconstitutional, they bound themselves to follow a policy of continuity and made it clear that they would not take a stance counter to the rest of the cabinet by specifically requesting defense cuts. The Japan Socialist Party, which had defended the constitution and opposed the SDF for many long years, had finally become part of the government, but they were powerless to do more. There could be no better opportunity for creating a new image of the SDF in the eyes of the Japanese public than in this transitional period to a post–Cold War East Asia, but the Japan Socialist Party didn't know how to take advantage of this opportunity.

With this mix of demilitarizers and advocates of the status quo, constitutional reformers and preservers, the new administration set sail. Prime Minister Hosokawa reined in the seven horses pulling his cart, but his political underpinnings were as insecure and confused as the rest of the post–Cold War world. The horses could hear the voices of the driver, but they refused to pull. All party heads called for defense cuts, but none of the parties wanted to initiate the effort. Defense Agency authorities violently opposed a change in defense policy given the uneasiness about the situation in China and the rest of Asia. Ultimately, the Defense Agency took the reins.

The fiscal 1994 defense budget was ¥4.6835 trillion, a 0.9% increase over the previous year. The new government continued all plans of the previous administration, including plans to buy airborne warning and control system (AWACS) planes from the United States. The Defense Agency described it as the slowest growth in thirty-four years, but the fact was that the defense budget continued to grow. Because Russia's military budget was plummeting, Japan's ranking in international defense spending climbed to second place, after the United States. The country whose constitution renounced war as a right of the nation had a larger military budget than Britain or France. The contrast between Hosokawa's promise to cut defense and the actual political situation was clear.

Suspicions that North Korea was developing nuclear weapons and the modernization of China's navy gave defense officials two strong arguments that the SDF should not be cut, despite the dissolution of the Soviet Union. Fear of North Korea's nuclear potential was particularly strong. The Korean peninsula has figured strongly in Japan's defense consciousness from ancient times and now did so again in the form of a nuclear threat. Reports of the firing of the Nodong I, a medium-range missile, followed reports of nuclear development and provoked a strong reaction within the SDF. As they saw it, the Soviet "evil empire" had vanished only to be replaced by a "little evil empire." The Defense Agency began to promote the need for theater missile defenses. It was reminiscent of a time when the Nakasone government joined in the development of the Strategic Defense Initiative upon the request of President Reagan to respond to the threat of SS-20 missiles. The concept of missiles to shoot down missiles was back.

The following February, in 1994, Prime Minister Hosokawa sought a new basic policy for defense by attending a consultative body reporting directly to him as prime minister, the Defense Advisory Council. At its first meeting, Hosokawa stated that "Japan's defense and security policies must respond to the dramatic changes in the world situation following the end of the Cold War. You have been gathered here because of your expertise in defense, foreign relations, economics, and finance, as well as for your international vision. It is up to you to find the framework of a new program." He asked the council for a report by summer. The aim was the first complete revision of the 1976 national defense program outline.

The nine members of the council included former ambassador to the United States Yoshio Okawara, former finance officer for the Ministry of Finance Toyo Gyoten, and Sophia University professor Kuniko Inoguchi. Asahi Beer president Hirotaro Higuchi was selected as the chairman, but the actual leaders in creating proposals turned out to be two men from the Defense Agency: former deputy director Seiki Nishihiro and former chief of the joint staff council Makoto Sakuma. Nishihiro was a graduate of the Defense Academy's first class who had risen through the ranks in the Defense Agency as a civilian staff member to become deputy director, while Sakuma was also a graduate of the Defense Academy's first class who was at the vanguard of his class, finally becoming Japan's highest-ranking officer. In 1957, three years after the Defense Agency was launched, they were chosen by the agency to be career staff members. It is an interesting twist of fate that after the end of the Cold War they should become responsible for creating the model for the Self-Defense Forces in the twenty-first century. Regardless of whether the Defense Advisory Council proposes continuity or change, status quo or defense cuts, its work will mark an important page in the history of the Japan's Self-Defense Forces.

1994 marked the Defense Agency's fortieth year. In 1954, two years after independence was regained, the Self-Defense Forces also began their history as a three-branch service. The Ground SDF, which began with the Police Reserve, was founded in 1950. Soon, the centenary of another important date in military history, the Russo-Japanese War, will be upon us. The year 1995 marks fifty years since the end of World War II. At this crossroads of history, Japan's decisions on its defense and security policy for the post–Cold War period will have a major effect not only on the Self-Defense Forces, but on all of twenty-first-century Japan and all of Asia.

Epilogue

I spent most of the 1960s living in the town of Sasebo in Nagasaki Prefecture. As a reporter on the police beat, the American navy's Sasebo Base and the Maritime Self-Defense Force Sasebo Regional District Command were part of my turf, so that the military and ships came to occupy a large part of my work activities. During the 1960s, the United States Navy, though heavily involved in the Vietnam War, began a transition to nuclear power and carried increasing numbers of nuclear weapons. Japan had its first encounter with this change when a nuclear-powered submarine visited Japan in November 1964. The nuclear-powered aircraft carrier Enterprise paid its first visit to Japan in January 1968. Since Sasebo had been chosen for both events, I was able to see and feel both events myself, walking the decks of the Enterprise and feeling the sting of tear gas in my eyes and the acrid smell burn through my nose at demonstrations.

At the time, the Maritime Self-Defense Force was a small organization, but it grew rapidly. The 1960s encompassed the Second and Third Defense Buildup Programs. The Model 61 tank (1961) and Model 64 rifle (1964) were built and paid for by Japan, and the last manned fighter, the F-104, was produced in

Japan under license. Shipyards laid down the keel of one new frigate after another. As I watched, the World War II–vintage Tacoma class patrol frigates and Livermore class destroyers on loan from the United States disappeared from sight, to be replaced by gleaming new antisubmarine frigates. The young officers of the first class of the Defense Academy became captains in the 1960s.

After forty years of existence, the Self-Defense Forces now stand at the most important crossroads of their existence. The advent of a new age of détente presents the Self-Defense Forces with a turning point in their reason for existence, because the Soviet threat was the food on which they grew fat. The Self-Defense Forces were originally created in response to a Cold War crisis, the Korean War. Now there is a certain irony in seeing them tossed about at the mercy of the Cold War's expiration. But for better or worse, the Self-Defense Forces have become Japan's new military. What to do with them is now a question not just for one faceless bureaucrat working within the Self-Defense Forces but for the entire Japanese people. It is pointless to ask where the Self-Defense Forces are going unless we know where they have come from and who they are. One has to know how the Self-Defense Forces have been shaped by the demands of the age and what they have done. From the start of the Cold War in Asia to the collapse of the Soviet Union, the actions of the Self-Defense Forces have been synchronized with the changing United States–Japan Security Treaty. It is that history I have tried to describe here. I hope it will prove of use in the debates sure to arise over the direction of the Self-Defense Forces in the 1990s.

Notes

Part I
The Birth of the Self-Defense Forces, 1950–1955

1. *Kodansha Encyclopedia of Japan* (New York: Kodansha, 1983), s.v.

2. For a good discussion of this often overlooked topic, see Michael Schaller, "The Workshop of Asia," in *The American Occupation of Japan* (Oxford: Oxford University Press, 1985).

3. General Charles A. Willoughby, quoted in William Manchester, *American Caesar* (Boston: Little, Brown, 1978).

4. Manchester, *American Caesar.*

5. Frank Kowalski, *Nihon Saigunbi* (An Inoffensive Rearmament) (Tokyo: Simul Press, 1969). This volume presents a very useful introduction to the subject of Japanese rearmament.

6. George Bruce, *The Paladin Dictionary of Battles* (London: Paladin, 1986), s.v. North Korean Army. Before the war's end, units from Australia, Canada, France, Greece, the Philippines, and the United Kingdom would see combat.

7. Douglas MacArthur, *Reminiscences* (New York: McGraw-Hill, 1964).

8. Shigeru Yoshida (1878–1967), Japan's longest-serving prime minister, guided the country through eight crucial postwar years. Yoshida entered Japan's Foreign Ministry in 1906 and spent his early career in China, especially in Manchuria. Although he was known at the time as a hawk, he soon became a critic of military engagement with Britain and the United States, which he regarded as folly. From 1936 to 1939 he was the ambassador to Great Britain. After his retirement, he worked with Fumi-

maro Konoe, Kinmochi Saionji, and Kijuro Shidehara to overturn the military dictatorship and stop proponents of war with the United States. After war began, he sought an early settlement and the overthrow of the Tojo cabinet, and was at one time imprisoned by the military police.

With this history behind him, Yoshida emerged at the center of postwar politics. The Occupation army favored him for his liberal views in foreign relations and his opposition to Tojo. He was appointed foreign minister in the cabinet of Naruhiko Higashikuni in September 1945. He then became head of the Liberal Party after the first general election and formed his own cabinet in May 1946. He cooperated fully with the Occupation troops to rouse Japan from defeat, and pushed Occupation reforms and the new constitution, which provided for an unarmed pacifist Japan. He believed that cooperating with MacArthur would be the best means of preserving the imperial system and maintaining the conservatism of the past.

Yoshida welcomed cooperation with the United States in foreign relations, but was cautious about too much American and Western European influence in Japan domestically. He favored traditional Japanese clothing and was aristocratic and nondemocratic in his attitudes. He was noted for episodes such as flinging a glass of water into a photographer's face and becoming so incensed at a questioner in the Diet that he called the man an idiot and dissolved the House of Representatives.

9. See Richard B. Finn, *Winners in Peace* (Berkeley: University of California Press, 1992) for an extensive discussion of this memo and its effect.

10. "The Origin and Development of the New Japanese Military," *Yomiuri Shimbun, This Is*, 11 October 1989.

11. Keikichi Masuhara, *The First Ten Years of the Self-Defense Forces* (Tokyo: Defense Agency, 1961).

12. Kowalski, *Nihon Saigunbi*.

13. When the Japanese empire accepted the Potsdam Declaration of 26 July 1945 and surrendered to the Allies, it was placed under the rule of General MacArthur. On the basis of the Allies' Initial Basic Ordinance, MacArthur began a sweeping reform of Japan's political, economic, and social structures. Laws and controls that had bound the lives of Japanese under the imperial system were discarded. GHQ released twenty-five hundred thought criminals and political prisoners, many from the Japan Communist Party. It enfranchised women and instituted land reform, giving many rural farmers their own land for the first time. It dismantled the *zaibatsu* (industrial conglomerates) as part of an effort to democratize the economy and encouraged labor and social movements as part of the process of democratization.

On 1 January 1946, the emperor renounced his divinity and declared himself a human being. His relationship to the Japanese people was redefined as one of mutual trust, respect, and affection. GHQ intended to use his influence to bolster the Occupation administration. The Japanese people welcomed the fall of the old system and the moves toward democracy. Although many conservatives and rightists opposed the changes, most of them were either defendants in war crime trials or had been purged, so they had little power. When Japan's constitution was passed in May 1947, the first stage of GHQ's democratization of Japan was complete.

14. Keikichi Masuhara, "History of the Self-Defense Forces and Japan's Security," in *Japan's Security* (Tokyo: Nihon Kokusai Mondai Kenkyusho, 1964).

15. Edwin O. Reischauer, *Japan: The Story of a Nation* (New York: Alfred A. Knopf, 1970).

16. D. Clayton James, *The Years of MacArthur* (Boston: Houghton Mifflin, 1970).

17. A total of 2,770 candidates from 258 parties ran for the Diet in the April 1946 general elections, but many of the candidates were members of single-person parties. Only eleven parties fielded ten or more candidates. The ruling party, the Progressives, was defeated, gaining only 94 seats to the Japan Liberal Party's 140 seats. Seventy-nine women ran for election, and thirty-nine were elected, as were ninety-two socialists and five communists. The first postwar Diet was rounded out by thirty-eight members of smaller parties and eighty-one independents.

 After the election, the Shidehara cabinet resigned and Ichiro Hatoyama was appointed prime minister for a brief time before GHQ purged him, paving the way for the secretary of the Japan Liberal Party, Shigeru Yoshida, to become prime minister. Except for a brief term of socialist government, Yoshida continued on as prime minister until 7 December 1954. His eight years as prime minister marked a transition from defeat and ashes to recovery and rebirth. Yoshida played the role of a faithful steward under MacArthur's successor as commander of GHQ, Matthew Ridgway, with the adroitness of a diplomat, and he set the course for postwar Japan.

18. Kowalski, *Nihon Saigunbi*.

19. James, *The Years of MacArthur*.

20. The purge of public officials was based on Article 6 of the Potsdam Declaration. It removed militarists and extreme nationalists from positions of political and social influence. The initial purge was based on the Ini-

tial Basic Ordinance, which was prepared by GHQ for the fall of Japan. Roughly two hundred thousand wartime political and social leaders were declared undesirables and were forbidden to participate in public life for a period of two years and four months. There were six classes of undesirables: war criminals; career military personnel; members of extreme nationalist groups; members of the Imperial Rule Assistance Association, the wartime political party; former colonists and colonial administration officials; and persons collaborating with aggressive warfare through word or deed. Eighty percent of the purged officials were connected with the military. They were dismissed and were barred from reemployment. Five cabinet members were purged, as were 260 members of the government party and the Progressive Party, resulting in the end of the government administration. The purged officials began to make serious moves toward getting the purge order lifted in May 1951, and then made furious efforts to institute a purge against the Japan Communist Party, a "red" purge.

21. William J. Sebald, *With MacArthur in Japan* (New York: W.W. Norton, 1965).

22. Kowalski, *Nihon Saigunbi.*

23. Kowalski, *Nihon Saigunbi.*

24. Kowalski, *Nihon Saigunbi.*

25. Masuhara, "History of the Self-Defense Forces and Japan's Security" in *Japan's Security.*

26. An elite officer of the Japanese army, Hattori had been chief of the operations section of the general staff. He instigated the Nohonman Incident, a severe and dramatic defeat for the Japanese, during May 1939, in Mongolia. This defeat did not harm his career. He was behind Japan's move into French Indochina, which helped precipitate war with the United States. Hattori directed the attacks on Singapore, Hong Kong, and Guadalcanal. He took responsibility for the defeat at Guadalcanal, resigned, and became Tojo's secretary. He opposed settlement of the war, lost his position after the defeats on Saipan and Okinawa, and finished the war as a regimental commander in China.

27. Masuhara, *The First Ten Years of the Self-Defense Forces.*

28. Masuhara, "History of the Self-Defense Forces and Japan's Security" in *Japan's Security.*

29. Eizo Ishii, "The Untold Story of the Birth of the Self-Defense Forces," *Japanese Military Review*, March 1977.

30. Hiroomi Kurisu, *The Hypothetical Enemy: The Soviet Union* (Tokyo: Kodansha, 1980).

31. James E. Auer, *The Postwar Rearmament of Japanese Maritime Forces, 1945–1971* (Westport, Conn.: Praeger, 1973).

32. Takeo Okubo, *Days of the Call of the Sea* (Tokyo: Kai You Mondai Kenkyukai, 1978).

33. Auer, *The Postwar Rearmament of Japanese Maritime Forces*, 1945–1971.

34. Okubo, *Days of the Call of the Sea.*

35. Okubo, *Days of the Call of the Sea.*

36. Auer, *The Postwar Rearmament of Japanese Maritime Forces*, 1945–1971.

37. *Defense Academy Friendship Magazine*, May 1969.

38. *Mainichi Shimbun*, 25 February 1953.

39. *Defense Academy Friendship Magazine*, May 1969.

40. "The First Class at Koharadai," *Mainichi Shimbun*, 12 October 1985.

41. Akira Matsuda, *The Defense Academy: The Heart of Its Education* (Tokyo: Origin Shuppan Center, 1989).

42. Shoin Yoshida was an imperial loyalist warrior in the nineteenth century who wanted to drive foreigners from Japan and plotted to assassinate a government councillor. He was executed in 1859 at the age of twenty-nine.

43. Yukio Mishima was a famous twentieth-century author known for his elegant writing style, right-wing views, homosexuality, and dramatic suicide at a Tokyo-area garrison.

44. *Cho-Un*, 7 September 1989.

45. James, *The Years of MacArthur.*

46. Shigeru Yoshida, remarks made at the first Japan–United States negotiations for the peace treaty, 25 January 1951.

47. Defense Agency, Ground Forces General Staff, *History of the Security Forces* (Tokyo: 1958).

48. Keiichi Miyazawa, *The Secret Tokyo–Washington Talks* (1956).

49. For an interesting discussion of this matter, see "Keiichi Miyazawa Talks About the Ikeda-Robertson Talks," *Mainichi Shimbun*, 3 May 1984.

50. *The City History of Sasebo* (Sasebo: 1959).

51. Ichizo Tsuji, *The Silent Port* (Sasebo: The Silent Port Publishing Committee, 1972).

52. For an excellent discussion of the immediate postwar period, see Finn, *Winners in Peace.*

PART II
The Development of the Self-Defense Forces, 1955–1974

1. House of Representatives, Cabinet Committee, *Minutes*, 25 March 1957.

2. According to Edwin O. Reischauer (*Japan: The Story of a Nation*), "Many Japanese felt mounting concern and indignation over the presence of American soldiers and bases. To such people it seemed that the greater safety for Japan lay in complete unarmed neutrality, rather than in a military alliance with the great capitalist nation."

3. The Potsdam Declaration was signed on 26 July 1945. It was intended to ratify the territorial division of Europe, as decided earlier at Yalta, and little of the declaration was meant to affect Japan.

4. The Keidanren is a very influential organization that coordinates the actions of several key economic organizations, manages some industrial competition, and funnels contributions from the financial community to politicians. Keidanren is often consulted by the government and the Diet.

5. The 260,000 American servicemen in Japan during the Korean War brought inevitable friction. Japanese were irritated by the appropriation of land for bases and housing, by the noise and damage caused by training, and by crime. Anti-American and antibase movements became very passionate, creating a difficult dilemma for the Japanese government. The Japan Socialist Party and the Japan Communist Party led the call for American withdrawal, claiming that American bases were unconstitutional. The government pledged to reduce the American presence by taking over some of the bases. There were no violent acts against American soldiers, however, and rather little bitterness, largely because the Americans kept themselves separate from Japanese society. More than a few Japanese have married Americans.

6. *History of the Mitsubishi Heavy Industries Nagoya Aircraft Factory* (Tokyo).

7. Yoshio Kodama, a right-wing activist, had been arrested and imprisoned many times before World War II for favoring direct action. He established the Kodama Machine in Shanghai to supply matériel to Japanese troops, and by the end of the war he had amassed a fortune estimated at ¥3.2 billion and had great influence among the military. His name surfaced whenever an influence-peddling scandal emerged within the Liberal Democratic Party, and he was active with right-wing youth. Kodama was taken to court for tax evasion and violations of currency exchange laws over the ¥2.7 billion that he had received as a consultant to Lockheed for the L-1011 Tristar, but he died before sentencing.

8. Matthew Ridgway, *MacArthur's Japan* (Tokyo: Shukam Shincho Henchubo, 1970).

9. Ichiji Sugita, *The Forgotten Security Treaty* (Tokyo: Jiji Tushinsha, 1967).

10. Sugita, *The Forgotten Security Treaty*.

11. Munetoku Akagi, "1960 and Me," *This Is*.

12. Kaneshichi Masuda, speech before the House of Representatives, 2 March 1968.

13. As early as 1978, Yasuhiro Nakasone had stated that the basic principle of Japanese defense policy was self-defense. For a discussion of Nakasone's views, see George Friedman and Meredith Labard, *The Coming War with Japan* (New York: St. Martin's Press, 1991).

14. Yasuhiro Nakasone, *My Private Life* (Tokyo: Kodansha, 1992).

15. *People's Daily*, 1 November 1970.

16. *People's Republic of China Press*, 3 September 1970.

17. The life of this unusual figure has spawned many books and articles. For very good analyses of Mishima's life, his work and his effect on Japanese politics and literature, see chapter twenty-seven of Donald Keene's, *Dawn to the West* (New York: Henry Holt, 1984) and John Nathan, *Mishima: A Biography* (Boston: Little, Brown, 1974).

18. Yasuhiro Nakasone, "Two Records of the Mishima Incident," *Bungei Shuniu*, February 1971.

19. House of Representatives, Cabinet Committee, *Minutes*, 16 May 1973.

20. Yukio Mishima, *St. Andrew's Review* 4, nos. 2–4 (1977).

21. Mishima was born on 4 January 1925 and saw no combat in World War II. From chapter 27 in: Keene, *Dawn to the West*.

22. Tsuji, *The Silent Port*.

PART III
The Self-Defense Forces from 1975 to the Present

1. Japanese exports rose from $55.7 billion in 1970 to $339.7 billion in 1992, *CIA World Fact Book* (McLean, Va.: Brassey's, 1994). Doves could be excused for concluding that prosperity and a small military were compatible, or perhaps even inseparable.

2. The Nixon administration also imposed a ten-percent surcharge on imports in an effort to bring down the yen's value against the dollar.

3. The wholesale price index rose thirty-one percent in 1974. Countermeasures were then put into place. For example, by 1985, nuclear power stations were producing twenty-five percent of Japan's power needs. For a good discussion of this issue, see W. G. Beasley, *The Rise of Modern Japan* (New York: St. Martin's Press, 1990).

4. "The Self-Defense Force at 25," *Mainichi Shimbun*, 15–16 August 1979.

5. The Joint Chiefs of Staff, *United States Military Posture Statement for Fiscal Year 1977* (Washington, D.C.: 1977).

6. "My Career," *Nihon Keizai Shimbun*, 21 January 1988.

7. *Shukan Post*, July 1988.

8. Shin Kanemaru.

9. House of Representatives, Special Committee for Okinawa and the Northern Territories, *Minutes*, 30 November 1970.

10. *Asahi Shimbun*, 29 August 1975.

11. "Statement by CINCPAC [Commander-in-Chief, Pacific] Admiral Maurice Weisner," *Asahi Shimbun*, 28 August 1978.

12. "Statement by CNO [Chief of Naval Operations] Admiral Thomas Hayword," *Asahi Shimbun*, 1 June 1979.

13. *Nikkei*, 22 August 1979.

14. Zenko Suzuki, speech before the National Press Club, 1 May 1981.

15. Funada, speech before the House of Representatives Cabinet Committee, February 1956.

16. Government Response Paper, September 1987.

17. Liberal Democratic Party Study Conference.

18. *Nikkei*, 19 January 1983.

19. Yasuhiro Nakasone, *My Private Life*.

20. Yasuhiro Nakasone, speech before Self-Defense Forces senior officers, 28 May 1984.

21. Ben Wattenberg wrote in the *Washington Times* issue of 18 June 1987:

> We should mention the central fact of Japanese existence: They are our wards. They live in a very dangerous neighborhood, close to some big bad countries who don't like the Japanese—Russia and China. The Japanese do little to protect themselves—spending just over one percent of their gross national product on defense, the lowest rate of any modern nation. The big reason they spend so little on defense, they say, is because their voters are afraid of resurgent militarism. Japan, after all, almost destroyed all of Asia, including itself, in World War II. So now the Japanese are the ultimate double free riders: They spend stingily on defense and yet

feel secure because the United States guarantees their security. The American guarantee is worth something because we spend six percent of our GNP for defense.

Chuma Kiyofuku presented an opposing view in *Japan Quarterly* (January/March 1989):

The reason most Americans still subscribe to the view that Japan is getting a free ride under the mutual security treaty is because they are largely uninformed. . . . The quality of Japan's defense force places it among the best in the world and Japan is one of the most openhanded American allies in terms of the amount it spends to support United States troops on its soil.

22. Edward A. Olsen wrote in *Collective Defense or Strategic Independence* (New York: Lexington Books, 1989):

The much vaunted surpassing by the Nakasone government in 1987 of Japan's self-imposed one percent of GNP defense spending limit was largely symbolic. Defense expenditures went from a tiny fraction under one percent to an equally tiny fraction over it. Though Japan's percentage of yearly defense budget increases often exceeds that of other United States allies, there is no sign that cracking the barrier means that Japan will move quickly to match the proportions of GNP spent on defense by other Western powers. It stands in dramatic contrast to neighboring South Korea's six percent of GNP spent on defense.

23. Defense Agency, *Opinion*, 11 December 1979.

24. House of Peers, Budget Committee, *Minutes*, March 1978.

25. The Cold War can be considered to have ended when Soviet people enjoyed free elections to their parliament in 1989.

26. International Institute for Strategic Studies, *Strategic Survey, 1989–1990* (London: Brassey's, 1990).

27. Yuken Hironata, "The Perspective of the Defense White Paper," *National Defense Magazine*, October 1989.

28. Defense Agency, *Defense of Japan* (Tokyo: 1992).

29. *Asahi Shimbun*, 1 December 1990.

30. *Clean Government Party Newspaper*, 5 December 1991.

Index

Konishi, Makoto, 88, 225
Konishi antimilitary suit, 88
Kono, Yoshikatsu, 180
Korean Airlines flight 007, 241
Korean War, 39, 83, 93, 158
  intensification of, 32
  Japanese navy and, 44–52
  minesweeping and, 44–52, 262
  rearmament of Japan and, 1–12,
   108
  thirty-eighth parallel, 12, 128
Kosaka, Masataka, 181, 182, 252
Kotaki, Akira, 97
Kowalski, Frank, 4, 7, 11, 18, 19,
  22–23, 25
Kozurof, Colonel, 239–241
Kubo, Takuya, 173–195, 209, 224, 231
Kubotani, Haomitsu, 28
Kuma, Tamotsu, 159–160
Kure, Japan, 82
Kurisu, Hiroomi, 35, 212, 216–228,
  223, 246
Kurogane, Hideyuke, 158
Kuroshima exercise, 262

L

Laird, Melvin, 200
Law Establishing the Defense
  Agency, 75
Law for Production of Weapons, 104
Le Carré, John, 240
Lebanon, Israeli invasion of, 225
Liberal Democratic Party, 79, 95,
  120, 122, 144, 145, 149, 178, 193,
  222, 224, 226, 246, 248, 253, 270,
  282, 283, 285, 288, 295
Liberal Democratic Party's Security
  Treaty Survey Group, 141
Liberal Party, 75, 95
Liberals (Japanese), xiv. See also
  specific parties
Line and staff. See Japanese military,

civilian control of
Lockheed F-104, 112
Lockheed F-104C, 114–115
Lockheed P3C, 189
Lost generation, 55

M

MacArthur, Douglas, vii, 279
  as commander of United Nations
   forces in Korean War, vii, 45
  response in Japan to Korean War,
   2–12
Maekawa, Kiyoshi, 55, 56
Magari, Nobuyoshi, 28
Mahan, Alfred Thayer, 231n
Mainichi Shimbun, 186
Maizuru, Japan, 82
Maki, Tomo, 53–62
Maritime Safety Board, 6, 44–52,
  142, 143, 175
Maritime Security Force, 47, 50–51,
  70. See also Navy, Japanese
Maritime Self-Defense Force, 47, 76,
  86, 105, 106, 110, 133, 157, 162,
  207, 259, 263, 307. See also
  Navy, Japanese; Photo section
  Nadashio accident and, 257–258
  sea lanes and, 230–243
Maruyama, Kou, 187, 222
Masuda, Kaneshichi, 124–125
Masuhara, Keikichi, 6–7, 25–35, 54
Matsuda, Akira, 60
Matsudani, Makoto, 60
McDonnell Douglas, 113
"Memo on Increasing the Japanese
  Police Force" (MacArthur), 5–6
Metropolitan Police office (Tokyo),
  126–127
Middle East, 202
Mig 25, 191–192
Mikami, Takashi, 126
Miki, Takeo, 178, 189, 193, 201, 202